I0814036

LANGUAGE LESSONS: VOLUME I

LANGUAGE LESSONS: VOLUME I

EDITED BY
CHET WEISE AND BEN SWANK

PUBLISHED BY THIRD MAN BOOKS
NASHVILLE, TENNESSEE

For information, address Third Man Books, LLC, 623 7th Ave S, Nashville, Tennessee 37203.

Printed, all material manufactured, and assembled in Nashville, Tennessee.

FIRST EDITION
Designed by Trent Thibodeaux
Cover photo by Brian Fuller
Back cover photo by Tim Kerr
Assistant editors: Joshua Gillis, William Miller, and Pamela Johnson Parker
The editors would like to extend their gratitude to C.D. Wright and Brian Barker. Both contributed more than words.

ISBN 978-0-9913361-0-4

A Poem is Everything

a Poem can be Words, letters and
even Numbers. but to Me it's a
Wondrous Place of Minds Places
of Wonder. amazing Thoughts. like
This: blue as the sky like a
robin bird going down but Never
going up. also White, Red and
orange. My Mind is a Thirsty
Garden   raindrops splash   a
Poem Through The Garden gate.

— Calliope Watford-Edelson

TABLE OF CONTENTS

Preface xvii

I.

Jake Adam York

Tape Loop 2

Cry of the Occasion 3

Te lyra pulsa manu or something like that 4

Letter Already Broadcast into Space 7

Postscript (Already Breaking in Distant Echoes) 10

Letter Written On A Hundred Dollar Bill 12

Dear Brother, 14

Cookin' With The Miles Davis Quintet 16

Adrian Matejka

Language Mixology 20

Seven Days of Falling 22

This Be The Verse 23

Wheels of Steel (Metal Face Villain Mix) 24

Tyndall Armory 25

Sampson Starkweather

I sense my own limit 26

from Flowers of Rad 27

from Flowers of Rad 28

from Human Week 29

from Human Week 30

our life, this temporary eclipse / to that other 31

C.D. Wright
Imaginary August 32
Imaginary Morning Glory 33
Imaginary June 34
Imaginary Waterfall 35

Joshua Marie Wilkinson
Afterparty 36

Pinckney Benedict
Joe Messinger Is Dreaming 40

Janaka Stucky
Recreating A Miraculous Object 55
Recreating A Miraculous Object 56
Recreating A Miraculous Object 57
Recreating A Miraculous Object 58
Recreating A Miraculous Object 59

Tim Kerr
John Coltrane 63

II.

Noah Eli Gordon
The Problem 65
The Problem 66
The Problem 68
The Problem 69
The Problem 70

Larry O. Dean
How To Defend Your Elf 71
Nixon Era Panda Dies 73

Nicky Beer
Mating Call Of The Re-Creation Panda 74
Nature Film, Directed By Martin Scorsese 75
Population 78
Scene 43, Take 1: Interior, Sushi Restaurant 79

Steve Stern
Swan Song 81

M-Dot Da Poet
"Fairytales" 87
Dear Mrs. Rashad 90

Russell Brakefield
I Want To Know About Anything 92
The Way Al Green Knows About Love
Nowhere To Run 93
Night Music 95

Gaylord Brewer
Being Lon Chaney, Jr. 96
Terminex 97
More Honored In The Breach: 98
Your Midnight E-Mails, the Morning After
The Martini 99

Carolyn Hembree
Old Sweetheart Slams White Russians 101
And Mudslides On Ditmars Blvd., Astoria
The Goner 102

Tav Falco
Chapter The Thirteenth: Discourse 103
Of Rage, Conjuration, & Exile

III.

Dan Boehl
emoemoji : dancing 149

Pamela Johnson Parker
First Person Plural, First Person Singular 161
Triage 163
It Pays To Increase Your Word 164
Power: Diminuendo
In Ictu Oculi 166
Some Yellow Tulips 167

besmilr brigham
Teachers, Masters in Their Places, and this 169
is a spirit world
The Song 172
Flood Rain (Wind 174
i remember the librarian throwing away 175
a magazine because it had the picture
of a Black man on the cover
the sign read: los hombres 176
/trabajando

Sheila Sanderson
Though the End Be No Mystery 177
Conspiracy in White 178
In the Temple of the Bulrushes 180

Andrew McFayden-Ketchum
Stormdraining 182
The Year Hyakatuke was Said 184

Stephanie Ann Whited
When Was Early 186
When the Cause is Lost 187

Joanne Merriam
Deaths on Other Planets 188
Presque Vu 189

Joshua Gillis
hot cop at iHop (w4m) - 190
Life is good I bartend and Love it (m4w) - 191
Our daughters are on the same soccer team. (w4m) - 192
Arbys cowboy (w4m) - 193
to the girl in the black shorts at kmart (m4w) - 194

IV.

William Miller
The Erection of Another Paschal Mystery, Nocturnal Emissions, and Immaculate Lady (Slight Return) 196

Nickole Brown
Fuck 222
Go Put on Your Face 224

TJ Jarrett
After Forty Days, Go Marry Again 225
A River Returns Emmitt Till to the Earth, 1955 226
Meridian, MS 1978: I Asked Her Late to Remember 227
Late at Night, I Go Hunting 228
Gaslight 229

Rachel Ballard
Independence Day Afternoon 230
New Year's Day at Whatcom Creek, Far from the War 231

Adam Vines
Anti-Aubade 232
River Politics 233
The Golden Years 234
After Warhol's *Rorschach,* 1984 235
After Tom Wesselmann's *Great American Nude #57*, 1964 236

Wayne Miller
Post-Elegy 237
The People's History 238
Some Notes on Human Relations 240
A Bit about the Soul 242
Allegory of the House 243

Chet Weise
An American Prayer for the Second Coming 245
h t i a F 246
In the Pines 247

Zachary Schomburg
The Killing Trees 248
Death Letter 249
The Reckoner 250

V.

Dale Ray Phillips
Creole 252

Spencer Connell
Yellow Fingers 256
Woman in the Shower 257

Sommer Browning
from Friend 258
The Whistler 259
Federal Holiday 260
The Meat from the Dream the Heart Knows 263
from Friend 264

Ben Mirov
Black Glass Soliloquy 265
from darklings 267

Paige Taggart
Starts in Herds 271
Poem With Scrutiny 272
Melatonin 273

Daniel Lucca Pujol
Getting Gas 274
N4 276

Benjamin Prosser
Moonlight in the Meadow 278
Fire Animal 280

Ben Burr
december 21, 2012; 11:23pm 281
july 19, 2013; 3:33am 282

Brooke McCarley
Age & the Beat 283

Richard Hell
My First Rehearsals with a Band 286

Kendra DeColo
Avocados 288
God is a Capitalist 290
After the Poet from Kentucky Tells me my Poems Are Not Considerate to Their Audience I Try to Teach Him What I Know About Etiquette 291
Places Where I Would Like to Conceive 292

Frank Stanford
Pits 293
Translators 294
For Those Who Sleep And Those Who Die 295

Antonin Artaud
Man is so afraid, 296
Cemetery Near the Sea 298

René Daumal

Brian Barker

Bats 299

Elk 299

Hippopotamuses 299

Turkey Vultures 300

Strong Man 300

Risk Management 301

Uncle Z's Toupee 301

Field Recording 302

Contributors 304

PREFACE

We knelt at the edge of the sinkhole and lowered the microphone down into the depths . . . fiddled with the dials on the reel-to-reel and pressed the headphones against one ear.

Ben Swank is a co-founder of Third Man Records, and I am an instructor at a local university. We are both writers, and we both come from the DIY, get-in-the-van-and-tour-rock-n-roll scene of the 1990s. Neither town where we lived during that time, Toledo, Ohio, or Auburn, Alabama, respectively, represented the cutting edge—to put it mildly—of music. To survive, we sought out the handful of like-minded music lovers within our local communities. Travelled to see the kinds of music we needed. Formed our own bands. Booked our own shows. Met more like-minded bands from out of town. Invited them to play our hometowns (house parties or whichever small bar on the brink of bankruptcy would have us), and, eventually, we became parts of the small yet potent music scenes blossoming in our corners of the world. It's a timeless story. Music and those who love it have continued to survive, thrive, and evolve because of an ever-existent grassroots and public forum.

It is by no coincidence that the evolution of *Language Lessons* is analogous to what Swank and I experienced with our bands. We never planned for this anthology. It was born from a community. It just happened.

A quick glance at any literature book or a trip around the Internet will show Nashville's rich tradition in poetry, prose, and music. Still, there existed room for another particular sort of reading series. In keeping with the early punk rock mantra, "Now start your own band," I shared with Swank my scheme to start that reading series. A reading series that would usually be curated, but sometimes be open mic, and would always showcase all types of language: poetry, prose, art, music, spoken word, comedy, a few instances of heckling, a thrown beer bottle . . . . (In time, Swank would read his confession there.)

Dino's Bar and Grill proved to be the perfect venue for this collision of arts. It was just the right size and shape to suit acoustic requirements, the need for intimacy, boasted nicotine-colored walls, and the owner—a dead ringer for Captain Ahab's long-lost cousin—flipped burgers behind the bar-top cash register. Dino's had welcomed all types through the years—bikers, punk rock bands, lawyers, a judge, hipsters, blue-collar happy-hour-ers, and country lovers. Dino's welcomed us, too. *Poetry Sucks! A Night of Poetry, Music, And All Sorts of Bad Language* debuted on November 3rd, 2011. (About the name: "Poetry Sucks!" is a cheeky, middle-fingered comeback. I mean, how many times have I heard someone dismissively say, "Yeah, I just don't understand poetry. It sucks." The name also is a literal admission of how difficult writing can be.) The first night featured the poetry of my friend and Auburn compatriot Jake Adam York. Jake attended more than one Auburn rock-n-roll house-show back in the day.

Swank played an integral part in this reading series from the beginning: helping with promotion and with recommending and contacting both readers and bands. We brought in free jazz, experimental music, punk rock, blues, . . . and even some country. As for the readers, we had everyone from award-winning, published authors to pizza chefs. All good writing. And we almost always included first-time readers, which infused the room with a special kind of energy. Dino's could never be mistaken for Madison Square Garden, but to have a line out the door for a reading, no matter how small the venue, in Nashville speaks volumes. The reading series had begun to grow and discover the larger community "out there."

Third Man Records would eventually invite *PS!* on a field trip away from Dino's. We had over three hundred attend. After the night came to a close, happily shocked, Swank and I felt there was something happening here. I suggested to Swank an anthology might be in order. He countered that Third Man Records had discussed starting a press, Third Man Books, and this might be a good place to begin. When Swank and I decided what *Language Lessons* should be about, we decided that, like the *PS!* reading series, the anthology should include all types of voices: from pens to keyboards, from vocal cords to guitar chords.

For most of us, poetry books should have section dividers at the local record store, next to all the rock, jazz, hip-hop, and blues. Likewise, our prose should sit next to the classical, folk, and experimental bins. The music of language grabs us, and we learn. I never saw the difference between posturing and rebellion until reading William Blake in high school. Nor did I know what metaphor really meant until hearing the three opening chords of The Stooges' "I Wanna Be Your Dog"; the phrasing and fuzz of those opening chords provided the perfect vehicle for the song's tenor. I never understood what beauty could be until James Wright's "A Blessing" or Son House's "Pearline." Or, what fear really meant until *Animal Farm* and Joy Division. What rhythm could do and convey until *Beowulf*, Robert Frost, Public Enemy, and James Brown. Or, the elegance of form until The Beatles' "I Want to Hold Your Hand" and Shakespeare's sonnets. Or, the ability to overturn conventions for the sake of message and expression until Sun Ra and Andre Breton. Or, the permanence of language until sitting with my roommates in college and watching the second plane smash into the tallest building in the world. Or, the existence of love, soul and the concept of heaven until Coltrane's "Love Supreme," Al Green, and reading Rilke. Or, the relationship between laughter and gut-wrenching misery until Plath, Bukowski, and Yankovic. Or, the universality of language until Lorca, Beethoven, Basho, and Guitar Wolf.

Even beyond these lessons, Swank and I discussed how the long-standing tradition of punk and language (Patti Smith, Exene Cervenka, Jim Carroll, Richard Hell et al) had ebbed in the last few years. It's frustrating. Sometimes it feels like we're living again in the shadow of the Industrial Revolution and its ideology of specialization . . . you're supposed to be a writer . . . you're supposed to be a musician . . . you're supposed to be a lawyer . . . you're supposed to be a teacher . . . .

Language Lessons represents a different paradigm. *Language Lessons'* horn players and teachers come from all walks of life. It takes a community of all kinds to make a scene. Almost 90% of the collection's contributors performed at *PS!* Many came from Nashville and a few more from out of town—some even toured in Ford Econolines, just like Swank and my rock-n-roll days, except boxes of books replaced the Fenders and Marshalls.

From editing this anthology more than anywhere else, I've learned to "kill your idols." When talking with our contributors, I've learned that they are taco-makers, teachers, librarians, mothers, fathers, students, stock-traders, software programmers, and bartenders. These are real people who have taken the time to speak, write, and even more, to listen, and all of whom share a love for the creation of language. In these pages we have authors recognized by the Pulitzer Prize and National Book Award alongside those experiencing the excitement of seeing their words in print for the first time. And there are guitar players and drummers too. All have shared many of the same experiences in both the world and their writing/music.

Together—audience, writer, player—we form an ensemble. We can sit back and listen to the array of voices, hear each word/note, read each emotion, let each image tell us about ourselves, the world, and the real person behind the voice. We're all students. I guess that's the real point of the anthology—a hope that the voices and sounds in this collection will engage both the reader and listener within ourselves. Nonetheless, you're not going to like all of it. You'd be a nutjob if you did. But maybe at least one or two of these voices will be welcomed into your community? Maybe, like a rare, good friend, one of these voices can create that moment of prodigious stillness, so needed in the modern world, not as an escape, but rather as a fortification of beauty versus all that is coming at you from out there. Maybe there will be that one favorite voice that empowers your day with joy, like setting the alarm clock to wake you with exactly the right song. It's all music. Lots and lots of music. And music is water. Blues singer John Lee Hooker said, "What do music do? It keeps the world turning." It keeps the world turning, more than the tallest building or the fastest operating system. A poem can save the world (or at least a Thursday night!). Now go make your own scene.

Chet Weise, 2014

I.

the word on the soiled

page here wants it out

with us

Tape Loop

—For Collis Marchbanks

touch the lip so silence
has a name neither of us
can pronounce
on midnight radio from Memphis
Houston Phoenix a beat
rattling in the valley
like the needle I am not
supposed to touch
between the trees in those
country songs my prayer
a sound that doesn't play
in this town I am
not supposed to click the button
so this gets dubbed
onto the ribbon in the black
cassette that gets dubbed
onto the ribbon in the white
cassette as the needle drops
the beat the head says
this town is a form of silence
waiting for the drum
of the tongue the lip
the sentence we're stretching
when we make our bodies music
we make an elsewhere
whose name reaches
toward the center and the needle's
caught it when the beat
slows between the tracks
your voice my voice
our elsewhere music
the groove never knew
it couldn't touch

Cry of the Occasion

John Earl Reese, shot while dancing in a café in Mayflower, Texas, October 22, 1955

so loud it fills the valleys
of even the fingers smeared
into a kind of quiet, the everything
you can't hear but hear through
the music every body in the room
still moving the beat gone erratic as a bat
juking the pines and chimney
swifts toward grace notes
of nourishment over the lake
I see in the perpetual lapping of water
in the lock groove of some cousin's
record I put my finger to
pull back the arm but it shivers
toward the moon thrown like a penny
from the engine's wheel like the sound
of a penny thrown from the glass
calling my name louder than I've ever
heard this part before a bird
whose name's so long
it has never finished saying it
holds me waiting for the end so I
can say something a little more blunt
like thunder a finger through the bone
peeling back the husk of the voice
opening like a bird called into
the wild answering but
like the bird I have not even seen
this music goes on forever the stars
blur the bottleneck against the bridge
swallows abandon for the water
cutting into the bank where I keep
trying to move the needle
to cut my answer into the night
I have to catch the bird and slide it
against my neck I have to carve
the guitar from the deadheads beneath
the lake and all its waves to sing

te lyra pulsa manu or something like that

As Ovid or Onomacritus—or was it Ike Turner?—said
music makes everything want to reach out of itself,
rocks forgetting their gravity, birds hovering
as if become part of the air itself,
and so the pines and the olives leaning over Orpheus
as he slid the bottle along the guitar's neck
gave up their sap and oil which is why he glistened
in the sun or the starlight and seemed to express
that brilliance, like a zoetrope or a planetarium,
and you couldn't tell if he was gathering
or giving it back, but that's music,
erupting beautiful and returning to itself at last,
Mercury's gift—the turtle's gut
strung across its desiccated shell,
a melody pulled from such concentrated silence
and returned to its bowl, making every ear
the parenthesis that separates us from persistence.
But we want to last, at least long enough
to grasp what we've just let go, so
the women, washing their clothes by the river,
hearing that song—its melody remembering
then forgetting every one they knew—
left their clothes to froth on the river's shoals,
to follow and catch and at last
to reach inside him for what they'd lost,
pulling everything out,
which is how music entered the human world,
a stain beneath the fingernails that tells
where you've been. His head, his guitar
floated down the Hebrus to the sea
where Apollo raised the strings into the night
making the turtle and the song immortal.
That, anyway, is how it was put to me
in a juke-joint in Mississippi, as if
from Onomacritus to Ovid to Ike Zimmerman,
who taught Robert Johnson how to play,
and when someone poisoned—or was it stabbed?—
Johnson, for something he said,
like *Won't you squeeze my lemon*

till the juice runs down my leg
or *I got a phonograph*... back, like a breath,
into the world, the water, the earth,
the light. There is always someone there,
Ovid should have said, to tear you apart
when you get beautiful enough, first just picking
at the skin, the fingernail or tortoise-shell
plectrum a kind of tease, but then more strident,
your corona zipped off and flattened to a disc.
This is how, in these moments, when music
coaxes everything out of itself,
when you become so attuned
you almost *hear* the light,
the pulse of the fluorescent tube
over the bar or the cigarette machine
or the star, 900 years away,
which is really two stars, eclipsing
then amplifying one another, this
is how I imagine William Moore,
after walking from Chattanooga to Gadsden,
with the sign, *Jesus Was an Alien*,
taped to his caisson, his letter for Ross Barnett—
Be gracious and give more
than is immediately demanded of you—
still folded in its envelope
when the assassin found him,
and this is how I imagine
Medgar Evers, not two months later,
the pulse of the kitchen light
reaching through the bullet hole in the window
to flicker on his skin,
the one struck down on the night
of the year's first Lyrids, the meteors
that seem to fall from the guitar in the sky
like change passersby have thrown
through the sound hole, the other
as the coins rang again on the dome of night,
and Zimmerman in the graveyard
where he taught Johnson how to listen,
looking up through the trees and playing
until the dew had fallen on him again
and he felt a music in his fingers

he hadn't known for years....
Maybe this is not what he meant,
Ovid or Onomacritus or Ike
or whatever his name was
when he told me the story
of the original bluesman
that night at the bar in Mississippi,
but this is how I remember it
when I see him, turning slowly
in the neon, as he reaches through the crowd,
everyone reaching, gathering
beneath the fingernails, this is what I remember
when he leans his head back
and I can see the beat of the artery
in his neck, this is what I hear
when I listen to the light
pulsing on his skin.

Letter Already Broadcast into Space

—To Sun Ra, from Earth

You are not here,

you are not here
in Birmingham,
where they keep your name,

not in Elmwood's famous plots
or the monuments
of bronze or steel or the strew

of change in the fountain
where the fire hoses sprayed.

In the furnaces,
in the interchange sprawl
that covers Tuxedo Junction,

in the shopping malls
they've forgotten you,

the broadcast towers, the barbecues,

the statue of the Roman god,
spiculum blotting out
part of the stars.

To get it dark enough,
I have to fold back
into the hills, into the trees

where my parents
planted me, where the TV
barely reaches and I drift

with my hand on the dial
of my father's radio,

spinning, too, the tall antenna
        he raised above the pines.

I have to stand at the base

                of the galvanized
pole I can use as an azimuth
        and plot you in.

The hunter's belt is slung again,
        and you are there

in the pulse, in the light of
        Alnitak, Alnilam, Mintaka,

all your different names,

                you are there
in all the rearrangements
        of the stars.

                        Come down now,
come down again,

                like the late fall light
into the mounds along the creek,

        light that soaks like a flood
to show the Cherokee sitting upright
                underground, light

like the fire they imply.

        Come down now
into the crease the freight train
                hits like a piano's hammer

and make the granite hum
        beneath.

Come down now

as my hand slips from the dial,
tired again of looking
for the sound of another way

to say everything.

Come down now with your diction
and your dictionary.

Come down now like the stars
and help me rise.

I have forgot my wings.

Postscript (Already Breaking in Distant Echoes)

—To Sun Ra, from Earth

Other sun among other suns,

clavinet wave
in the Moog sine of the stars,

tell me, Uncle Elsewhere,

when I lift my prayer into the night,
how far

does it have to go, how far back,
Alnitak, a millennium,

or Vega, twenty years away,

how long past
this future I await,
and how old,

if it returns, your music,
your answer, your wave?

If you are there,

in the light, behind it, if
you are there,

tell me

how to turn the dial
or the dish

or the tall antenna my father raised,

tell me how

to turn my head to listen,

and how, at last,

to tell the past from the future

if they both arrive.

Letter Written on a Hundred Dollar Bill

—To Howlin' Wolf, from Mississippi

Did your right hand itch when I transcribed your *O*
don't you hear me cryin? phrase I'd pay a hundred dollars
to raise my voice into, cause you got money for sure,
not like Son House in the nightclub film, drunk
as a goat glutted with rotten apples and waving a sawbuck
like a flag, but stacking up in a New York office
like a locomotive's chimney if I keep this going
and then I imagine raining down into the world below
or uncurling on a magnolia only you know
how to find, my hundred plucked, still crisp,
then rolled up in your pocket as you walk again
from White Station and West Point to Grenada,
Ruleville, Rosedale with a guitar on your back,
where you meet Charley Patton again.
You pull out the bankroll and count off a Cadillac
so y'all can cruise to Memphis, St. Louis, Chicago,
unpack at the 708 or Silvio's and maybe House
is already there at the bar, rediscovered
and thirsty for oblivion, when Sumlin walks in
with Dixon and you're ready to pitch it again,
and the microphones are humming so you can invent
rock-and-roll or whatever it is Eric Clapton
tries to play in that London session when you take over,
showing him that music is a kind of language,
you just say this, you just call roosters and cats
and airplane pilots into the club, the whole
Wang Dang Doodle of the afterlife catching your notes
like undampered pianos and sounding long after
you've gone down the blue highways back to Jackson,
Nashville, Lebanon where your girl stands in the door
of the house you kept together as peaceful and bright
as the day you met, you're gathering everyone you know
and rolling down to Natchez where the fire
hasn't ashed the Rhythm Club and the whole town's
waiting for you to take the stage, maybe costumed
like an engineer or busking like a janitor,
the mic taped to a broom handle, the sheet-metal walls
shaking when you let out your *O*,

O there is no sound like this in the world above
except the one you engraved in the great disc of the night
that spins above us, through the hole of which
every C-note floats to bud from that one magnolia
somewhere in east Mississippi where this sound was born.
When you walk down the dirt roads each night,
when you pull your hands from your pockets, the lint
turns everything first-Spring green,
and when you open your song you light the underworld
with a throat and a mouth full of gold.

Dear Brother,

Hank Williams dreams the unknown grave of Rufus Payne

You can keep on knocking
but you can't

make a sound. The door's
been torn and only

a hole's been left in the frame,
the sound of one hand

keeping time against the air.
Keep on till the knothole

or the bung falls out and all
the beer, all the spirit

spills to the ground, for all those
who can't be here anymore.

Come Tee-Tot, come teeter
ridgepole and spine

to watch the crawdads scumble
in the mud, riverboats

knocked slow in the river's groove,
scuttles wider

than the mouth on a 45
or a gun or a whiskey bottle

that only spills out tea.
Keep on knocking

till the roof falls open,
a song as old as anyone alive

shambled off the edge of a dime
        on a doorstep in Georgiana

to my own once-shy ears.
        Come home, Tee-Tot,

come and answer the door,
        the chimney, this hailstorm

of singles with that Storyville
        song once spilled

from the holes
        in Jelly Roll's face.

Shut me up with the bucket
        and the washboard and the harp

and the cymbals on your knees,
        then set me to sing again.

Come home, dear brother,
        or tell me where

to meet you in that city
        where there is no pain.

Cookin' With The Miles Davis Quintet

You've seen it in pictures, in photographs
        I mean, Davis wreathed in smoke
that hangs like jasmine or kudzu or silence
                in the listening air,

        in the studio or the felt-
curtained night-club or the cookhouse
                with its yellow bulb
and its fly-strips and its stereo so old

it still plays just the old LPs, needle
                delicate, tender,
tentative, it seems, in the groove, Davis
        leaning in to the microphone

                or the cigarette
or the flame on the cover of *Steamin'*,
        the match striking heartwood
and hickory, a needle over its groove,

as if time forgot itself in that peregrine
        stare, as if Davis was about to
tell time to take the night off, tell time it
                had been fired, had been replaced,

        about to tell time, when he got
around to it, when the cigarette was gone
                and he took his breath
and raised the horn to his mouth, the smoke

still etched in air, as if to say,
                there are all kinds of time,
there are many kinds of time, my funny
        valentine, I can hold this

                moment all night long.
The smoke is sweet. Fireflies and stars
        have broken twice since the match
first tongued its word to wood, since

the pit first spoke, and now salt,
vinegar, pepper barb the shoulder's,
the brisket's savor. The smoke is sweet,
and it hangs in the air

like memory, like history,
like childhood's first flavor, childhood's first
mouthful of not enough,
and it may seem the smoke has sweetened the air

ever since you were born, since you learned
to breathe, because
all the lights are low, it's after midnight,
and you've been here since yesterday

and you've been cooking since
yesterday and the yesterday before,
and even then it seemed the fire,
it seemed the flavor had had no beginning,

that you woke, that you were born into this smoke
before the first tree fell, before
the first tomato blossomed, before
uncelebrated hands

rubbed chili into the meat, before
the first hog was slopped, the first ear of corn,
the first acorn folded
into the future, it was already late,

already early, you were, you are already
in two places at once,
in the corn-crib, in the crib, at the pit,
in the stye or the feed-lot

or the field watching
yourself watch the pit, and it may seem
to anyone else that the smoke
isn't moving, that you aren't moving,

but you know you're listening to the wood,
the embers breaking down like
Philly Joe Jones on the skins on "Airegin"
and "Blues After Five"

when everything will be done,
when the flavor will be clear, will be one
perfect note with all
the other notes inside it, opening

on the tongue, opening so quickly
anyone would turn
to the clock and tell it to take the night
off. There are all kinds of time.

The smoke is sweet,
you've seen it in the films, in the photos,
the light caught within it just before
it burns away, like music, as Eric

Dolphy said, after you hear it, it's gone,
in air, the air become music,
become smoke, become a history
of flavor, a book

of memory waiting to be read.
When that smoke is gone, it's folded
into the tongue
that can tell the story again, the smoke

that gathered honey on the tongue, a story,
a ghost, ready to flame
over the tongue, over the pit, as you keep
your face to the light, your back

to the camera, keeping
your quiet so still it may seem
you've fallen into sleep, but, you know,
there are all kinds of time, and you're just waiting

for the moment to ripen into right
so the flavor of all that waiting,
so all that time can flower on the tongue
like language, so every word

will be yours, so you will know
just what to say, you will know why your tongue
is weighted, you can tell
how eloquence smiles in quiet.

Language Mixology

Half brother of the same halves,
simulacra is fancy for "absent."

Like banging means "good"
or off the chain means "good."

The same way off the hook forgets
the phone, I'm forgetting the space

between Oregon and North
Carolizzay, daylight savings time

and the addition of the "-izzay."
So silly that suffix, verbed blackface

for black folks. So here you are
bouncing verbs without the face

paint like an empty room bounces
echoes: "The Mulatto Question,"

a question of remixing our name
or re-envisioning our cliché

like Bonz Malone saying, *Life*
is beautiful. It's just the shit in it

that's fucked up over vocals keys
looped like a fishhook. Didn't he know

piano is necessary in any mulatto blues?
Black key for one woman or white

key for two women. You should
be writing and that combination

is feminine. We've got a disputed
lineage, like Arizona before

Estevancio named it. We've got all
kinds of folks acting like Estevancio,

get it? Mixed man, mixed man,
states weren't called states, even though

the pedigreed mountains, the high-
styling lizards were already in place.

Seven Days of Falling

Today, I'm assimilating like margarine
into hotcakes. I'm getting down

like Danny LaRusso after the against-
the-rules leg sweep. So low,

I'll be a flower in common decency's
lapel. Factual, the same way "Zanzibar"

means sea of blacks to anyone who isn't
from there. Where is Juan Valdez,

his burroesque dependability when
you need him? I had a friend who minted

t-shirts with Juan front and center,
an afro instead of a sombrero, a power

fist in place of a smile. The inscription:
100% Colombian. I'm going the way

of skin—radio waves, thoughts
like ear-to-ear transmissions grounded

into the ozone on the way from mindless
space to forgetful Earth. Man, my skin

doesn't need me any more than mold
needs cheese. On this day of cellophane

lunchboxes and hand grenades reshaping
my palms into their own militaristic orbit,

there are only oceans to catch me.
On this day, something needs

to catalogue me: a hall monitor
doubled wide by ambition,

a goldfish with thumbs hitchhiking
toward a fishbowl full of dub.

This Be The Verse

It is the 21st century.
—Radiohead

This is the skin they put me in,
my mum and dad. Remixed melanin,

olio for the asthmatic and colorblind.
See how it bronzes on command.

See how my hybrided daughter looks
darker while on the beach with me.

If my skin was a chicken wing,
I'd lick my eyebrows before

code switching inflections.
If my skin were a woman, I'd check

my leopard print steering wheel
at the door. I'd transform my crust

of rust and sea salt into something
more 21st Century. Borges said,

Things belong to the past quite quickly,
so I'd throw some butane on my funk

transistors. Face paint my brown
band aid convocation. Toss my sweaty

"Free South Africa" muscle shirt
to the crowd at the recycling bin.

I'd leave it to the ghetto fabulous
to ID the magical backspin of skin.

WHEELS OF STEEL (METAL FACE VILLAIN MIX)

I got me two songs instead of eyes—
all swollen & blacked out like the day

after a lost fight. Two chop saws spinning,
buzzing the backdrop for woodshop or emcee,

bar mitzvah or afterset. *I read the fine print*
& be like, "What's the big deal?" I spun

wheels-of-steel since broke wheel Big Wheels
with shined up rims still spinning after the ride

stops. Dubs kind of grind like me in their perpetuity
because *a little grease always keeps the wheels*

a spinning, like sitting on twenty-threes to get
the squeelers grinning. I'm the Wizard of Oz

if Oz was a fish fry in July. Call me Master
of the Cracked Fingers. One song spins forward,

the other back to repeat itself: *"Doo-doo-doo-*
doo-doo!" That's a audio daily double." Doo-

doo-doo-doo-doo!" That's the audio daily...
Baby, I'm the layaway payment on a Ferris wheel.

My songs orbit parking lots & rent parties
like the crazy lady's eyes when she finds out

her lover man already left: she be like *Tripping*
off the beat kinda, dripping off the meat grinder.

Tripping off of my song spinning backward,
while the other plays forward like sugar mixing

in to make the grape. My joints are the pinwheels
in this parade of moonwalks & uprocks: *I'm like*

"Hi, there." Y'all play the rear. This whole year
my year. This whole year my year.

Tyndall Armory

Public Enemy had no idea of what
to do on a stage in 1987, but we
didn't know what to do as rap crowd either.
Attendance was mandatory, jammed
into the Tyndall Armory, one night
after amateur boxing and one night
before bingo. A bunch of homeboys
kenti-ed together with African medallions,
graffiti spray-painted jeans—all of us
mad at the conspiracy of conspiracy,
staring each other down with a circular
anger only black men can justify.
Terminator X—his one-handed power
fist cut and scratch already perfected—
was the only thing keeping the revolution
from starting right there. Bass lines, warning
sirens transformed into samples refusing
The Wop like the black maître
at the Highlands Country Club refused
to seat black people. My friend Richard
was determined to be the first black
president, refused wine coolers and weed,
white women and white lines because
the man could hold anything against him
during a campaign. As president,
he would buy Highlands and turn it into
a black thing. Terminator X had Rich
ready to say *peace* to the presidency
and Nat Turner the first patch of white
he saw. And when Chuck D mugged
the stage, African medallion swinging
like left hooks, baseball cap pulled down
so low his eyes were the idea of eyes,
the heat in that room was enough to make
any Tom reconsider his friendships.

I sense my own limit

when I die
will someone please
keep me alive
in Second Life
my password
to all things
is *pipedream!*
don't forget
the exclamation
point and feel
free to bring
flowers
fuck
the sniper
in the mall
I leave
a hole
in everything

FROM FLOWERS OF RAD

two trailer park girls go round the outside
was all I took from that decade
that saccharine blip
in which I was supposed to become a man
I still wonder how something that stunning
was flung from the torpor
but there they are
the language and those two girls entwined
like certain trees I remember
or the faces of adults during sex
tortured and sublime at the same time
the way some storms seem to call you
and all you can do is sit on the screened-in porch and watch
letting its power settle over you
until it ceases and the Earth smells like a secret
me vs. the 90s
equals a bloodbath of mistakes
churning out this man-cherub
full of debt and poems and friends
ill-equipped to deal with the world on its terms
but pretty much riding it like a wave on mine
I was a supernova
a girl in a field
a pink bull full of arrows
angelic if you call perpetually falling a trait
fairly invincible by super-hero standards
my superpower would be
to be loved by everyone
all at once
my trailer park girls
let me see your lighters in the air

FROM FLOWERS OF RAD

I want to write a poem as long as California
like lying on a couch forever
as a serious man takes notes on your dreams in a little book
maybe I mean I want to talk forever
but is there even a difference anyway
like my uncle who went walking
and never stopped
or that day on the LA Freeway
when a horse got loose, people freaking out
cars honking and skidding
and me and my sister rooting for the horse
who I still imagine, 20 years later
trotting around the freeway
a living argument against time
as people drive right past her
without even noticing a horse
she keeps on, at home in the gridlock
a phenomenon in the smog
we want to think she is looking for something
but she is past panic now
content, her heart a part of that freeway
unaware that I
am the one telling this story
and in this version
no one listens to anyone's dreams
and that couch is the one we came on
while your parents were gone
blood on the cushion
which wouldn't come out
no matter what we tried
so we gave up
and just laid there, sweating
in the bliss of thinking nothing
and somewhere
a startled horse
is not smashed by a semi
on the LA Freeway
on a summer day in 1988

FROM HUMAN WEEK

wrap a t-shirt
around my head
and head
into battle
the kitchen
a necropolis
of knives
and pale apologies
butt-dials
to co-workers
and my blood
on the cutting-board
better believe
I do more
than spread
cream cheese
with these
civil war swords
now put down
that iron
and kneel
to the fucking king
of forgetting

FROM HUMAN WEEK

stuck between
wife &
goddamn
I take
the road
with the most
dust
wires crackle
and hum
the grackles
disband
in a black fan
shot-through
with sun
I pretend
is you
heading
south
without a shirt
feeling lonely
but brave
because
you can't forget
the way
to
no home

OUR LIFE, THIS TEMPORARY ECLIPSE / TO THAT OTHER

at the party I say
a bunch of historical shit
that never gets recorded
the world felt
as a presence
reminds me
of a field
of pool tables
due to a deficiency
my friend
thinks the ocean
is green
he is a genius
plumber
in the Times
people die
of sadness
it is beautiful
outside
yo clouds
what the fuck
is up

Imaginary August

If one stood perfectly still. Even in the withering hours

of then. Hair down to here. Being alive and quiet.

One could forget oneself. Forget what one didn't even recognize.

How mad it felt. Subliminally. One could pick out goldfinches

and mourning cloaks among the dying stalks of cosmos,

and across the ditch of grey wastewater they use to irrigate

the burial ground, a young man in a late-flowering tree

taking our photograph.

Imaginary Morning Glory

Whether or not the water was freezing. The body
would break its sheathe. Without layer on layer
of feather and air to insulate the loving belly.
A cloudy film surrounding the point of entry. If blue
were not blue how could love be love. But if the body
were made of rings. A loose halo would emerge
in the telluric light. If anyone were entrusted to verify
this rare occurrence. As the petal starts to
dwindle and curl unto itself and only then. Love,
blue. Hallucinogenic blue, love.

Imaginary June

Night: wears itself away   clouds too dense to skim
over the sheer granite rim   only a moment before
someone sitting in a mission chair   convinced 101%
convinced   she could see into her very cells
with her unassisted eyes   even into extremophiles
even with the light dispelled   until the mind sets sail
into its private interval of oblivion   a hand falls from its lap
a pen drops to a carpet   a stand of leaves whispers as if
to suggest something tender   yet a potentially heart robbing
sequel: to a dream in which faces flare up   fuse   dissolve
but there is a lot of color before their vanishing   and a name
for such phenomena   that comes from the belly of a lamb
rather   not a lamb anymore   from the stomach
of a particular canny but kind: blind-from-birth ewe

Imaginary Waterfall

You could ask any one of them up by the lake
It had presence

Fold of coldness folded over cold

The rumors of what was beyond
mostly worthless

You had to take into account who was telling
the story and

for whose ends

Against the dark of her intuition
an unrelenting stream

of light starting to set like cement

some mildew tingeing the dream since

its uniform had not been
properly kept

Where her love stood

until he stepped behind the overhang
the synesthesia of his name

a silver helmet ringing
when struck

Afterparty

for Abelardo, Amber, & Mindy

It's the frost's decade to loose a shadow

down from the bridge above

to supply the cut of our looking

with some method to freeze it.

So felled and it's fleeting

but the word on the soiled

page here wants it out

with us, not to be known

or said aloud among friends

but to induce a look into

desire's stony grasp

on our own dreaming.

Or to simply shut up by speaking

through a word to the lisp

of the wet world, dozing off

on a northbound train

however much we're faking the way

we had wanted others to touch

what's left of what we think

needs it.

It's a good, bad, limpsey night

& that's probably got to do with

why you want to get inside it

while you're standing in its hollow.

Some call it weather or getting there.

Maybe it's a delay or a botched departure—

I call it music coming up through

the flooring, the pleased work of

touching at the car keys in your purse

while you're standing there in

the jetway corridor, watching somebody

watch somebody talk softly

at another who's not there.

Though what's missing is not the dead

as they're in the words spoken out

now ventriloquising us, happily

jawing to a slaver with drinks

under nice light, more music.

Maybe it's not us versus the dead animals.

Maybe it's us versus what we've learned

to tamp down or stave off like so much coastal water.

That unfastening from whatever lay beyond
the word might yet hope to expose
just what was risked in hoping to find
ourselves in another.
& that what I called missing was only
steeping or unbuttoning itself
like a song from one on a bus to
another, a strange moment between
strangers, because the song's words' rhythms'
ineluctable force was dripping between us
like so much dripping.
The story I'd held onto in private
went something like this:
The phone in the motel rings
as I'm in the shower & there's a knock also
on the wall or door & children
from the parking lot are crying out in
laughter at a game or suspended humiliation.
When I come out, there's nobody but a couple
of drunk teenagers in the hall quarreling.
Desire's a bit of gleaming in the decanter,
some nickel of lust set before you

with nothing left to operate that still functions much.
As if to say we probably shouldn't touch the top
of this lake with our hands or discuss the very coin
of what opens
want's passage seemingly out of our own bodies
and directly at another, namely, you.
But we might as well go ahead and split apart at
the almost of it, to court the ruler of it, right?
Some modicum of untoward commands
from an elsewhere we have only three or four hundred
thousand scant, dusty words for:
spilling forth like a child's clumsy wish
as if uncoiling a secret from a photograph
of a cross-cut trunk of words to stifle
the peculiar gap between what you want
& what you wanted & what it's like
to get to dance to some old music
in the dark with some choice activating
from without. & like there's somebody standing there
next to the doorway, not actually awaiting some other,
& still wanting it.

JOE MESSINGER IS DREAMING

This is the highest step in the world.

That's what it says, the hand-lettered sign that the engineers made. They've set it at the bottom of the short flight of metal stairs on the gantry of the cramped gondola of Excelsior III. It's 1960, and Excelsior III is an extreme high-altitude balloon. It's a weather balloon that's been repurposed for carrying out near-space experiments, in preparation for manned space flight by U.S. astronauts. The stairs lead nowhere now. The balloon, with the gondola dangling below it like a sack of groceries, has departed. It departed at five a.m. sharp. It's now just a little past eight in morning. 0800 in military time. Joe Messinger rides in the gondola.

This is the highest step in the world.

~ ~ ~

Joe Messinger, as a boy of nine, stood without trembling at the edge of the great limestone cliff that overhung the Seneca River near his house. His parents lived on a sixty-acre farm nestled in a bend of the broad, shallow river outside of the town of Mount Nebo, the county seat. The rocks that lined the river's bottom, worn smooth by years of the water's running, by decades and centuries of it, shone like coins in the last of the day's light, from where Joe Messinger looked down on them. The cliff was four hundred feet tall.

Joe Messinger, with his toes at the crumbling edge of the cliff, gazed on the river and its gloriously smooth stones, stones lapped one over the other in the river's bed like the scales on a snake's back, and he felt as though he might be four hundred and four and one-half feet tall. He felt like the greatest giant ever to walk the earth.

He could see clear across the Seneca Valley, across his family's place, which sat at the base of the cliff, which looked tiny from so far up, a series of tidily-arranged squares and rectangles, some planted in corn, some in alfalfa, some in succulent timothy grass, some populated by strolling sheep. His collie dog trotted to and fro among the sheep, keeping order. In the smooth air over the valley, suspended between heaven and earth, the great birds, the vultures, went gliding on supple wings.

He could see all the way to the ridges on the western edge of the valley, which he knew marked the county line. Beyond those ridges bulked others that were higher, and others even higher beyond those, in dull-edged rows marching off to the curve of the earth. Above them, the rolling sky, the unbroken clouds as serene and friendly and slow-moving as the sheep in his father's fields. He was aware that such vistas made other people afraid. He was aware that heights frightened his father, who wasn't frightened of much of anything. It seemed odd to Joe Messinger, who wasn't particularly brave in other ways, that he should feel no fear of falling. It seemed wonderful. He closed his eyes and stretched out his arms and imagined leaning forward into the wind that blew straight into his face, a wind of ten knots, perhaps fifteen, brisk up here at the edge of the precipice, bracing as the flat of a hand against Joe Messinger's cheek. He imagined leaning out into the wind, imagined that the wind would hold him up – that he could lean out, how far? A few degrees? Twenty? Forty? Until his entire body hung hovering over the abyss, and nothing visible to hold him there.

If the wind were strong enough, and if he leaned far enough, could he float? Could he fly? Like a predator bird? Like an angel? He had no thought of dying, and no fear of falling. He had climbed up the narrow trail to the cliff-top by himself, a strong little boy, determined, compact and muscular, with clear, far-seeing eyes.

Joe Messinger's father was the county constable. He wore a big Colt's .44 revolver on his hip when he did the county's business, and a brown, wide-brimmed hat. He wore a badge on the lapel of his long brown coat. In the county, if you had a problem, he was the man to see. But his authority ended at the county line. Past that, he was just a good strong man who lived in a poor little valley in a poor little state in the poorest region of a wealthy nation. Joe Messinger looked to the west. Past that first ridge line was a world that didn't know his father.

Between that first ridge line and the next, he surmised, there must be a valley very much like this one. Maybe there was a man who lived in that valley, like Joe Messinger's father, who was important there and unknown beyond the ridges. Maybe there was a boy there, looking eastward from the ridge's summit. Maybe that boy was looking at the place where Joe Messinger stood at the edge of his cliff. Maybe they were looking at each other. He wished he could see the boy across all that distance. He wished he could hear that boy's voice, which was likely quite like his own, reedy and ready, soon, to break.

This is the highest step in the world.

Step out into nothing, Joe Messinger.

~ ~ ~

Air Force Captain Joe Messinger perches stoic and immobile in the gondola of Excelsior III, his expression serene and deeply serious behind the glare shield of his helmet. He's a handsome fellow, though it's impossible to tell that from looking at him in his bulky environment suit. He looks as ungainly as the Michelin man. He looks comical, but he's never been more solemn in his life. No sane man could do what he is about to do. No sane man, fully awake and aware, could undertake the task that Joe Messinger is about to undertake, to step out of safety and into the air.

Joe Messinger is awake, but Joe Messinger is dreaming.

~ ~ ~

Colonel John Paul Stabb wears his full dress uniform, and he grips the sides of the podium before him, referring liberally to his notes as he speaks.

"I recruited Captain Joseph A. Messinger for Project Man-High five years ago, in 1955," says the colonel. "It's an Air Force endeavor to test the limits of man's endurance in, or at the lower limits of, outer space. At the moment, Captain Messinger occupies the gondola of the Excelsior III, floating above the earth at its peak altitude of one hundred and two thousand eight hundred feet. It has taken him just over three hours to reach this altitude."

Joe Messinger is dreaming, and in his dream, he can hear the colonel perfectly. He does not need a radio to know what is being said about him on the surface of the earth, unimaginably far below.

"Joe Messinger will stay with Excelsior III at peak altitude for approximately ten minutes. And then he will jump."

Do you hear him, Joe Messinger? He says you'll jump.

Joe Messinger blinks. When a man leaves the congenial atmosphere of Earth behind, apparently, he leaves behind human chronology and physics as well. He can see across the gulfs of time and space. He can hear the voices of those who love him. He can dream without sleeping. Are these the effects of increased radiation at extreme high altitude? These are just the sorts of things that he is here to experience. He will have to report to the colonel on these anomalies. When he reaches the ground, in just a few minutes' time.

"Captain Messinger will free-fall for four and one-half minutes. He will fall eighty-five thousand feet during that time. He will reach speeds of over six hundred miles per hour, nearly the speed of sound. Without an airplane, ladies and gentlemen!"

In Joe Messinger's dream, the colonel sounds remarkably like a carnival barker. Joe Messinger has always liked and admired the colonel, but he finds him faintly ridiculous when he waxes bombastic. "At approximately seventeen thousand feet, he will deploy his main chute, after which – it is profoundly to be hoped – he will float safely to the ground."

Do you hear him? He says you're going to fall.

"Let's all applaud the bravery of this singular man, Air Force Captain Joseph Messinger, shall we, ladies and gentlemen?"

~ ~ ~

Years after he stood at the cliff's verge, on one of his first solo cross-country flight in the little yellow rented J3 Cub, Joe Messinger passed over the rectangles of his father's farm, swung the plane over the boxy farmhouse. With him was his current girl, the beautiful Margaret, who later that night will give herself to him entirely, her body, her spirit. She will become pregnant. They will marry. Margaret had never been in an airplane before, and the sight of the places she knew so far below her thrilled and terrified her, left her helpless and adoring of her pilot, her Joe.

Joe's mother, still lovely, the skin still firm and tight on her bones, looked up from where she knelt digging in her garden plot and waved at him, at them and their tiny wooden plane. Joe waggled the Cub's fabric-covered wings flirtatiously at her.

His father sat in a low chair, his hat – the one he wore when he worked

– pulled down over his brow. He had left the valley for the South Pacific, Recon Marines, a few years after Joe Messinger stood on the cliff and looked across the valley, and there he got blown up by a Jap hand grenade. Lost his left leg from the knee down. Couple of fingers off his left hand. His left nut. He waved at Joe too, with his good hand. It made him happy to see the bright yellow plane pass over his place. It made him happy to see a plane that wasn't trying to shoot at him, that wasn't trying to shoot at anybody. Any day where nobody was trying to kill him was a good day. He watched the cruciform shadow of the J3 as it passed over his neat fields on its way to somewhere else.

He was still the constable, Joe Messinger's father, but they had hired a deputy for him. County commission hired the guy. A young fellow, served in the European theater and didn't get blown up. Didn't get a scratch. He was on his way up. He was going to be somebody in the Seneca Valley, someday soon. Joe Messinger's father was glad to have the help.

Joe Messinger pointed his plane to the west, circling and climbing, climbing and circling, until he passed over the ridge that he had spied from the cliff's edge years before. He made sure to pass over it right at the spot where he had imagined that other boy, the one just like him, the one that was looking at him. He wanted the boy to see the airplane. He wanted the boy to see his girl, to see Margaret: the melting expression on her face as they passed through the wisps of cloud, her lush figure, the desire written on her face.

One day Joe Messinger would go to war in an airplane, but that day was not this day. The engine of the Cub strained and whined. The wings thrummed. He was gaining altitude as he departed from his father's county.

~ ~ ~

"You're all clapping for my father, aren't you?" asks Katherine Messinger, called Kitty, sixteen years old and pretty as a picture. Joe Messinger can see her clear as day from the gondola that hangs beneath the converted weather balloon, twenty miles above the earth. He can hear her as clearly as though she were in the gondola and speaking right to him. More clearly, in fact, because her voice is not muffled by the thick helmet of plastic and metal. "People clap for him a lot. I don't know why, exactly. He always tells me that what he does is classified."

She's a painfully good-looking girl, slender as a young birch, with strong slim legs and a narrow waist. Her skirt is prim and swirls stiffly around her calves when she moves. Her face is flushed with excitement and worry. Is she a virgin? Joe Messinger can hardly bear to think about the answer to that question. It's not possible to stay pure for long in this world. He wasn't a virgin at her age, though her mother was, he believes. He was a dashing fellow, a burgeoning pilot, a good-looking kid, the son of a powerful man in the county. Clearly headed for someplace else, clearly going beyond the narrow confines of the Seneca Valley – but where?

If he had told them then, those high-breasted little damsels who gave him what he wanted, if he had told them that he was going to fall to earth from more than one hundred thousand feet in the air, fall from the very edge of space – would they have believed him? They would have laughed and slapped at him in a playful way as he tugged at their clothes, and they would have sighed and gone ahead and surrendered their virtue to him, dreaming (while awake) of something well outside of that place, and never imagining the truth, never imagining how far away the truth would take him. Kitty's mother Margaret had been just such a one. He had been her first. And her only. So he believed.

"When I told my history teacher what my father did for a living," Kitty says, "that he did classified things for the Air Force, he said my father was a hero."

Did you hear that, Joe Messinger? A hero!

"But that's in 1960. You're all living in the future." Who could she be talking to? She's speaking to the future. Her own children, perhaps? He struggles to imagine her married, his innocent little Kitty, imagine her pregnant, imagine her telling stories about him to her children, his grandchildren. Is that who she's speaking to? Or to some posterity that lies beyond the confines of his family? It occurs to him that it may be that, once a man has left the atmosphere, once a man has learned to see through time and across space as he has, perhaps all men are simultaneously freed from the bondage of the standard dimensions. He has been liberated, and his liberation has freed the world. What a discovery!

"You've never heard of my father," she says. "You've never heard of Joe Messinger. Probably by now… Probably in the future everybody's been to outer space. It's probably no big thing anymore."

That's what they promised us, those men in sterile white lab coats and horn-rimmed glasses, unamused under their flat-top haircuts. The men who wrote the sign: *This is the highest step in the world.* They promised us flying cars. Personal submersible watercraft. Robots and ray guns. X-ray glasses, so that we could conveniently see through the clothes of good-looking girls. All the items offered in the ads in the back of the comic books: they were supposed to have come true by now. Where are they, Joe Messinger? Where is my hovercar?

~ ~ ~

"Eight minutes!" cries Colonel Stabb.

And on the earth far below you, Joe Messinger, the earth that hangs like a lamp at your feet, in the year 1960, when your daughter is sixteen and maybe still a virgin: great adversity between the nations, and perplexity, roaring like the sea's mighty waves. Those mountains that seemed endlessly tall when you were a boy, the cliff that it took you hours to scale, the valley that seemed so broad – they are invisible below the clouds that blanket the planet, as far as the eye can see. If you could see those mountains, that cliff, they would barely register in your vision. What is a mountain that's three thousand feet tall, four thousand, five, when you are a hundred thousand feet in the air? That cliff on which you stood, on which you were a giant – it wouldn't make a footstool for you now.

Still the voices come to him. He is dreaming in the air, and they are dreaming of him far below: his daughter, and the colonel. The tops of the clouds – they are so like the cloud bottoms that day on the cliff. They seem to be moving peacefully across the face of the earth, but he knows that the winds down there are wicked and violent and may well shortly tear him to pieces. Joe Messinger is looking down, and he was looking up on that earlier day, but the view is quite similar. Rising and falling – if the distance is sufficient, they are much the same.

"When I was a kid, there was a war in Korea," says Kitty.

"Joe Messinger will fall through a layer of clouds more than a mile thick!" bellows the colonel.

Fearful sights and great signs will appear in the heavens when the end times come. Do you see them dancing around you, Joe Messinger, where you dangle in the sky? Are you one of them yourself?

"They say there will be another war soon," says Kitty.

The Colonel continues, his stentorian voice nearly drowning out Kitty's soft soprano. If he keeps on shouting, Joe Messinger will awake. Joe Messinger very much wants to remain asleep. "And after returning safely to the surface of the planet, Captain Joe Messinger will fly nearly five hundred missions, in three combat tours of Vietnam. Which is a country where there is not yet a war in which we are involved. That's in the future, like the forgetting of Joe Messinger's name."

Kitty will not give up. She means to be heard. "They say this next war will be fought with nuclear bombs. They say this next one will kill everybody in the whole world."

Famines, plagues, and earthquakes. Much better to be up here, yes, Joe Messinger? Where it's quiet, and calm, and unfrightening, for at least a little while yet. The thought of falling cannot frighten you. What comes after the fall, the return to earth, boots on the ground again and looking into the faces of those who love you – yes, that can make even a man like you afraid. But the sleep before the fall, and the fall itself, those are sweet as milk with honey stirred into it. What you used to drink before bed, warmed by your mother. Before you climbed into the upper bunk in your room, there to sleep until morning and the crowing of the cock.

"Except for the cockroaches, which will survive," says Kitty. "I hate cockroaches. The cockroaches will become gigantic and intelligent, and they'll be the next species to inherit the earth, they will be the next race of men, because they're hardy and they breed so fast." Cockroaches! Where do kids get this stuff? She is describing some movie she has seen, he supposes. She has quite the imagination, his little girl.

He pictures her in the movie house, and it's not the movie house near their suburban home. It's the old Princess Theater in Mount Nebo, the one from the 20s, the only movie theater in Seneca County. Decorated like the tombs of the ancient pharaohs, golden columns and twelve-foot-tall statues of half-nude gods and goddesses, Osiris and Isis and Anubis and Ra – unreadable faces with high cheekbones and mascaraed eyes. It's been shut down for twenty years, but still that's where he pictures her, her figure dimly lit with the flickering of the projector's arc lamp. Is she there with someone? Is there a boy slouching in the seat beside her? Is his arm across her shoulders, is he touching her? Is she resisting or is she yielding?

Recall those nights in the upper bunk, far above the floor of your humble room. Where it is very quiet, and no one can reach you. Where you have a few moments to think.

"Do you imagine cockroaches can fall in love?" Kitty wants to know. Is she asking him, or the listeners from the future? She used to ask him all manner of things, and most often he knew the answers, and when he didn't, he made them up and she was satisfied with what he told her. How to answer this new line of questions? Cockroaches and love. He knows as much about one, he supposes, as he does about the other. "Intelligent mutant cockroaches," she says. "Maybe they wouldn't breed so fast, if they had to love somebody first. Love another cockroach."

"Six minutes!" shouts Colonel Stabb.

"I think I'm in love, Daddy!"

All these are the beginnings of sorrow, Joe Messinger, and the love of many will turn cold.

~ ~ ~

Margaret Messinger isn't out of her bathrobe yet. Eight in the morning and it looks like she has just rolled out of bed. Joe Messinger always rises at first light – sometimes, frequently in fact, before first light – but Margaret likes her beauty sleep. This is how Joe Messinger likes her best, warm from the unmade marriage bed, housecoat barely covering her sumptuous figure. She's not young, but she's still a great tumble.

She snaps a smart salute toward Joe. She can't know where he is, can she? His mission is highly classified. No man can make such a jump when others are watching. It's a private thing, this leap from twenty miles up. Beyond the atmosphere, though, it seems that nothing is private anymore.

They can see him, and he can see them, and it's as if there's no distance between them at all.

"Love you, Captain. Love you … Joe," Margaret says. Her voice surprises him. It's full of static and echoes, and there are gaps in the transmission. Data loss.

"He goes to the Air Force Academy, Daddy." Kitty interrupts her mother. It's something she does frequently of late. Sorrow, to those who bear children in those days! "The boy I'm in love with. Mother adores him."

She is still a virgin. He can hear it in her voice. But she won't be for long. He can hear that too. He has the sense that he's watching his own life from on high, watching it repeat itself. The boy, the girl, the Air Force. The leap that's coming.

~ ~ ~

"Joe? Where are you, Joe?" Margaret asks. Why, of all these people, is she the least able to apprehend him, where he is, what he's doing? "I know you're high in the air. You're always high in the air. Can you see me from where you are?" She's calling out as though she's blind. He can barely hear her, barely understand.

Of course I can see you, Margaret. I can see all the world, I can see everything, and you are at the heart of it.

"I know you'll love him too," Kitty tells Joe in a whisper.

Margaret says to Kitty, "A father can't ever really love the man who marries his little girl, you know. He can like him, he can respect him, he can even admire him – but he can never love his rival."

"That's silly, Mother," Kitty says. "Rival?"

"Yes, baby. Don't you know? The man you marry will be your father's greatest rival. His rival for your love. You're the great love of his life, Kitty!"

"But that's you, Mother. You're the great love of his life."

Margaret laughs, and the laughter is tinged with bitterness. Joe Messinger's cheeks burn with shame.

"Captain Joe Messinger will kill many men in his three tours of duty," calls the colonel. "Men who killed that many of their country's enemies – in the old days, they became kings."

"What do they become now, Colonel Stabb?" Kitty wants to know.

"Now? Now, they become… colonels," says Stabb, shooting his cuffs and straightening his shoulders. He is gleaming and magnificent and covered in medals, lean and muscular and fierce as a hawk in his crisp blue uniform. Joe Messinger wears a clumsy suit of canvas and rubber and buckles. "Now," says the colonel, "they become me."

"When you were just a tiny baby girl," says Margaret into Kitty's small pink ear, "I would ask you, I would ask: 'Where do you have your daddy, Kitty-kins? Where have you got your daddy?' And do you know what you would do?"

Kitty holds up her right pinkie and encircles it with the forefinger and thumb of the opposite hand. Margaret grabs her linked hands and raises them high.

"That's right! That's right! Wrapped around your little finger. You were so precocious."

"Five minutes!"

"Five minutes until what, Colonel Stabb?" Kitty asks. She wrests her hands away from Margaret.

Margaret makes a shushing noise. "Don't ask the colonel that, honey," she says. "It's probably classified."

"I'm afraid that information is classified," the colonel admits.

"But I'm his daughter. I think I deserve to know."

"I'm his wife!" Margaret says. "Do you think I ever had him wrapped around my little finger? Joe Messinger the brave? Joe Messinger the stoic? Joe Messinger the hero?"

Joe Messinger is dreaming. The hero is dreaming.

"The killing is all in the future, though," says the colonel.

"Is the future classified?" Kitty wants to know.

"He loves me," says Margaret. "Oh yes, he love me. But not like you, little Kitty-kins! He loves no one the way he loves you."

The colonel resumes his air of professionalism. It is important to remain professional, even in the face of powerful and potentially unsettling emotions. Especially then. "Right now, Captain Joe Messinger is hanging over one hundred thousand feet above the earth, peacefully and contentedly waiting for the moment to come when he will jump from the gondola. He will set a free-fall record that will stand unbroken for nearly fifty years! That's what I can tell you about the future."

~ ~ ~

Joe Messinger dreams about the dog he had when he was a boy. The dog was a great big collie that guarded his father's sheep. It was named Grenadier. He smiles at the thought.

"Do you love my daddy, Colonel Stabb?" Kitty asks.

Margaret flutters her hands in the air. Her peignoir comes slightly untucked, and she moves quickly to fasten it again. "Kitty! What a question to ask."

"No, no, Margaret, that's a very good question," the colonel tells her. His tone is as reassuring as his words. He is not afraid of sincere sentiment, in its proper context. "Let me answer it."

"It's not classified?"

"I honor your father, Katherine."

"Everybody calls me Kitty."

"I honor your father, Kitty."

"But do you love him?"

"I honor him because it's possible for him to do what other men cannot. No one could order another man to do what your father is doing today, right now… in four minutes…"

"Is it possible that he'll be killed?" Kitty's face is strained, but she's prepared for the answer, whatever it might be. It shocks Joe Messinger a bit, to see his daughter so prepared to hear that he will die.

"Yes, is it possible that he'll be killed?" Margaret asks. Joe Messinger cannot hear through the static what her attitude toward the question is. Does she want him to die?

"I have ordered men to their deaths in battle, many times, in more than one war, but I could not order a man to do what Joe Messinger, what your father, what your husband, Margaret, has volunteered to do."

Joe Messinger is dreaming of his great fluffy collie dog Grenadier, he's dreaming that he and his dog are playing out in the great meadow of timothy grass out behind the house where he grew up –

"Should his stabilizing chute fail to deploy correctly," the colonel says, his voice calm, " it's entirely possible that Captain Messinger will enter an irrecoverable flat spin, which could quickly accelerate to as much as two thousand revolutions per minute."

"Oh my!" cries Kitty.

"What then?" The look on Margaret's face is bland, her inquiry practical. The belt of her robe has slacked again. She's a voluptuous woman, and the colonel has a difficult time keeping his eyes on his notes, the bland notes that rest on the podium before him.

"He will be … liquefied."

"Daddy!"

"Joe!"

"Two minutes!"

Joe Messinger dreams that his mother is calling him in from the field, and that a glorious meal awaits him and his mother and his loyal dog Grenadier, a great groaning board laden with all the foods that he loved as a boy. Fried chicken. Green beans. Mashed potatoes. Silver Queen corn, on the cob, dripping with butter.

Joey! Jo-ey! Time to come in now! Supper's waiting!

Best of all, his father will be waiting at the table, and he will hold young Joe's hand, and his father's hand will be whole, as it was before the Japs took his fingers; and he will hold Joe's mother's hand, and they will say grace together before they eat. And afterward young Joe will climb upstairs to his bed, and he will lie down to sleep, and to dream, and it will be peaceful and quiet and he won't have to jump out of anything until morning.

"Should his stabilizing chute fail to deploy correctly, and should he enter such a flat spin as I have described, I imagine he'll return to earth as a light rain, all along the slopes and ridges of the Alleghenies. He will have – even in failure – a glorious return to the land of his beginnings."

"He'll turn into rain?" Kitty asks. It's the sort of transformation a girl such as she can understand and enjoy. Cockroaches into men. Men into rain.

"You know why he loves you best, don't you? Best in all the world?"

Margaret again, her voice edged with fury.

"Why will he turn into rain?"

"It's in the best tradition of the military, and in service of the highest calling of science. We must know!"

"What must we know?"

"The answer to the question."

"He loves you best," Margaret says, "because you remind him of me. When we met. When we fell in love. We were just children. Children! He went to the Air Force Academy. He was so handsome in his cadet's uniform. I looked just like you then! I looked just like you, Kitty!"

Kitty ignores her mother. More and more these days. "What question?" she asks.

"The one that your father, Capt. Joe Messinger, is hanging twenty miles above the earth in order to answer."

"Why doesn't he love me that way anymore?" Margaret demands.

"One minute."

Joe Messinger makes his way to the open hatch of the Excelsior III. Below him, the earth is covered in a blanket of clouds. Soon Joe Messinger will be falling through them.

Joe Messinger's fingers drum against his legs.

"He will feel no sense of acceleration as he falls. Only a man who is dreaming could do such a thing." The colonel.

"I was beautiful." Margaret.

"Thirty seconds. Count with me, Kitty. Twenty-nine, twenty-eight…"

Only a man who remembers the prayers of his youth, his bedtime prayers, could do such a thing.

Now I lay me down to sleep –

Kitty and the colonel count together. "Twenty-seven, twenty-six, twenty-five…"

I pray the Lord my soul to keep –

"Come on, Mother. Count with us! Twenty-four, twenty-three, twenty-two…"

If I should… If I should…

All three of them now. "Twenty-one, twenty, nineteen…"

Die.

"Eighteen, seventeen, sixteen..."

If I should die before I wake –

"Fifteen, fourteen, thirteen..."

I pray the Lord my soul to take.

Count with us.

It occurs to Joe Messinger that he could easily just stay where he is. Distant. Omniscient. Holy. He could stay aloft for all time, drifting from place to place above the globe and dreaming the world. Dreaming it without pain or pleasure. He could become a legend, a ghost. There is no one to insist that he walk through that door.

This is the highest step in the world.

"Five, four, three..."

He must return to the ones he loves. He must fall and fall and fall until he is with them again.

Zero.

Joe Messinger leans forward. The wind once again slaps his face. How can such a thing be? He's wearing the heavy helmet, but nonetheless the stiff cool breeze of his youth touches the flesh of his cheeks, caresses his forehead. It is the current at the top of the cliff, and he can lean into it, and he will be borne up. That evening comes back to him whole. The boy on the opposite ridge – where is he? He must be on the earth. He must be grown. He must be waiting for Joe Messinger, back at the border of Seneca County.

Joe's gloved fingers brush the edges of the doorway. He forces himself to relax, not to grab hold. If he does, he will never let go.

Below him lies the farm. Below him lie the valley and the mountains that surround it. Below him his family has gathered. Below, the return to conventional time, conventional space. His center of gravity shifts forward. His balance, always excellent, suddenly deserts him. Unaware that he's falling from the gondola – it seems to him that the gondola has left him, that it's shooting up into the sky at an astonishing rate of speed – Joe Messinger tumbles head over heels into the great blue void.

Recreating a Miraculous Object

Belonging not to winter but to another
I face the face that made me

And lie all my hours
Upon your reckless hands

Make myself a prisoner
Of the sky

The sweet vermouth
Of your teeth

Shaping me
Like a spectre

In the attic of my flowering heart

I hear the parade of mouths
Beating upon my sleeping head

I hear the thieves rising
With their fingers full of moon

I hear the ocean I gave you
Waving back against the black

Uniform of the earth
And the saint children marching

Like blood

I hear your memories of me waken
And glisten

And rise in the hollow
Of my muscled dread

Treading through the unlatched snow
Here they come

Here they come
Here come my betrayers

Recreating a Miraculous Object

I have lived through every war in my lifetime
Like everyone I am

A vessel that takes the shape
Of what it contains

If you feed me to fire
I will become fire

Place your teeth upon me and I will be
The sound from your mouth

You see that axe that axe
Is me

Cleaving myself from my self
In your hands which are
Also me

When you arrive
I become you coming

The snow you came in
The next great war

I live through

Recreating a Miraculous Object

When I was a boy I was made
Entirely of salt

Silent with the silence of adoration
For what had come

Before me

Like a father

In the belly of a great whale
I lived in myself

Waiting to be
Illuminated by your arrival

At night I pray
For glaciers of salt

Now I wait
I have waited
I will wait

I eat your footsteps in my sleep
I wake from my animal dream a legend

Recreating a Miraculous Object

The world pisses on itself and takes
A million forms

The way winter melts and reminds
Us we're alone

Each drop of water punctuating
Our open mouths

Broken by absence but more
Beautiful for it

I want to be a part of all
Things I am apart of

Weave my nest from the teeth
Of laughter

And place it like a crown
Upon your departure's giant brow

I am less
Than an insect moving

From judgment to awe in all things

I am dust
On a moth

The whole universe
Printed on the wings of a moth

Recreating a Miraculous Object

Thus I perish in amazement
At the ruthless curve of your delicate hip

Thus I perish in amazement
At the suggestion of your wrists

Thus I perish in amazement
And am recreated by the aloe of your eyes

Thus I perish in amazement
In your tongue's candied skull

Thus I perish in amazement
Drowning beneath your flowering feet

Thus I perish in amazement and am preserved
In the formaldehyde of your impossible breast

Thus I perish in amazement
Salted in your blood and consumed with milk

Thus I perish in amazement
Dashed to shreds on the glimmering bergs of your teeth

Thus I perish in amazement
Like a flame devoted

Thus I perish in amazement
In the thundering honey of your wake

Thus I perish in amazement
And sink fathomlessly down with all your masks

Thus I perish in amazement
And am born into your favorite laughter

Thus I perish in amazement
Kissing your elemental hands

Thus I perish in amazement
At the ecstasy of your itinerant breath

Thus I perish in amazement
My bones liberated by your wolves

Thus I perish in amazement
Pinned to the axis of your innumerable eye

Thus I perish in amazement
At the matrix of all possible narratives

Thus I perish in amazement
In the mushroom of your every deadly atom

Thus I perish in amazement
A sobbing angel hung in a tree

Thus I perish in amazement
An azure column touching the alabaster sky

Thus I perish in amazement
Plucked like a berry from your trellis of blood

Thus I perish in amazement
In the ribbed lightning of the next great ice age

Thus I perish in amazement
Am magma

Thus I perish in amazement
Am lice

Thus I perish in amazement
As the flowers sway in myriad lysergic awe

Thus I perish in amazement
As you wasp the abyss between my ribs

Thus I perish in amazement
And am made whole by the white mud of your ambivalence

Thus I perish in amazement
Drowning in the black orchard of your hair

Thus I perish in amazement
Eating the poison from your reverential sleep

Thus I perish in amazement
With wings with planets with fingers

Thus I perish in amazement
At the dawn of your surrendered eye breaking on its lid's horizon

Thus I perish in amazement
And am greatest when I know nothing

Thus I perish in amazement
Living for centuries on the freckled hours of your neck

Thus I perish in amazement
Living for centuries on the freckled hours of your neck

Thus I perish in amazement
Strangled by the glorious gesture of your abdomen rising to meet mine

Thus I perish in amazement
Alone in my aberration and still I have not ceased to weep

Thus I perish in amazement
Within the pure lie of mystery we walk

Thus I perish in amazement
My perfect veins crumbling to dust on your fingers' perfect tips

Thus I perish in amazement
The swishing sound and that is enough

Thus I perish in amazement
This rose bursting delicately out then rising

Thus I perish in amazement
A half-open door in a glass of darkness

Thus I perish in amazement
In the gruesomeness of your embrace which no one can take from me

Thus I perish in amazement
Amid the uncurling tides of your wandering

Thus I perish in amazement
Broken by the enormity of a future apart

Thus I perish in amazement
And return to rest my head on your immortal thigh

Thus I perish in amazement
And become the sapling tree that

Centuries from now still bends in the wind
Of your uncertain longing

Thus I perish in amazement
Thus I perish thus I perish still I have not yet ceased to perish

JOHN COLTRANE

was - IS - ever shall be
    everlasting
Sound of Sound
second to none
second sight
INFINITY
light everlasting ever lasting
LIGHT
FOREVER and ever and ever
from then to NOW
always now
every step small or giant
always now
RIGHT NOW

II.

Distortion for the sake of distortion is a dead end. Distortion is an application . . . as applied to something that is free of distortion, hence something unusual results. Or distortion is an inherent condition that can be made more distorted, but only in degree . . . then when distortion is removed or taken away, the condition changes in kind and something unseen is revealed.

The Problem

The first person the social networking website suggests you befriend is the one most responsible for your obsessive compulsion to check for friend suggestions. This is the problem with the first person: the first person is too selfish; the second person, too accusatory; the third person—just plain distant. It's like a train whistle without a train, this barbaric act of writing poetry after the internet.

The Problem

He feels a strange, superficial obligation to say hello to his neighbor when they cross paths on the porch, pass on the stairway, stand, amazingly, at the front door together, keys awkwardly in hand, walk by each other in the back alley, exiting the laundry room, taking out the trash, picking up the mail, anywhere, really, just on the periphery of public space, in those transitional places between the private security of one's apartment and all the exits and entryways it abuts, all the blurred edges around what constitutes being at home, but never, no matter what, and herein lies the problem, never when they're both out on their respective balconies, even though only a slight partition—a two-foot tall railing really—separates them, even though they could almost touch, almost be page turners for the symphonic quiet of the personal space they're both intent on maintaining. But maybe I'm wrong; maybe it isn't a problem at all. Maybe they've exchanged pleasantries on numerous occasions, even become fast friends, sharing chitchat and dinners, commiserating, drinking, eventually moving in with each other as lovers. I couldn't say for sure. I say hello when I have to, but only in passing, only outside, near the front door, or the steps, but never out here, out on the balcony, where the treetops are so close, so goldenly comforting.

le Edit View Insert For
Send
OPTIONS
HTML
FROM...
To...
CC...
Bcc...
Subject...

The Problem

If he sleeps with the windows open, the noise of morning traffic wakes him several hours too early. If he sleeps with the windows closed, the heat of the stuffy apartment makes for a restless and difficult night. Between these two options, as between the unconditional love of two exemplary and devoted parents, the problem sleeps like a baby.

The Problem

First, there were a lot of gods. Then there was one, but a lot of ones. Can I tell you that what I most admire about the arachnid is the mechanics of so many legs in motion? After a while, the problem adds up to something infinite. And then, then there's just us counting it.

THE PROBLEM

Between a woman who wants to retrieve her hiking boots from the sun porch where several wasps are hovering expectantly and a camp counselor who attempts to stifle his amusement with the teenage girl's complaint about what she calls a *scorpio* in her cabin, the problem oscillates continually, refusing the finality of a decision, no matter how ominous or innocuous. In this way, it is like a Dutchman who doesn't know French, who speaks a little English but certainly can't read it, and who happens to be staying at a decidedly Americanized hotel in Paris, watching what turns out to be a Dutch film that has been dubbed into French and given English subtitles. Even in his uncertainty he seems so relaxed and sure of himself. To the west the sun begins its slow descent. The wasps deposit themselves on a window. Mercury is in retrograde.

How to Defend Your elf

First, keep the little guy
off the ground—he could easily
be trampled there, the way
people hurry nowadays; put him
on your shoulders,
                    like a child
at a parade, but remember—
your average elf is above-average
smart, in any event smarter
than a preschooler, so never
condescend and make no assumptions
either.
          If you're driving, don't
buckle him into a baby seat,
he'll just slip through and out
—believe me, it's been known to happen;
clean out the glove box and put
a towel in there—they adore
enclosed spaces and he'll feel safe.

Never slip your elf into a pocket,
even if he asks (and he may ask),
there's no reinforcement and you
might forget he's there;
                         it's been
known to happen—in fact, it did,
to a close personal friend of mine
and he still wakes up screaming,
I won't go into the details, this
is not the time or place for it.
Maybe later.
                 One more thing—
your elf is your elf but
remember, he's his own elf too
so the best way to take care of him
is to give him some room
—if not his own room then a spot
behind the couch and near

the furnace grate; he'll love the heat
        and maybe use it to cook
his favorite foods, things
you or I could never imagine
as edible (but they are), they're delicious
but only if they're prepared a certain way.
He'll know what to do, he'll offer you a
taste. Believe me, I know.

Nixon Era Panda Dies

He was 28, an extraordinarily advanced
                    age for a panda.

Unresponsive to his keepers,
nearly blind, plagued
with arthritis
and barely able to rouse himself to eat,

zookeepers gave Hsing-Hsing
a lethal injection
after deciding
that irreversible kidney disease
had made his life
too painful to endure.

His final meal
consisted of a large
blueberry muffin,
boiled yams, a bit of rice
broth, and some bamboo.

Gift from Mao to Nixon
        in April 1972,
with his longtime female denmate Ling-Ling,
who died in 1992 of sudden heart failure.
The pandas mated frequently,
                on their own
and with the aid of science,
but left no survivors.

Mating Call of the Re-Creation Panda

Re-Creations are defined as renderings which include no natural parts of the animal portrayed . . . For instance, a re-creation eagle could be constructed using turkey feathers, or a cow hide could be used to simulate African game.

—World Taxidermy Championships rule book

after Melissa Milgrom

Cleanliness is my only real fault:
I could have done with a little faux shit
yellowing my rump, something to make it
seem like the bamboo I'm chewing will end up
somewhere. I bear the bodies
of seventeen grizzlies on my back alone:
peeled, dried, Clairol-dyed and quilted
into the whole of me. I know that my ears
were done with great tenderness,
and one quiet evening, my maker even
briefly held one in his mouth.
That I have no memory is hardly his fault:
I'm not even a ghost, since this requires both
life and death as precedent. Says the poet:
What is more precise than precision? Illusion. I am more
precise than the clockwork of your own
expiring mitochondria. Come closer.
Try to guess the provenance of my claws,
gently blow the dust from the smoked snifters
of my eyes. Imagine from what, or whom,
your own body could be collaged, whose
lips could be stitched into an homage
of your smile. Take my lie in your arms.

Nature Film, Directed by Martin Scorsese

Juvenile Barn Owls, Cornell Lab of Ornithology Nest Box Web Camera

Our young hero's a mixture of glamour and horror,
though Glamhorror sounds like a quaint
village in coastal Scotland famous for its
driftwood crucifixes and inbreeding. But yes,
glamour and horror, all bony yellow scrawn
and expensive-looking white down,
Hieronymous Bosch meets Ginger Rogers
(they say the feathered dress she wore
in *Top Hat* ruined dozens of takes
because of how badly it shed & gave Fred
the sneezes). His initial approach
to the dead rat was leisurely, careless even,
picking out the twangy threads of innards
one by one in a dank taffy pull, bowing
his head again and again in hungry reverence
to his feet. His body's kinked up so it appears
that his haunches are on backwards, and if
you've ever looked at a barn owl you know
that one of the more unsettling things about them
is their heart-shaped, almost human faces, likely
similar to the eloquent aspects of Circe's pig-men
moments before the autumn slaughter...
So the scene here is really that of a man, perhaps one
you might know, say, the myopic bartender from Sal's,
dining on a rodent nearly the size of his head
with his ass facing the wrong way. He turns
occasionally to consult with his brother juvenile

in the nest box, who's bobbing his head in time
to the tune of that universal pop standard,
"Are You Gonna Eat All That?" But while
Brother's in mid-bob, the feeding owlet
suddenly turns abruptly from him with the rat
suspended in his beak, facing the camera,
his expression unnervingly inward:
clearly, he's about to have his De Niro moment.
But not *Taxi Driver*—although wild-eyed,
skinny-ribbed Bob preening with his firearms
makes for a fine raptor in his own right—
no, it's *Goodfellas*, that great, wordless shot
of a smoke-hazed Bob at the bar, his glance skewed
slightly offscreen, dragging the cigarette, and as the slow
zoom starts, the opening chord of "Sunshine
of Your Love" kicks in like a death sentence
for the fat, mouthy gangster dangling under
Bob's gaze. We're watching the man decide it.
It's done. In those few seconds of film, Bob's already
swallowed him. Which is what
the barn owl has decided to do with the rat
carcass, yanking his head *down*, surprisingly,
to negotiate torso into beak, now stretched
aria-wide, an emphatic YES-YES-YES!
to the rapidly-approaching hindquarters, the tail
riposting with a coquettish *Th-th-that's*
all folks! as it disappears into the dark maw's
aperture. The brother, in his bid for Best Supporting
Owl, has backed watchfully into the corner,
looking ready as a *Raging Bull* Pesci,
poised with towel, stool, and spitbucket,

nodding *I gotcha kid, I gotcha. Stay*
in the ring. The bird staggers back a few steps
to accommodate its newly-packed gullet,
then stands there, his heavy, flurried shoulders
heaving mightily, the breastbone stretched now
as if filled with extra hearts. Chucks his beak roofward
with an expression that seems to say *Never*
has anything ever been so possessed by anyone,
not even you. Yes, I'm talking to you.

Population

After the surgery, I placed my wisdom teeth in a small blue box, and every time I lifted the lid, I felt a great surge of affection for them, those shapely, miniature Brancusis I'd grown myself. Ten days later, I discovered that four teeth were now six; two new molars, slightly smaller, and not quite as yellowed, lay in the box. After the twentieth day, ten teeth. For a while I allowed them to flourish, feeling like Mendel observing the inheritances being passed on: the tendril-esque twist in the root of the maxillary molar, an insouciant slope in the mandibular's crown. Soon they took over my small apartment—several dozen spilled out of my sugar bowl, scores of them overtopped an old boot, and countless pairs had worked their way into the back alleys between my sofa cushions. Eventually I rounded them up, and placed each in its own jar. I stacked them flush against the walls, and they rose in giant grids like a beehive. Sometimes at night I can hear, scattered from room to room, the sounds of lustful little clicks against the glass.

For Carsten René Nielsen and David Keplinger

Scene 43, Take 1: Interior, Sushi Restaurant

The actor does his best to put death in his eyes.
He holds the live, fist-sized octopus before
his face and murmurs *I am sorry I am sorry*
before the cameras roll. *Action.* He stuffs
the squirming animal in his mouth. *Tear.*
Tear it a bit more, the director says. The actor jerks
the tentacles in his hand to the right
like a grotesque typewriter. *Ping!* he thinks
as he grinds his jaw. One tentacle slings itself
about his nose like a drunken friend.
He wonders if the animal, before it suffocated
in the dark acids of his belly, would catch a glimpse
of the thing that had made people want to use
his face—or rather, the lack of a thing:
that he was completely empty. Not stupid,
or cold, or cruel, but a windy place in which
everything that was not him always fit
with great ease. He was less of a man and more
of a storage space, suitable for personalities
ranging from Businessman with a Terrible Secret
to Homosexual Trapeze Artist-Detective.
He looks at the bluish knuckles of the key grip
and already knows how to play him
on his deathbed. When the actor stares at him-
self in the mirror, he thinks of snowfall
on the ocean, flattened spoons, the empty
column above the mercury in a thermometer.
He suddenly wonders if the octopus is female,
if he's doing something unseemly. Perhaps he'll be

able to play women, too, and summon the complicated
geometries of their saddest smiles. Sometimes
he worries that he'll run out of lives. The remaining
tentacles cling to his chin in a comic beard, a few
rearing up to gesture back to his face, as if to say
Him, him. He's the one, Officer.

after Park Chan-wook & Choi Min-sik

Swan Song

As Morris Silverman, a retired salesclerk for Lipsky's Discount Shoes, plummeted toward the sun-dappled river, he thought that this was a stupid way to end such a cautious life.

It happened on a perfect Sunday afternoon in April, when his son Nat and daughter-in-law Miriam had come to air him out in their sporty new Dodge sedan. They'd driven across the shuddering bridge into the bottomlands beyond the river, cruising along the flat roads among rice paddies and cotton fields. Then, after the hour it took for his father's chronic complaining to wear his patience thin, Nat turned the car around and headed home. They were back on the old cantilevered bridge, which Morris had contended for years was falling down, when the blowout occurred.

"Gott in himmel!" cried Morris, as if the gunshot sound of the puncture had penetrated his own rickety person. Fortunately, given the snail's pace of the Sunday traffic, Nat had no real difficulty in maintaining control of the sedan. But as the other vehicles were backed up and honking behind him, the situation was somewhat tense. Nor was the tension reduced by Morris, who hung on to his fluttering heart in the backseat, cataloguing calamities they'd narrowly escaped— "No thanks to my meshugener son!"

Nat was removing the jack from the trunk, placing it under the bumper.

"Miriam," he called out in a singsong voice that implied his temper was being tested, "will you help Papa out of the car?"

Holding her straw hat with silk violets against the wayward breezes, Miriam got out and opened the backdoor. She took hold of Morris's arm and began gently, then not so gently, pulling him to his feet. You would have thought she was dragging him over a precipice.

"What are you doing?" he demanded, his sallow eyes sprung from their sockets. "Vildeh moid, leave an old man in peace!"

From behind the car Nat shouted, no longer disguising his aggravation, that Morris must get out. Sulking, his father stepped uncertainly onto the sidewalk, tethered to Miriam of whom he'd never approved. "You see how she manhandles me," he moaned, inviting heaven to witness his treatment. To Nat he barked, adding his voice to the chorus of curses and honks,

"You should of been more careful how you buy a new car. Shmo, you let them take you for a ride."

Then it bothered Morris the way the accusation redounded upon himself. He looked about, suddenly aware of his tenuous situation on the trembling span, and began to complain of vertigo and imminent peril.

Nat was muttering between clenched teeth that flat tires sometimes happened. Looking up from his labors, he called over his shoulder to Miriam to come please and collect the lug nuts. Before complying, Miriam took Morris's bony fingers and folded them one by one around the rusty guard rail. Morris stared daggers as if he were being marooned.

"Comes a big wind and Silverman's a goner!" he wailed, stealing a peek at the swollen river that turned him green.

Then came a big wind. Blown off his already precarious balance, Morris clung for dear life to the railing, at—as it happened—its weakest point. The corroded castiron came loose under the pressure of even the old man's slight weight; and before he could appreciate his sudden gift of prophecy, Morris was gone, falling headlong toward the moiling water.

He fell for a very long time.

Before he'd fully appreciated his predicament, he saw, receding above him, the bewildered faces of his son and daughter-in-law, summoned to the broken rail by his forlorn cry. He saw a zephyr take Miriam's hat like a tossed bouquet.

Then he was tumbling head over fallen arches, the wind like a flock of mice running wild in his clothes. The rush of his descent rearranged the creases of his face and forced a grin, unknitting the ashen tufts of his brows. His throat and bowels played pitch with his delicate stomach, which made him indignant; he was doubly irate at realizing that the fear by which he set such store had abandoned him here where it should have been most intense.

Feeling cheated here in his extremity, Morris could have demanded a refund of all the years—which were passing swiftly (all seventy-six of them) before his eyes, a long life though you couldn't have called it happy. You'd have had to stretch it to call it a life.

There was a childhood spent, come to think of it, watching other boys throwing themselves off of high places. They jumped from fire escapes and trees, from bridges, leaping blindly into the future; while Morris, whom they guessed was born old, cautioned them against breaking their fool necks. They should think of the consequences; they should, for the sake of their poor mothers and later their wives, keep themselves in one piece. They should follow the example of Morris, who, in the employ of his old friend Lipsky, kept his head down and watched a procession—four decades long—of other people's feet. Then came retirement and the passing of his joyless wife Annie, after which, out of habit, he'd kept himself in one piece for the sake of...

Death, maybe?—which, in the shape of a river that glistened like a dragon's tail, was rising up to slap the daylights out of Morris Silverman.

But with respect to such an anticlimax, Morris could feel only contempt. Wasn't he, even as he dropped into oblivion, a survivor? Hadn't he come through this world unscratched? Disdainful of his brittle bones, he wanted to fling what remained of his caution to the winds. He wanted to spread his arms like the boys he used to warn against diving headfirst off the high board.

Then the wind stopped its shrill battery; the water kept its distance, as if he'd faced it down. A funnel of blackbirds whirled about him and Morris hung suspended in the eye of their storm. Then they'd risen above him, leaving the old man to float miraculously in mid-air: an extraordinary fellow after all, not only fearless but able to fly!

With some minimal adjustment to the horizontal and an occasional flap of his stick-like arms, Morris began to glide on a raft of air. Through his gaping jaw the inpouring gulf stream seemed to cleanse his creaking innards of age. What impressed him most (in a way that would have formerly made him fearful of a stroke) was the naturalness of his buoyancy, as if he'd come home to the element in which he truly belonged. He was born to the air, shikkered with vitality, sailing against the current above the turgid river they called the Old Man.

Clearing his throat of catarrh, he hooted obscenely, tore open his shirt to stretch the tails into wings, kicked off his shoes. In no time at all he had the hang of it; he was aerodynamic, a regular Peter Pansky, somersaulting as he clutched his ribs to savor the joke. An exotic and fantastical creature, he was SILVERMAN—the bold letters emblazoned across his spangled underwear as he barreled down out of the heavens, scourging Nazis in every walk of life.

Cunningly maneuverable now, Morris took in the sights. He hovered above a sandbar that featured, like a decaying snail shell, a beached paddle wheel. He swooped down over a forested island with a hermit's shack in a tree, over garfish like a school of torpedoes, a barge upon which a little man leaped and pointed at the flying landsman—yet another joke. Then having seen what the earth hereabouts had to offer, Morris aimed his tussocky beak toward the clouds—which were turreted and onion- domed like holy places, like palaces where maybe God kept his harem.

He lost his bearings among fleecy corridors embroidered in golden sunlight, caught (he could have sworn) fleeting glimpses of soaring alabaster wings. Then feeling a nosebleed coming on, he changed direction, doing a kind of pigeon breast-stroke down through the billows until he rediscovered his southern city perched on its bluff. With his moist eyes sharpened from gazing at impossible distances, he was delighted to see that life still carried on. People were fishing from the cobbled levee, window-browsing along the sidewalks, scattering doves in the fountained square. And north along Main Street, the sinking ship to which some of his neighbors still clung, Morris thought he could make out a couple of acquaintances.

Wasn't that Seligstein the druggist in his drooping suspenders, shambling across the street between a tin facade and a jungly vacant lot? And that freckled pate seated on marble steps leading up to the rubble of a collapsed synagogue, didn't it belong to Abe Plesofsky the jeweller? And there, leaning out of a window above the boarded up front of Lipsky's Discount Shoes, wasn't that Morris's longtime boss, old sourpuss Lipsky himself? These were the boys who had long ago thrown themselves from high places instead of keeping themselves in one piece until they were old enough to take flight.

In his own variation on barnstorming Morris made a megaphone of his hands, frog-kicking above old North Main.

"Hey Lipsky, you fossil," he bawled, "this is Silverman! I'm flying and I don't care who knows it!" But Morris's neighbors, even as his shadow passed over them, were not in the habit of looking up.

He wanted to tell them how the neighborhood looked like a bombsite from his vantage. Whereas, beyond it there was modest but respectable housing; there were shimmering bayous, far-flung blue pastures, three hundred and sixty degrees of promising land. There was snow somewhere to the north and to the south, New Orleans and the sea. Morris had a sudden yen to see New Orleans, a fun-loving and romantic city he'd been led to believe. And while he was at it, why not solo on across the ocean, dropping benedictions on the heads of the crowds who would wave from the Eiffel Tower and the Wall of China; then continue his travels, island-hopping the South Pacific, stopping long enough to cure his constipation with fresh fruit. Who knew but he might fly off to the evening star, which winked a come-on in the cobalt sky over Morris's right shoulder? While on his left the sun, extinguishing itself behind mauve Delta fields, leaked flames into the smoldering river.

But Morris was growing tired. His lungs, unused to such exertion, wheezed like tuneless bagpipes in his ears. He'd developed a stitch in his side that was causing him to veer downward with a limp. Windmilling his arms in an attempt to tread thin air, he panicked at the thought that he might never be able to land. The flying landsman, he was maybe condemned, for having been always so earthbound, to bobbing about like a fugitive kite till kingdom come.

Eventually, however, he managed to alight by labored degrees on a gravelled rooftop. Immediately his knees buckled under him. The dizziness, unexplainably deferred during his flight, caught up with him now he was stationary, so that he felt he might lose his lunch. Over by a cracked skylight there was a torn canvas deck chair that someone must have once dragged up to enjoy the view. With the same effort it had cost him to land on the roof, Morris made his way to the chair and lowered himself groaningly into its sling. Dabbing at runnels of perspiration with a shirttail, waiting to catch his breath, Morris had to admit that this flying stuff was for the birds, or at least for younger men.

"So I'm a late bloomer," he considered, though the howling of his joints argued against it.

Already the memory of flying had begun to fade. No match for his aches and pains, it was dissolving, like that sunset across the river whose only surviving trace was a warm scarlet stain. Good riddance, thought Morris, who in his exhaustion had no more use for nostalgia than for dangerous fun. The thing was to watch your blood pressure and keep your health, such as it was. Only, what if he'd fallen off the bridge, say, seventy years earlier? With a lifetime in which to practice, he would have been some aerodynamic person, a thing of beauty able to stay aloft for days, to run a shuttle service between here and paradise. What a waste that his talent had been neglected for so long, that his own nebbish flesh had kept the secret from him all these years. What a crying shame.

Then it must have been his fatigue that prompted Morris, who didn't put up much of a fight, to succumb to a fit of sobbing. The tears welled up from his gut with a furious force, not unlike—if he weren't mistaken—the surge he'd felt upon receiving the gift of flight. For a moment he had the hope that such an eruption might lift him once more into the air, but instead he was only shaken to the roots of his feeble frame. He was wracked with lamentation until his false teeth chattered and his heart, tossed in the flood, could no longer keep itself in one piece.

"Fairytales"

I once read somewhere that imagination was the weapon in the war against reality.
And that made me wonder...
What if unicorns were real?
Would it kill the childhood of all my siblings—
Forcing them to realize that not all dreams come true.
What if groundhogs had access to the internet too?
Would they google the latest dance moves?
Lacing up their shoes,
and straightening up their ties—
Hoping for when that day arrives when shadows would play harps with distant sunbeams,
They might scream.
However...
They won't choke.
What if the toothfairy went broke,
And she was no longer able to feed into your candy obsession.
Pawning every tooth in her earthly possession—
Cause believe it or not...
She's afraid of the dark.
What if?
What if Cupid had no heart?
Would he pierce our souls with bullets of hate?
Exchanging his arrows for pistols—
His holster for missiles—
What if the loudest person in the room only knew how to whisper?
I'm thinking...
Would you be able to interpret their stories?
What if expressing yourself was termed as being corny?
Would you hide behind your fragile state of trying to be cool—

Losing yourself behind a pool of others.
No longer to be confused as an individual...
But only to be acknowledged as a wave.
Why...
Are we such slaves to falling generations of failed expectations—
Trusting and believing should be a nation that we carpool to on Fridays.
Maybe,
Saturdays wouldn't be so bittersweet to us anymore.
Realizing that our early morning cartoons have been transferred into mid-afternoon naps.
I wonder,
What if Atlantis could be located on a map.
Would it force dreamers to no longer dream—
Realizing that it's not as colorful as Disney made it seem.
I wonder...
What if Rapunzel was lazy?
What if Mr. Rodgers was actually crazy?
What if Spider-Man got arrested for drinking while hanging—I wonder...
Would this poem even exist?
Or would our childhoods get lost in the mist between late nights and early mornings.
I failed to realize that after I stopped wanting to be a Power Ranger,
Life would end up so boring.
I wonder...
What if Trayvon Martin would had been seen as Batman instead of a young man in black—
Would that bullet had been just as quick to heal as it was to kill—
I wish that men like Zimmerman would go back to wanting to be Superman
and not the men of steel—
You know...
The first time i stopped believing in Santa
was not after someone first told me he wasn't real,
But shortly after i started believing that they were right.
It's time for us to start turning our pillowcases back into superhero capes...

And get out there and fight.
Cause this world...
This world needs us now more than ever.

Dear Mrs. Rashad

Dear Mrs. Rashad...
Hi.
We've never met before. Though, I feel like I've known you my entire life.
See, when I was younger—
While flipping channels between Nickelodeon and Disney,
Your beauty hit me like two runaway trains blindly slamming head first into each other.
You...
A woman of color like mine—with grace that before that time
Had never before been seen on screen.
Mainstreamed to the world to be displayed on a weekly basis.
No foolish dances or painted faces—
Just you.
A successful, educated mother of five and a loving wife, too.
Like glue, I was stuck upon your every word.
Hanging-dangling along upon each and every syllable—
I, just a kid...was pitiful...
And in love.
I didn't even know what an OB/GYN was.
Yet, I wanted to be one when I grew up
Just so I could one day have a life and a wife like your husband.
I liked how he pretended to be in charge,
But we all knew that he wasn't.
You were the one who held everything in the palm of your hand.
For 8 seasons, I watched you stand firmly beside that of your man.
No talks of divorce or even separation.
I wish I could express how watching that marriage was preparation for my own.
Taking insights and values and installing them within the walls of my home—like...
Teaching my kids to be respectful and always putting education first.
Mrs. Rashad, I've rehearsed my reaction

for meeting you since you've danced off my tv screen—
Hoping that one day, I could ring the doorbell that never worked
and you would open the door. With that glow
in your face as if to say, "Welcome home." So in close,
I just wanna say thank you, I love you and I'm forever grateful
for being witness to your grace. Sincerely...yours truly...aka Mrs. Huxtable's
long lost mate.

I Want to Know About Anything the Way Al Green Knows About Love

How to sew, to string together the cheeks
of some soft skin, like let's stay together.

How to be a man, man. How to be still, and still know
the world is a caught mouse

gummed by some fur slacked mouth. I want to know
about anything the way Al Green knows about love,

knows that the true beast needs the blood more
when it's warm and new.

How to stand accused, but really
how come not being able to see her eyes

feels as though I've slowly peeled back
the swallow's wings until I have heard the hollow crack.

I want to know love like... or I want to know like like...
or no, I just really want to like anything about knowing love.

I want to know about anything
the way Al Green knows about love.

The reason for the angel's dirty feet above the rooftops,
how to squeeze the slick rub of time, her eyes

or the pain slain dead aves, or a day's deep breath.
I want to know you against me

against the world if it must be. I want to know about anything
the way Al Green knows about love.

Nowhere To Run

Today is a fine day at dawn.
A great green settles here—

the weight of the air. Each strand
of each thing living

moves of its own accord—
the leaves are audible, some subtle

croon settled down here in the valley.

Along the fence line on Main Street,
the fans in the lofts of the old mills

spin in the slow wind—
propellers turning quietly

the memory of industry. *Ghosts
must do again / what gives them pain.*

Maybe the best day I ever lived
was that day in Detroit

when I danced with Martha Reeves
to "Dancing in the Streets."

Even if we weren't in the streets
but at a Union rally, a musty canopy

hung like wet net above our heads.
Me and a dozen people thanked God

and Lake Eire for the rain and for sweat
and for touching hands to waists.

There are hundreds of bad stories
hung like masks on the buildings

across the country, but in this

quiet town, this maze of narrow streets
set down like a bowl full of hallways,

and those steeples piercing the sky,
miles from Wayne County,

I hold out as the day opens
for the slow sound of rain
over the ridge, the rage of the quarry
down south to build into a soft chorus

of "Come and Get These Memories,"
or that last cold coda

from "Nowhere To Run." Time,
try to take from me a place

I once knew well and I will hold it
like an old song

inside the failing foundations
of this little town.

I will tuck its edges beneath these
skinny streets and shout

all the old truths I know
into every open space I see.

Night Music

In the quiet darkness of the evenings, my body
        is made into a light falling snow.

I want a bright, bright day

                to blow the night out from the stars

like dust into a pan,
                        like those huge lights

along the sides of the frozen highway.

Made small   by distance   through a window

I stand.

A single black bird upright along
the prairie's edge
                        an anchor
                        in the wind.

One or so days of every man's life
is lived like the water at the bottom

of a well—

                voices gone, echoes caught.

Being Lon Chaney, Jr.

No ankle manacled to bedpost,
although hair swoops away and eyes
twitch with terrible revelation.

The sun is sinking (*the sun is sinking!*)
behind breezes like Bavarian streams
cooling an unlucky man's hot flesh.

Thank God that innocent girl, innkeeper's
daughter, escorts the Baron tonight.
Let the carnival run late, let no one return
while the moon hums its bloated anthem.

You tremble like an animal startled
in its skin, shoulders hunched, teeth
beginning to grow as the whole dark world,
even Gypsy wagons, tense to see what
you'll do next, you and your sweet curse.

Terminex

I shuffle along the wall of my nest,
sniff at the door. Muted conversation out there
in the big outside, maybe laughter.

The bug man has the hots for my wife.
She, a cold eye for me. Neither would cry if I were
found on my wings, abdomen still, thorax shut,

every leg stiff in the air.
I dash for the kitchen. There are bugsy
and wifey drinking coffee. I hear him

declaim his longing for "the Bordeaux region."
He sees me and his thin mustache twitches
at something repellent.

How blinding the room! The woman frowns, disgusted.
I've learned to keep my palpus shut,
scurry back to a world quiet and small.

But when the fist on the door comes, what can
any creature do? Fate erect on two legs—
cropped hair, white shirt, silver keg of poison.

I wave an antenna and tell him to help himself.
I'm spineless, but hard to kill.

More Honored in the Breach: Your Midnight E-Mails, the Morning After

Take your time flossing, brushing, rinsing.
Take time with the razor, all the time
you need with the razor.

Then go ahead, go in and have a look.
Before coffee, before dry toast
and boiled egg, before juice and Tylenol.

Sit down at the screen. Remember to breathe.
Get on with it: "sent" files, to set the stage.
Breathe. Bring it up. "Inbox."

Maybe it's not as bad as you don't remember.

The Martini

4 oz. premium gin
3 drops extra dry vermouth
olive or, occasionally, lemon twist

H. L. Mencken recognized the Martini, that most elegant and powerful of drinks, as "the only American invention as perfect as the sonnet." What civilized person would disagree?

A proper Martini, despite (or arguably because of) the apparent simplicity of its preparation, is deucedly difficult to make. It will take you several years to master, and this dedicated time will be well spent. Your small 8-oz. metal shaker, Martini glass, and bottle of gin should be kept in the freezer *at all times*. As soon as your finances afford the opportunity, upgrade to a premium gin (Bombay, Bombay Sapphire, Beefeaters, or Tanqueray). You won't ever return to Gilbey's, Gordon's, or worse. In fact, come to think of it, don't even bother to begin until you can afford to have a bottle of good gin consistently in the freezer. For the vermouth, stick with Martini & Rossi or Noilly Prat. A bottle lasts for months, so the cost is negligible.

To make the Martini, fill your cold shaker with medium-sized ice cubes and then top with the cold gin, about 4 oz. Add 3 drops of dry vermouth, cap the shaker, and shake vigorously 10-12 times. Don't shake it to death. (If you're attempting to use warm gin, then of course you'll need to shake more to achieve your diluted and inferior result. Also, I've no intention of getting into some rhubarb about stirring gin to avoid "bruising" or "over-chilling" it. Please.) Pour/shake into a chilled Martini glass into which you have already placed a single olive—speared on a sturdy, turned toothpick—or a squeezed twist of lemon. If you have a "top" freezer with a wide lip when the door's open, I recommend making and pouring the Martini right there, to keep the ingredients as cold as possible. This may not seem energy efficient, but as your skill level increases so will your speed.

Raise the frosted glass by the stem. (Invest in graceful and thin Martini glasses, with seductively long and narrow stems, and always in clear glass.) Admire, wide-eyed, smiling, aroused and anticipatory, the gentle shards of floating ice. Bow your head slightly and bring lips to the glass. There is no other sensation in the world like that first sip. You will feel and know its transformative power immediately.

Old Sweetheart Slams White Russians and Mudslides on Ditmars Blvd., Astoria

First words out of my mouth he say: My, my you're not from around here.
Every bone cry *hie you hence* but in uniform he's out of this world.
Brass chicken hawk on brick wall exposed read fifty degrees.
Truly, I want a shortcut to the innermost workings of one other.

Says: You take your chances running night operations. I say goddamn.
Bird's eye view of his fingers spread out on his crown, flesh
wound. Through three shot glasses the waitress' fingers loop.
Clappin' off the beat he guffaw: You dance like a country girl. Flush.

To the beaten path of his hand in the pile of my skirt go
towards the southernmost row houses, turn at the spicy restaurant
its awning ruffling—there one woman lends another her rabbit fur.
Dream a man at the N station at the crack of dawn to sing and flaunt.

Now whether to sing or tell it other ways.
Leastways, atop the gratings a man dance with a puppet life-size
its arms to his waist tied. Hot little number, he say and has it
say *caramba* while the train skates in and speakers crackle live.

My sheets snapped flat and train-case crammed,
I never answered you (losin' your mind, scramblin' in the grass down)
asking me years hence: Why don't you sound now like where you're from?
No, you just looking hard at me—the voice is from elsewhere thrown.

THE GONER

They'll read something like it somewhere—
wronged one longed all along for the long gone wrong one

wool over this one's eyes, steel wool
in that one's mouth, a half-eaten blood orange

on the floor of some abode, some dust
devil of angel dust, where, half-senseless

in a half-slip, a drama mama fans herself
with an automatic, strung along

by this mind reader, that peter
meter, another string bikini'd string bean

who in a string of bad language unstrung
my mind—a gripe a gulp a growl a glint a goring

Chapter the Thirteenth: Discourse of Rage, Conjuration, & Exile

from *Ghosts Behind the Sun: Splendor, Enigma & Death*

Under the spell of a Herschell Gordon Lewis movie, *She Devils on Wheels*, I watched Falco and his coterie of hangers-on, stymied students, losers, and thwarted artists merrily embark on another road to folly and disillusion. This time the idea was to form an all girls sister group to Panther Burns. The band was named after the theme song to the Lewis movie about a gang of female motorcyclists: *the Hellcats.*

We are the Hellcats nobody likes,
Maneaters on motorbikes,
When you hear the roar of our cut-out exhausts
Get off the road or you'll get your rear-end tossed.

Before the posse of felines self-destructed – as any self-respecting sorority of hellcats are apt to do – both groups made a trip to New York during a particularly intense heat wave by invitation of Central Park Conservatory Summerstage. Again I acted as gopher on the journey and had promoted Cordell Jackson's addition to the bill. Both bands delivered as righteous a performance as they were capable of, but Cordell stole the show. While the Panther Burns rode in their new replacement to the Thunderbird, a long black 1963 Chrysler LeBaron limousine, Cordell had driven her canary yellow Cadillac up from Memphis, and stayed on in Gotham for a few days promoting herself as the 'Rock n Roll Granny'. A tireless self-promoter, the efforts of the lady from Moon Records paid off in spades. She was ecstatic to be offered two Budweiser commercials, a shot at Letterman and another of those nameless late night yak shows. Cordell returned to Memphis a jubilant rocker in full glory.

Not long after the Central Park Conservatory triumph, the next time these two incestuous wildcat groups appeared together was the LSU, Louisiana

State University, graduation party on the USS Kidd naval destroyer docked in the Mississippi River harbor at Baton Rouge. More babies were conceived on that saturnalia and more graduates jumped overboard, were pushed, or fell into the harbor, than on any other party known in the annals of the university.

Shortly after the USS Kidd bacchanal, Midtown was stunned one Friday when the jejune husband of Amy Gamine, bass player of the KLITZ, was shot down in broad daylight as the couple were leaving Pappy and Jimmy's Lobster Shack on Poplar Avenue at Hollywood. Amy and James Starks were darlings of the art scene – she herself bearing a striking resemblance to Natalie Wood, and James a promising artist and painter employed by the prestigious Dixon Gallery and Gardens.

Amy's grandfather, Julius Gassner, served as *maître d'* of *the* Sacher Hotel in Vienna before he too moved to NYC where reigned as *maître d'* for the New York Athletic Club for over 30 years. Francis, Amy's father, had gone to school with Andy Warhol at Carnegie Tech on the GI bill. Andy had a crush on her father who also was the apartment manager of a Victorian pile called the Castle. Andy lived there for a while and that's how she came into possession of an early, quasi-cubist Andy Warhol painting of a saxophonist, which her father bequeathed to her. Twenty-five years later she sold it for a pittance during the depths of a distraught lifestyle.

Francis was eighteen when he married and Dolly, seventeen. He studied one summer under Frank Lloyd Wright and then the couple moved to Greenwich Village for several years where she worked in fashion and he practiced architecture and gigged on stand up bass in a jazz combo. In 1959 they moved to Memphis when Francis got a job with architect Al Aedilott. They immediately were drawn to the academic and to the architecture crowd: Francis Mah and Roy Harrover (who designed the Art Academy and Memphis Airport, and who is married to Stephanie, the sister of Bill Eggleston). The couple also traveled in the sphere of Marcus Orr, the historian, novelist Shelby Foote, and faculty from the Art Academy. They worked with actor George Touliatas at Front Street Theater: Dolly on costumes, Francis on sets. Structures that Francis designed included the Library at LeMoyne Owen College – for which he commissioned artist Ben Shawn to paint a mural – the Theater and Music building at the University of Memphis, Sears Building on Poplar Ave, Temple Israel, and the obliquely *avant garde* C&I Bank downtown with the angular glassed-roofed tropical garden in the lobby.

Francis Gassner was well liked and lived on the cutting edge in his love of flying, fast cars, audio equipment, musical evasions, equal rights, and eventually younger women. On his baby grand, he played hours and hours of Chopin and Beethoven. He traveled in Europe, Africa, and South America and spoke several languages. Architectural junkets took him several times behind the Iron Curtain to Russia and Hungary.

The stress of replacing Main Street with the creation of a pedestrian mall and the tribulations inherent in dealing with city hall politicians and building authorities affected Francis' health, not to mention the cigarettes and the nightly routine of beer, manhattans, wine, and aperitifs. For the Mid- America Mall, he commissioned a monumental organic sculpture called, *The Muse*, designed and executed by John McIntire. It was cast by the artist and Randall Lyon in white concrete and marble chips. A champion of civil rights, Francis marched with rabbis and clergy to end the sanitation strike the day after King's assassination. Then worked with civic leaders to help secure and dedicate land for Martin Luther King Park in South Memphis adjacent to the Chaucalissa Indian Mounds beside the Mississippi River.

On that payday Friday afternoon in September of 1984, Francis' daughter and her husband, James, were walking out to their car in the parking lot after a fine meal at the Lobster Shack, when three youths strolled by and one of them brushed against Amy's jeans. The couple kept on walking and as they turned the corner of the building they noticed that the black kids were running after them. The three imps were pursuing them pointing guns. Beside their car the boys were trying to get Amy in the car with them. She was able to calm down the boy that was pointing a gun at her; he was the youngest and she gave him her money. Unfortunately James decided to fight back and refused to cooperate. First he was pistol-whipped, then as he attempted to approach Amy's side of the car, he was shot through the back with an expensive chrome-plated pistol. Amy screamed maddeningly, and the knaves quickly ran away.

The couple managed to get back into the restaurant and call the ambulance. Their favorite waitresses were now only complaining about the blood that was falling on their carpet. By this time Amy was hysterical. The ambulance drivers saved James' life by keeping him awake on the drive to the hospital. The bullet grazed his heart as it traveled through several organs. He spent six weeks in intensive care with a 50% chance of pulling through. The night he was shot a chaplain came to tell Amy that James probably wouldn't make it, but maybe prayer works.

The adolescent offenders were summarily caught because the next day they went to school and in their art class at East High School, they bragged about shooting a white boy. The police then had a good idea who had done it and the shooter was quickly apprehended. Just a few days previous, the *Commercial Appeal* had published a lengthy interview with James that featured his paintings, so the art schoolteacher at East High was aware of him. At the trial, the assailant licked his lips horribly when he saw Amy in the courtroom. The juvenile served eight years at the penal farm, while James Starks miraculously survived and went on to bring forth many more paintings. His injuries, however, have caused him tremendous residual pain and he engendered more than his share of psychological duress.

The Memphis Music Heritage Festivals in May began to leave wider and wider gaps in the cultural landscape, especially concerning the alternative art scene. To address this sense of neglect felt by an emerging weed patch of artists and musicians, Falco got the stubborn idea in his head to present the best and the worst of them in the setting of an alternative festival. He and Alex dubbed it COUNTERFEST. In 1985 the first Counterfest was held at 96 S. Front St. back in the same cotton loft of the original Panther Burns show, which had for quite some time languished in disuse. It was a two-day event with artists and musicians working together in utter anarchy and with no support other than what personal resources they might conjure up. Bizarre environments were constructed; psychedelic lighting and diffraction gradients were fabricated and installed in the wide-open rooms. Stage risers from the Cotton Carnival warehouse were again dragged up the stairs. Suddenly there was a waiting list of participants eager to join in. Again the TV news crews came to capture another Falco-instigated *art-action*. Their cameras happened to catch the precise moment when Falco wielded a wood-chopping axe over his head and brought it down full force, crashing onto and splintering an electric can opener he had placed on the makeshift stage, while spontaneously invoking an incendiary manifesto for the stodgy ears and perceptive faculties of the Midsouth viewing audience:

LOUNGERS, RAKES, LOAFERS, FOPS, EXHAUST QUEENS, MIDINETTES, PUPPET HEADS, IMPERIALIST RUNNING DOGS, & BACKSLIDING HEIFERS – WE ARE THE NEO-RUMORIST FESTIVAL – *COUNTERFEST*!
WE ARE THE DITCH-DIGGERS IN AMERICAN ART AND MUSIC – UNDER THE PSYCHOTROPIC RED GLARE OF THE AUGUST MOON,
TONIGHT IS THE NIGHT TO FORGE A TRAGIC ALLIANCE WITH THE UNDERGROUND! TONIGHT IS THE NIGHT TO *CRACK* THE IMPERIALIST BLACK EGG!
TONIGHT IS THE NIGHT TO GET YOUR ASHES HAULED!
WE'RE NOT TALKING ABOUT PIE AND CAKES, CLUTCHES AND BRAKES, OR THE HIGH SOCIETY SCHOOL OF THE ARTS –
ALL FRANKING PRIVILEGES ARE REVOKED! *PANTHER PHOBIA, PANTHER PHOBIA, PANTHER PHOBIA! BURN, BURN, BURN! – BURN, BURN, BURN!*
REMEMBER, THE PANTHER BURNS ARE THE ONES WHO *ALWAYS* HOLD OUT A HAND TO THE ENEMY…!

Then Falco swung the axe head around again and plunged it through the picture tube of a waiting and useless TV set stationed on the other side of the stage from where the once intact electric can opener had so naïvely stood. This guy Falco was continually coming up with absurd ideas and gestures. I'm not sure anyone truly understood what the heck he was doing… I'm not sure he even did.

COUNTERFEST events were mounted for five years on an annual basis. The last one was held on an industrial barge floating at the dockside of the river harbor. I had been out on the road with Panther Burns filming their concerts, and when we returned to the Bluff City we found Jim Jarmusch winding up the production of his movie *Mystery Train*. A friend from the East Village named Red Rockets was acting in the role of a night clerk in the film, getting gunned down in a 7/11 – Rockets fell like an avalanche when he took the bullet. Jarmusch was filming in the abandoned Arcade Hotel at Main St. and Calhoun, where I had filmed the opening sequence two years earlier for the Panther Burns short, *Memphis Beat*. Jim brought the entire cast and crew down to the barge for COUNTERFEST. Meanwhile he'd come by our place and looked at our short films, and somehow Falco got him interested in the rebuilt Triumph motorbike sitting next to the Norton in our living room. Next thing I knew, Jim Jarmusch had bought the Triumph with cash from his production office. Often I've thought Falco would have made a better salesman than a singer.

One day I was stretched out on the porch swing with the newspaper, reading the help wanted ads. Some people like to read crossword puzzles, but I read the tightly spaced help-wanted columns for the same reasons. There's no danger of getting hired or of even trying to… as it's extremely unlikely a disaffected white boy has the ghost of a chance finding any sort of job in the Bluff City other than the most menial of tasks. Such perplexing youth do not look, talk, or smell good to the eyes, ears, and noses of sanctimonious Dixie-fried Baptists who drive the markets of the petty bourgeoisie in this citadel of the Bible Belt. On the page behind the help wanted there appeared a truncated column under the rubric: Houses For Rent. Usually there were not more than five or six listings in that column, but that day I saw a curious listing for a *farmhouse* in Binghampton = $150 monthly. As the quarters were becoming a little cramped, shared with Falco and his burgeoning entourage who kept all kinds of bizarre operational hours, I decided to call up about the 'farmhouse'. The price was right, although a bit more expensive than the Cox St. duplex.

The call proved a perspicuous stroke of Fate. The wife of the farmer who owned the house gave me the address, and I hopped on the Norton and rolled over to Binghampton to scope out the place. I parked the bike on the natty front lawn that fronted an otherwise dilapidated bungalow. The porch was rotten and the roof over the porch was just as rotten, as well as the bathroom floor, which I would find out later was rotted out due to a standing pool of water under the house. All in all though, it looked like a good deal. Yet the more I poked around the sagging old house I felt a strange twingeof *déja vu* ... like I had already been there once, had in the distant past already encountered the moldering old bungalow, had already seen the forlorn streets around it, and the sullen trees that overhung its peeling white walls. In a couple of days the farmer came to Cox St., driving an extra long pickup truck; we piled all my junk onto it and headed over to Princeton St. in Binghampton, looking like a couple of Arkys fleeing to the Promised Land. The Cox St. duplex and the Thunderbird I left to the custody of Falco and his seething camarilla.

It was twilight when we unloaded the last two boxes of books onto the coruscated front porch. That peculiar feeling came over me again that somehow, at sometime in the foggy past I had known this spot in Binghampton. Perhaps it was the heavy fragrance of the petals from a gardenia bush set at the northern corner of the house that had fallen on the dewy earth in a perfect circle that evoked this necromantic reverie. The blooms of gardenia, yellowed from their whiteness, last only a few days before dropping from the bush, which will remain barren for the rest of the year. As the old farmer cast off into the murky light, I thought I heard the high timbre of an indefinable voice... yes it was a voice. Someone was speaking in the half-light, in the shadows. It was not an effeminate voice, yet not masculine, nor was it the utterance of a child. The intonations were emanating from the side driveway between my bungalow and a high homemade clapboard fence, much higher than the height of a grown man. The odd hodge-podge fence surrounded a colossal, decrepit farmhouse. I peered into the veneer of darkness toward the direction of the waggish voice, and discerned the outline of a wrinkled truck fender of a gray color that blended perfectly with the evening dusk and with the dirt of the alley. The door of the truck appeared open and two reclining feet and forelegs were sticking out from the truck seat. I drew closer to the apparition and saw that one of the feet was not actually a foot, but was a bandaged nub.

Suddenly the brute hulk of a man swung up on the seat. A gnome in short pants and Coke bottle eyeglasses darted around the side of the truck, carrying a set of wooden crutches which she handed to the bearded, glowering creature. The leviathan lunged forward and rested his armpits on the crutches, looked up at me with cold white, narrow-set eyes and his narrow face split into a wide grin. He introduced himself as Sammy Lee, and the gnome as his daughter. He lived in the fenced-in compound next to my bungalow with his daughter, his dwarfish wife, and a pack of ornery hound dogs that he had trained to attack the front fence line whenever someone walked past. The rubes were from the hill country in Mississippi, I learned, and were friendly as could be for new neighbors.

Sammy Lee, like Charlie Feathers, was part Indian and he could mimic all the bird and animal calls from the forests and swamps. He was perennially attired in farmers' overalls, and usually wore a soiled red-plaid hunting cap on his pecan-shaped head. Sammy's wife kept Sammy Lee's head of hair close cut with a pair of old fashioned, Sears buzz clippers. My new friends invited me into their compound on that first chill autumnal evening on Princeton St. The daughter gnome opened the wide-boarded gate and ushered us in while the hounds growled and yelped and leaped all around me higher than a man's shoulders. I was sure the dogs were going to take off an arm or at least a few fingers before I got in the door, but upon the entreaties of their masters, they obediently forebeared from tearing me to pieces.

Inside the barn like structure, there was a wood fire burning in a small iron fireplace of the kind once used in Memphis for burning coal. The glowing embers were cheery, and Sammy Lee was hoisted onto the middle of a king size iron bed by his minions of dwarf and gnome. He said, "Now walk *lightly* in here, son. I got two cases of live grenades sitting under the bed. When the lid blows off, they're not going to get us out of here without a fight, I'll guarantee you that!" Sammy Lee spent the next hour demonstrating how he manufactured his own bullets by pouring molten lead into metal moulds. There was an arsenal of antiquated rifles that he had stacked on racks against the walls of the bedroom. Of the few decorations around the room, there were a John Deere tractor calendar on one peeling wall, and over the bedstead was a red-robed Christ figure pasted on a solid paper fan with a flat balsa wood handle of the kind ladies fan themselves with on a hot summer's day at evangelical revival meetings. The hound dogs would repeatedly run through the bedroom vying for Sammy Lee's attention, but he brushed them away with a vigorous swipe of his crutch.

The philosophy of Sammy was that of a survivalist. His sole ambition in life was simply to survive on his Ponderosa with his brood and his pack of hounds: an illustrious example of the robust individualist. Although Sammy Lee looked studious when he wore his wire-rimmed eyeglasses doing precise tasks like pouring bullets, he could neither read nor write. He eked out a living of sorts as a junker, meaning that he and his family collected junk and debris discarded on the streets and in the alleys of Memphis. A good part of this scavenging included Genie, his wife, and their daughter diving into industrial dumpsters scattered around the area and retrieving choice scraps of copper wire and junk metal. Then the loot would be sorted through, gloated over, and recycled and resold to junkyards on the edge of town.

To transport these raw materials Sammy Lee had a fleet of three derelict pickup trucks of which at least one was operational at any given time. The trucks had high side panels that the three of them had fabricated from cast off scraps of lumber, so the truck beds could be piled with junk to the point of such top heaviness that the whole rig seemed ready to topple over at the slightest provocation. Yet, when Sammy drove these behemoths, he showed no mercy and no fear of driving at top speed with the accelerator mashed to the floorboard. Due to the carburetors on the truck motors being totally worn out, top speed was rather limited. When Sammy gunned the motor of his truck on the street in front of our houses just to show everyone what his truck could do, he would hang out of the driver's window with his elbow over the door sill and look back in glory at the plumes of smoke spewing from the exhaust pipes as his rig sputtered, coughed, bucked, choked, and lurched ahead. The color of the exhaust smoke, of their clothes and skin, and of the truck bodies were of the same color of the asphalt upon which they rode.

The foot of Sammy Lee was lost in a motorcycle accident. He told me that he was riding a 400 cc Honda down Poplar and when he got to Highland Avenue, the little motorbike carrying this gargantuan junker tangled with a bob truck. The encounter resulted in him getting completely run over by the bob truck. He said when the ambulance came the paramedics put him in two body bags, sure that he was dead. Sammy Lee survived, but when he woke up in the hospital he discovered they had taken off his foot. That had happened some years before I met Sammy. The problem was that after the foot was amputated, the nub that was left had never healed. The doctors had him back in the hospital a number of times to drain it, pack it with antibiotics, cauterize it, yet nothing proved effective. The gauze at the end of the nub was continually wet with redness, and Sammy Lee told me, among other repugnant stories, that once when he was out on the compound in his wheel chair supervising his wife digging a post hole, he removed the bandage from the nub for a moment and a little white worm wiggled out and fell on the ground. Even he was sickened by the sight of it.

When Sammy Lee and his wife and their gnome weren't out in the pickup truck scavenging and junking, Sammy Lee had them building the surrounding fence of the compound higher and higher and reinforcing any suspect pickets. Crowning their protective barrier were strands of intertwined barbed wire they had scavenged from here and there. Sammy Lee ruled over the toil of his two laborers like a fractious, crippled tyrant. When their handiwork did not meet the expectations of their lord and master, a cruel crutch would whip through the air and knock them to the ground. More than once I would hear the gnomish girl squeal with the pain of the oafish battering, and I would come to the window to see her weeping and running to escape another blow.

When Sammy Lee had some distance to perambulate, he rode in a wheelchair pushed by either Genie or his daughter. He was not without his own brand of good humor, and was often amusing simply because he would find *himself* so amusing. Falco even took a liking to the hillbilly. Once he came over with the band, and handed Sammy Lee a camera to take album cover photographs. Sammy's first effort behind the camera was a success, and his pictures of the group were accepted and distributed by the Parisian record label. Seems the French dote on anything authentically bizarre. Falco then cast Sammy Lee and his family in a short film called, *Shade Tree Mechanic*, which a student from the San Francisco Art Institute had come to town to make with Panther Burns. The prodigious brio of Sammy Lee shone on celluloid with exultant triumph. Falco was dabbling around a lot with films and pictures. I still think he would have made a better salesman – used cars or something.

Once after a gig in Oxford, Falco and his camarilla rode the Thunderbird into a ditch on their way back to Memphis. They hitchhiked back to town, but they couldn't remember where they had left the car. Sammy Lee drove me down to Mississippi to find the T-Bird, which we found about ten miles north of Will Faulkner's stomping ground. Sammy had a log chain that we tied to the front bumper of the T-Bird and hauled the heavy barge out of the ditch then on up the highway to the Bluff City. Even though I had advised there was no pay on this mission, once on the road Sammy Lee insisted on two cheeseburgers. We stopped at a roadside burger joint, and while he munched the burgers, he asked me if I had ever taken someone out in the woods and tied them up. I admitted that I had not. Sammy Lee proceeded to describe in lucid detail how he had tied up two hapless individuals to a tree deep in the woods, and had molested and violated them until it wasn't funny anymore. His mirthful, yet livid eyes betrayed his straight face in telling me that no matter how much they screamed and hollered, there was no one and nobody to hear them except disinterested animals and birds hiding in the silence of the forest.

After an extended sojourn out of the country, I came back to Memphis at one point and learned that in my absence, while a section of the protective fence was being reinforced, Sammy Lee had been knocked over in his wheelchair by his wife and his daughter during a fit of mutinous rebellion, and the Draconian hillbilly had died there in the dirt of a heart attack. His hounds howled all night.

BOMB magazine called up from New York one weekend and set up a lengthy phoner with Falco. Before they called back, I coached Tav the best I could, and I had to give him some ammunition from my own background to round out the interview. In the end I don't think the magazine published much of the extended, overwrought discourse.

BOMB: From where does this confluence between 'hillbilly' music indigenous to the South and extremely dark, European-style Gothicism spring? What is its origin and why do you believe it's one of the dominant and recurring motifs of roots music? It seems to run from the paradigm of Robert Johnson meeting the Devil at the crossroads to the murder ballads of Hasil Adkins to the skulls and coffins of Screamin' Jay Hawkins. What is it exactly about the music of Panther Burns that so often aligns itself with the terrifying and the exotic?

TAV: There was a notion afoot that America was an extension of Europe. As in most such aphoristic statements there is a particle of truth in it. More than other Americans, Southerners, the closer you get to New Orleans, seem more connected, consciously or unconsciously, to European legacies. The lineages are there to be traced and ruminated over... the persecutions, the migrations, the witch-hunts, the hangings, the burnings, the exaltations, the apostasies, the betrayals, the avarice, the peonage, the enslavements: themes elaborated in the writings of the Virginia bard, Edgar Allan Poe. Paralleled in the last century, further sinister and distortive evocations from devastated lands in Europe entered our consciousness in the shadowed form of Expressionism. The South is a land of lost causes, brother against brother, burning mansions, of splendor, twilight, and exile... sharing an affinity with similar regions of central Europe. Burying ground ballads, hellhound blues, ghostly military waltzes, vigilante gavottes were played by Southerners who picked up European instruments and pressed them into the service of music and song that was reflective of analogous events, and of a spiritual nature shared with their European ancestors and brethren. The Panther Burns are only a mirror of such disenfranchisements, torments, and ecstasies.

BOMB: While Panther Burns was steeped in the tradition of the blues, the band also went well beyond mere revisionism, reinventing obscure songs of the past rather than simply performing old classics.

TAV: This is the literal part of our mission and how we approach it. While deconstructing formal harmony and pattern, we embrace a merry/sinister Gothicism in lyric and melody that harkens back to the dark mythologies not only of the blues, but also of parallel genres like mountain balladry, tango, and funeral marches.

BOMB: Your music has its own sonic palette, using heavy feedback and distortion, synthesizers, and incorporating other kinds of exotica... the experimental-meets-traditional. Traditional country, soul, and blues didn't delve much into atonality, feedback, and dissonance.

TAV: If your eyes and ears were open in the 60s, one could not help being exposed to everything at once. Histories and glyphs from the European avant-garde overlaid with strains of gypsy violins, Transylvanian harpsichords, and with gradients of noise generating devices of the Italian Futurists, were laid out on a mosaic gestalt of tapestry side by side with country blues traditions, hillbilly hollers, and motorcycle exhausts. It was an expansive, holistic, ever expanding, mind flogging 'magic carpet' for you to go stomping around on. For example, the Velvets had the experimentalist, John Cale, and a fashion model, Nico, with a German background. The group once played an unauthorized gig on the lawn of the HL Hunt mansion in Dallas, Texas, that was more of an art/ noise happening than a RnR show.

BOMB: From where did the decision to incorporate more of these dissonant and experimental textures into Panther's music come? Was it a result of Alex Chilton's and Jim Dickinson's influence? I'm automatically reminded of tracks like 'Kangaroo' from Third/Sister Lovers, which used mellotron and guitar feedback to similar dizzying effect. Did your earliest gigs meet a lot of resistance from Memphis purists for these reasons?

TAV: The "Kangaroo" track I've heard somewhere along the line, but the recollection is foggy. "Bangkok" I recall vividly and here one can savor the jaunty dissonance and distortion that Alex was cultivating at the time. Later during his tenure in Panther Burns, he attained even more heightened transports of feedback and crafted spontaneous, atonal electric guitar fugues that were astounding. A taste of this can be heard on the Rough Trade single of "Train Kept a Rollin'". Jim Dickinson was more into a bag of extreme electro/acoustic distortion and pink noise which was oblique to the thrust of Panther Burns... the influence derived from him was focused more along the lines of dramatic content and theatrical intervention. During those early gigs in Memphis, musicians who knew better than I, warned me to turn down the volume, turn down the reverb, drop the hideous feedback, and learn to play in meter, if I were ever going to become a musician. I am afraid that I was unable to heed their council, and have yet to attain the stature of an honest or earnest musician.

BOMB: As the 80s underground music scene expanded beyond punk, many of the stylistic and musical cues of Panther Burns were used by bands like Primal Scream, Spacemen 3, The Gun Club, The Meat Puppets, Big Black, Pussy

Galore/The Blues Explosion. Some like The Gun Club and The Meat Puppets merged country-blues and punk while others assimilated a wider range of soul, psychedelia, and garage- rock. They were all essentially necrophagists, consuming and digesting the music of the past into new product. This methodology reached its apex in indie music by 1986 with Pussy Galore's bootleg cover of Exile on Main Street. The album is a track-by-track recording of the classic Rolling Stones LP but their translations are nearly unnerving blasts of noise with bits of Stones' lyrics thrown in. It is an intense listening experience. However the whole concept seems to be an extension of the Panther Burns/ Cramps' method of recontextualizing old lyrics and melodies to form an entirely new composition.

TAV: There are different kinds of noise, e.g. white noise, pink noise, brown noise. Some forms of noise have little redeeming value. Hence groups who produce useless and misguided noise are no better than the racket they make. Just because a group can manage to blithely savage an existing opus with unnerving blasts of unmitigated noise cannot be construed as elevating, revealing, extending, or even deconstructive of anything of more significance than a Coke bottle. If you are going to deconstruct something, you have to go on to reconfigure it and *add* something to what is left... or you end up with a worthless heap of meaningless fragments. *Nothing* is left in such operations except traces of anger and frustration that sooner or later fade into oblivion. It is misguided to make cases for such actions. Distortion for the sake of distortion is a dead end. Distortion is an application... as applied to something that is free of distortion, hence something unusual results. Or distortion is an inherent condition that can be made more distorted, but only in degree... then when distortion is removed or taken away, the condition changes in kind and something unseen is revealed. The dynamic of NOISE operates the same. Noise is what you find in a sack of *gris gris*, and although it can be dispensed with abandon, it must be used carefully. As applied, I embrace the term 'necrophagist'. Panther Burns *are* 'necrophiliac', and purveyors of pink noise specializing in 'Live Excavations'.

BOMB: These bands also did much to literally dismantle and destroy the traditional timbres of the guitar in order to record the death shrieks of guitar music, very reminiscent of your chainsaw debut. Do you think this type of music took the guitar to its limit or signaled the end of a certain kind of guitar experimentation? Could you foresee the end of the guitar as the focal pop icon?
TAV: Before the guitar became the focal pop icon, it was the tenor saxophone... esp. in jazz and jump blues which are essentially popular music forms. Out of destruction comes rebirth. Out of the death rattle comes the fresh wailings of the newborn. Out of dichotomy and annihilation comes the *Pantherbourne*. Whether the device is a guitar, or a saxophone, or a string of baling wire strung up on the side of a cabin, or a humble fife cut from a stick of cane... it is the hand that plays it, the mouth that blows it, the mind that perceives it, the soul that feels it, which matters in the end. There is no limit.
BOMB: I find it interesting that you have had the quasi-technological element of 'TONE SCIENCE' added to the Panther Burns moniker. What was your reasoning behind that decision?
TAV: Not unlike other artists, Panther Burns draw from a palette of tones and colors and gradations. Underlying an array of 'found' noises, drones, musical tonalities, and noise effects are two fundamental wellsprings of the din of Panther Music. The traditional musical aspect is drawn from the Devil's interval and chordal syncopations of African-American deep gospel instrumentation; the other aspect is drawn from unintentional, often industrial sounds, e.g. noises and syncopations of trains running up and down the rails... both tonalities overlap and both enchanted me from an early age when steam locomotives came chugging and puffing through the remote Arkansas railhead near where I grew up, and covered our town in huge clouds of coal black smoke. Later when I was working as a brakeman on the Missouri Pacific railroad, the reiterative and cadenced sounds of riding the rails were running through my head night and day. In the evenings the train might be dragging a cut of freight cars past a country church, or a sharecropper's cabin, or saw mill worker's front porch where electric guitars were being picked in the groove of

Jimmy Reed, or church chords were heard coming out of distorted windows hung on unpainted clapboard walls. Until this day I am still entranced by both layers of this tonal palette and thus comes music as heard by a swarthy and dusty Panther as he rolls over in his slumbers under the palpable shade of a pine grove not so far from the R/R tracks.

BOMB: I've found that so many innovative 'noise' musicians (whether they be electronic, electro-acoustic, or electric) tend to have a fetishistic relationship with their gear that borders on the scientific; namely, they are very precise on what brands of instruments they like and what kind of 'sound' they are searching for. Are there any particular types of guitar (Fender Telecaster, Silvertone surf guitars, etc.) and playing methods (strange tunings, how you play your feedback, the ever-present twang of a tremolo pedal, etc.) that you've married to the overall Panther Burns sound? Do you believe these kinds of textural components are as essential to your music as the more traditional elements of rhythm, harmony, and melody?

TAV: The thrust of Panther Burns as a group has always been an electric two-guitars sound. Early in my development with Panther Burns, I made a transition from black Silvertone guitars to the black 1963, violin-shaped hollow body, six-string Höfner with the built-in, push-button active, factory fuzz tone unit. Since then I've played the same guitar, and I am not sure that another instrument could ever achieve the sonic thrust of the Panther Burns as well and as faithfully. I eschew all types of intermediary effects devices, and plug directly into a Fender tube amplifier equipped with a long, three-spring reverb tank and with dual or quadruple 10-inch speakers. Occasionally I have campaigned a National tube amp running 2 x 12-inch speakers – the model with the chrome icebox door handle on top – with sterling results. Using a flat pick or three National steel finger picks and a thumb pick, I often attack the instrument with a "slide" tube of chrome steel over my finger. Lush echo and a splash of reverb are essential to the vocals of Panther Burns... I cannot see committing to a Panther Burns performance without the aforementioned. As for the complementary guitar, we prefer a hollow body Gretsch, or Gibson, or National, or Burns of London powered by likewise amplification. When we can get it, we employ an amplified stand-up contrabass or Fotdella, otherwise a hollow-body electric bass guitar is acceptable. A trap drum set is required outfitted with tambourine and a long cowbell. Added to these essentials can be any number and configuration of ancillary instruments and sounding devices, depending on the application, from Theremin to bandoneon, to singing saw, Leslie oscillator, etc. It is with these tools that we evoke the rhythms, (dis) harmonies, and melodies of Panther Burns.

BOMB: While most pop music historians look to the mid/late 60s as the earliest flirtations between rock and experimental music (the aforementioned elements of feedback, synthesis, an emphasis on the 'sound' of production) it still seems as though the 50s were chockfull of studio invention. From Les Paul to Joe Meek's earliest space opera. The 'Memphis' sound appeared to be a hotbed of experimentation, particularly in its use of echo/delay and gospel multi-instrumentation to low fidelity distortion. Looking back over the vast catalogue of rockabilly classics, from labels like Sun to King to Meteor etc., do you have any particular favorites that you believe made seminal contributions to 'noise rock'?

TAV: Worthy of mention is the innovative fuzz guitar used by Pat Hare on songs like, "I'm Gonna Murder My Baby". Certainly the sonic universe concocted by Joe Meek extends beyond the pale of invention and far ahead of his time and far into the future. *No one* has really matched the impeccably fastidious dynamic contours of sonic brilliance and atmospheric elegance that he achieved on his recordings. In Panther Burns we did the best we could with recording his anthem of teen angst, "Have I the Right?" (upon careful scrutiny, essentially a rockabilly song), yet we hardly attained the unearthly and divinely inhuman ferocity of the vocalizations recorded by the Honeycombs. If only Joe Meek could re-materialize and produce Panther Burns as we are ready to prostrate ourselves before the altar of his cosmic wizardry.

BOMB: I wonder if you'd consider the 'slap echo' the very first psychedelic studio effect, the way in which its undulatory gradations would simulate hypnotic propulsion throughout the background of the track, e.g. its eerie use in Charlie

Feather's "Jungle Fever"? To me, it bears an uncanny resemblance to the 13th Floor Elevators' later use of the electric jug. It's also completely organic to the song, c.f. the 'novelty' effect of certain modulators in 60s psych songs like "Baby Your Phrasing's Bad" with its cheesy phase shifting.

TAV: Well, I adore funky 60s effects. I had no idea 13th Floor Elevators made use of an electric jug! I am mightily impressed to hear this about a group that I've already held in the highest esteem. 'Slap back' tape echo is surely a psychedelic effect, and it has existed since the advent of tape recording machines. What is significant is *who* applied it, and *how*, and to *what*... as much as when. It is thought that the radio engineer, Sam C. Phillips, and his early colleague, Charlie Feathers, were perhaps the first to apply tape echo to actual tape recordings as an aesthetic device. When Charlie Feathers finally got in a position to apply the effect to his own material, as evidenced by the hauntingly exquisite echo he produced on "Jungle Fever", an erotically thrilling new threshold was achieved in sonic reverberation. To attain the maximum, aesthetically pleasing delivery of the effect on a track, as Charlie explained it, required considerable experimentation, finesse, and delicate fine-tuning.

BOMB: I am not a musician per se, but I am fascinated by the style and image of the studio musician – the Electric Warrior as Marc Bolan put it so beautifully – as a kind of scientist or alchemist who sat in his laboratory channeling unknown forces through various alembics. Of course, in their time alchemists from Nicholas Flammel to Gilles de Rais were feared as magicians and occultists – in the same way, certain musicians who played bagpipes, the hurdy gurdy, and other drone instruments were executed for invoking evil spirits. Do you see a connection between the status of the noise musician and, say, the Outlaw or the Witch or the Alchemist? Do you think there is still a general cultural aversion to the experimental nature of noisy or distorted music as somehow verboten?

TAV: The image of the artist or musician as alchemist is utterly fascinating. Music – an unseen force – magic, the occult, and alchemy all seem to be interconnected. One cannot deny that the spell of music is mysterious. I had friends from Dubrovnik who were in a band called the Scientists. Mercurial individuals, whose music was strictly alchemical. The first thing I do when I go onstage is to cast a spell. When people surrender to our rhythms without inhibition and dance, they go home thinking about it the next day, and the next. I have also witnessed Panther Burns polarize audiences – those reaching out in ecstatic embrace side by side with others spewing howls of contempt and derision. Casting a spell in the crucible of a recording studio, where there is no live audience, is another matter. In that case, one must rely on *conjurations*. In Venice one day I saw a strange man in the shadows of a portico playing bagpipes constructed with white flour sacks and with long pitch pipes. Part of the instrument he drove with an extended foot pedal. The Italians were captivated by the atmospheric droning he was generating, as was I. He was not entertaining with his deadpan grinding as much as he was saturating us with ancient, penetrating and ominously wheezing tonalities that could not be easily evaded or dismissed.

BOMB: How important a component is dancing to your music? After Panther Burns' initial forays into rockabilly, your albums tended to incorporate elements of tango and samba. Interesting because so much of early rock 'n roll was based on its ability to incite these massive audiences into flailing dervishes, whether it be at the juke joint or the Sunday social.

TAV: *Bien sûr*, Panther Burns is above all a dance band. Dancing is the response elicited by Panther Burns... other considerations are residual. Dance is an essential form of expression, and one that cannot be overlooked literally or in its profounder manifestations. Argentine tango, for instance, is reflective of passionate sensual, yet philosophic relationships between men and women, although its origins are derived from more primitive forms of human contact and cadences.

BOMB: But after the punk days of pogo-ing and gobbing, traditional rock audiences rarely danced beyond the occasional rigid shuffle which makes a song like "Tina, The Go-Go Queen" all the more anomalous. In your opinion what is it that has changed the rock audience from 'movers 'n' shakers' to merely spectators?

TAV: Popular dances and dance crazes in America ranging from *fin-de-siècle* Cakewalk and 1920s Black Bottom to the Madison and the Hully Gully of the early 60s were predicated on the blatant sensuality and syncopated structures of blues, ragtime, and jazz rhythms. When rock music, as a product of these forms, shifted toward heavy instrumentation and mind-expanding psychedelia, the body was left to re-orient itself within a tribal context, rather than to interpret musical cadences within the refined structure of paired couples and defined lines of dance. What had been a dance on Saturday night became a rock 'n' roll concert or free-form revival meeting. What had once been a house party with Fats Waller grooving at the piano while couples danced the shimmy became a sit down concert with Thelonious Monk at Birdland. Music makes its own demands. Though personally, I have no trouble dancing to the chording of Monk. The body is esoteric and holds its own mysteries and collective memories. What is evoked from it, as movement, is more like phenomena. The mind has thought; the body has movement. When they get together under the spell of music, the phenomenon of dance appears. Unless it is a complicated form of communal solo dancing like flamenco, dancing in couples is more demanding than dancing alone and brings with it a certain degree of socialization and acculturation. Dancing alone or head banging at a rock concert is free expression. When the music changes, the feet change accordingly. When hemlines on skirts come down or go up, the style of dancing changes. When music contains more intellectual import or becomes ultra cool, audiences tend to sit and ponder rather than get up and dance with each other. Audiences become introspective when listening to protest music or music with a message – when they are too occupied figuring out meaning to do anything other than tap their foot. Dancing before such thoughtful music might seem frivolous... but when the music gets hot and sexy, people are seen cutting scissor steps between each other's legs. Of course, when a performance becomes nothing more than sheer spectacle, the audience becomes nothing more than spectators at a circus. Dancing in couples is ritualistic and reflective of more stratified rites of courting and mating. Unstructured dancing alone or alone within a group is more like free jazz. Infused in the gaucheries of Panther Burns are aspects of all these forms of music and dance. Personally, I find dancing in couples most rewarding. I would be bored stiff at a rock concert unless it were the Doors or Suicide.

BOMB: Do you think there has been an elevated sense of intellectualism infused in pop music over the last twenty years, i.e. the birth of the indie rocker, which has shifted the focus away from becoming a part of the 'ritual' of the live gig to a theatrical distance, in other words, observing it?

TAV: The ground is always shifting underneath the artist... and Theatre takes many forms. Intellectual gradients do not necessarily preclude ritualistic sensuality and movement as in dance. Bob Dylan embodies a certain balance between these elements. On the other hand, what form of dancing are people doing to Nine Inch Nails...? Or to Marilyn Manson? No doubt these groups are eminently danceable.

BOMB: Not sure if you are a follower of the electronica sub-culture, but do you think with the last decade's popularity of electronic dance music – rave, hardcore, drum 'n' bass, grime, 2-step – that there has been a real 'shift' in 'common' cultural/musical experience from melody/harmony back to rhythm? I say 'back' because, in a sense, rave and electronica audiences seemed to return to rock's traditional primacy of R&B and the beat, Bo Diddley, Chuck Berry, Howlin' Wolf, Link Wray, all of which have been part your focus for decades?

TAV: Has the two-step come back around again...? If primal rhythm is withdrawn, melody and harmony are depotentiated and robbed of their throbbing pulsations. What you have left is Third Stream jazz or 12-tone structures of Arnold Schönberg... which I can groove on. I adore heavenly arrhythmic arias and atonal fugues, yet I live to throb = *andante, adagio, o larghetto.*

BOMB: In several of your past interviews, you mentioned your influences/ connections with female rockabilly musicians like Jesse Mae Hemphill, Cordell Jackson and Memphis Minnie. However, the contribution of women, and, in a larger sense, the feminine mystique seems scarce in the rough 'n tumble world of rockabilly. Similarly, in interviews I'm currently conducting with noise-rock and electronic musicians, I've pointed out that the role played by women in the history of 'experimental' music seems to be overwhelmingly minute (exceptions of course, Pauline Oliveros to Delia Derbyshire to Laurie Anderson to Poison Ivy to Kim Gordon)...

TAV: Jesse Mae Hemphill and Memphis Minnie were country blues artists, while Cordell Jackson was more of a rock 'n' roll player than rockabilly, yet she was one of the most noisy, spontaneous thrashers of electric guitar (a red Hagstrom) that I have seen on stage anywhere of any gender. Extraordinary. She attacked the guitar like a field hand driving a posthole, while her femininity remained intact and uncompromised. What matters most, may be the quality of that which is contributed by the few, rather than the quantity of what may be dished up the many. Sheer numbers ultimately have little significance toward validating the role of women in these genres. Certainly no male has outstripped the stature of the women you have cited.

BOMB: Do you think there is an 'elemental' disconnect between women and noise music, whether it befeedback-drenched rockabilly or atonal electronica? Why do you think these kinds of music, with their emphasis on dissonant textures and droning harmonics, have remained by and large a boys' club while other genres like acoustic folk, country, and melodious pop have expanded to include larger numbers of female artists and female audiences?

TAV: The gender distinction between these genres is due to notions of confused femininity. The more traditional music forms have attracted female adherents whose femininity are never threatened and are often, by conventional standards, enhanced. In the area of generated tone and noise music, we find technologically and aesthetically experimental mind sets at work. Outside of computing and scientific fields and notables like Mme. Curie, we do not find so many women tinkering and toiling in sound labs. This is a pity because of the fertile contributions women are capable of making to any field. Women ought to be attracted to experimental activity with promise that is not sexually subtractive. There is so much to be derived by their inclusion. Much ink has been spilt, for instance, over the role of women in rock 'n' roll, and the nature of their playing. I love to hear women playing rock n roll instruments; it sounds so different from men playing – irresistibly different to masturbatory impulses of men.

BOMB: I'd read that you started your career as a film documentarian in a group called TeleVista, traveling around the South in search of blues and country figures of the past before deciding to pick up the guitar yourself. Would you mind telling me some of your more interesting experiences while on the road?

TAV: Before Panther Burns, there was TeleVista – an art-action group with a video-making thrust. The Arkansas poet, Randall Lyon, was its president, and I was the secretary and videographer of TeleVista. One TeleVista mission was a trip to the mountainside home in the Ozarks of former governor of Arkansas, the Honorable Orval E. Faubus. This controversial politician proved to be a suave, cordial, highly articulate, cunning, and utterly charming individual who embodied a number of unexpected complexities and inconsistencies, especially involving his origins and background. Randall made the interview and I made the camera, but before we could start we had to wait for his new girlfriend's teenage son to finish band practice. The kid had his rock 'n' roll group set up in the middle of the living room. His mother was an approving shapely and busty Madison County brunette.

We stepped out on the terrace overlooking an expansive range of the Ozark mountains, turned on the camera, focused in the Swiss lens, and learned that the father of Orville Faubus had been a pacifist and had been arrested in the county seat of Huntsville for passing out seditious anti-war literature during the first World War. When the young Orville became of age, he was sent to Commonwealth College – a communist institution of higher learning in Mena. During this period Arkansas cultivated a tradition of acceptance and tolerance for sects, movements, institutes, churches, and temples of various and extreme religious and political persuasions.

Even though Faubus will be remembered as the populist leader who was the first governor in the South to dispute the 1954 Supreme Court decision to enforce racial integration, the story does not end there. In some very nasty and sad confrontations at Central High School between his constituency and federal integration officials, Orville stood his ground and was quickly summoned to Washington by Eisenhower. There he refused to concede any compromise and maintained his contrarian stance until Ike was forced to send in Airborne Federal troops to Little Rock to quell the situation so that nine black children could attend classes in the white school.

Still, he knew that no one could be governor of Arkansas without winning the black vote, which represented 30% of the electorate. Orville knew how to get the black vote. Black voters knew where he stood, they knew they could trust him, and he got their vote... going on to enjoy four consecutive terms as governor of the state. Yet Orville Faubus always thought of himself in the perspective of an American liberal, and during his tenure as governor did much to improve conditions in the state especially in the area of education and opportunities for blacks and whites alike.

BOMB: Who were the musicians you encountered and who eventually turned you onto making music yourself? Was it R.L. Burnside? Did you find something more primary in making the music that simply videoing it could not provide?

TAV: Once I was introduced to the charismatic, magical individual known as Rural Burnside in the backwoods of Panola county in north Mississippi, and I heard his haunting, trance-dirge guitar and filmed him through an interminable night in his honky tonk, I fell then completely under the spell of his snaking, swamp infested rhythms. I had never heard anything quite like these darkly melodious strains of erotic yearning and torment that seemed to flow effortlessly from his body and from his battered, de-tuned electric guitar. His honky tonk was like a secular church. Sharecroppers and their women came there for serious merrymaking, for the voluptuous guitar sounds, and howling vociferations as heard from the seemingly farthest reaches and corners of hell itself. The tenant farmers and tractor drivers came for the camaraderie, for the chicken frying all night in an iron skillet, for the endless cases of cold Schlitz, and they came for miles around to wager on the vagaries of the tumbling dice shaking in a leather dice horn, and for the girls working the back room. At some point during this period I began to see no separation between what was in front of the camera and what was behind it... between being behind the camera and being in front of it, no separation between the observer and the observed.

As a youth I had acquired my first Sears Silvertone guitar, but never learned how to really play it. I only made sounds on it, in part because in my isolation, I had no live models to learn from, and I learn from people's hands. Eventually I traded the guitar for a Webcor open reel field tape recorder. When I encountered Burnside and Charlie Feathers and others, I had models playing before me for the first time. And I had made films and tapes of them playing, and could now playback sound and picture of their playing *ad infinitum*. It was then, and it still is, just as natural to reach for a funky guitar, as it was to pick up a film or video camera.

BOMB: Similarly, I've always thought the most imaginative music had an inherent synaesthetic component in the way that it could blend visual 'tones' and 'colors' with aural harmonics. I've found this to be particularly true with rockabilly, where the heavy use of echoed vocals and reverbed guitar yields an ethereal, nocturnal lament and a perfect mood 'soundtrack' for late-night listening. Do you think your music was influenced by filmmaking or particular genres of cinema, for example, the works of Fellini, Jodorowsky, Lynch, Waters, etc.? Do you write or record your music with any cinematic perspective for the way guitar timbres or textures might be mixed?

TAV: When I first started listening to electric blues records as a youth, I used to lay back and close my eyes and experience visual hallucinations orchestrated by and syncopated with the musical tones and phrases. This form of synesthesia is cinematic in abstract form. For me, pure cinema *is* visual music. Yet in my mind, pure cinema is mute – it is silent cinema. Still, it is quite apparent that sound and picture go together very well... and it is the strength of an art form regarding how well it interfaces with another form or medium. As Marshall McLuhan pointed out, new art forms or technologies have the characteristic and capability of 'wrapping around' an earlier art form or technology. Like, for example, television wrapping around film. Then there is music arranged especially for film, often called soundtrack music, conversely film is also conceived for illustrating musical pieces.

Admittedly, I am captivated by Italian movie music from the 60s, which is a genre in itself. For instance, the music to the *La Decima Vittima* is irresistible and totally integrated cinematically. We have produced short films illustrating our songs. The atmosphere of B&W appears most suited to Panther Music, as exemplified by the piece entitled, "Born Too Late." Before we filmed it in Budapest at the 19th century Club Fésék, I had met Alejandro Jodorowsky in Paris and was invited to his home one evening. I had the notion of asking him to direct the film. He demurred, but not before giving me a number of his ideas for realizing the song filmically. In the end, we used none of his rather Dadaist visualizations, but I perceived how his mind worked in terms of a moving picture treatment of musical and lyrical content. When I conceptualized the Panther Burns album, *Hour of the Shadow Dancer*, I thought of it as music designed for a feature film. After recording the album, I collaborated writing a scenario, *Shadow Dancer: the Movie*, with Rainer Kirberg, the scenarist in Berlin and director of "Born Too Late". In the process of creating our films, I found that syncing tones, sounds, and music to picture and to moving images produces an intriguing visualization and a very dynamic one with unlimited dramatic possibilities of montage.

BOMB: In another interview you said, "The influence of William Eggleston on my work is in being introduced to a symphony of color and sound while looking at seemingly mundane objects." Would you mind elaborating on what exactly it was about Eggleston's photography that inspired you? Was it exactly the kind of nocturnal, shadowy tone mentioned above? While your music always coaxed a stark black- and-white mood in my mind, were you more inspired by his color or non-color photos?

TAV: To elaborate on that impression of the Eggleston *oeuvre*, not only color relationships but innovative *de*compositional aspects and Expressionistic distortions drew me into the Egglestonian cosmos – a visionary realm of ambiguity and ironic, and unresolved consequences presented on a fabric woven with the most literal and prosaic of objects and icons and with the people – whether seen or unseen – who are attached to them in often alarming ways. Before Panther Burns, I assisted Eggleston on nocturnal missions, filming in color with stroboscopic lighting and yielding images of unearthly spectra...as if Edgar Allan Poe had been dropkicked into post-modern Virginia wielding a Leica lens. As much as his color compositions, his earlier, lengthy B&W essays enthrall me. You are right to perceive our music in black & white imagery.
In my own 16mm and 35mm short films, I am most drawn to those filmed in B&W, and all future filmic work I intend to be done in monochrome. On the contrary, in his personal work Eggleston long ago lost contact with the genre of B&W.

BOMB: At the time of Panther Burns' formation in 1979, what was the general vibe of Memphis music culture? With Sun and Stax Records along with numerous other soul labels like Hi, etc., gone or on the decline, I'm curious whether or not there was still a strong sense of identity to the city's music? What else was happening there at the time? Were the city's other 'forward thinking' musicians looking elsewhere at NY or LA punk for inspiration?

TAV: Even with Gospel groups, the nature of music in Memphis has over the years been ostensibly a commercial enterprise. Even before Panther Burns, my comrades were fed up with the status quo. One of the groundbreaking events that brought attention and focus on indigenous musicians and their music was the annual series of Memphis Country Blues Festivals held in Overton Park Shell. Here the great artists of the non-commercial world of country blues and gospel were presented before a new generation eager to experience and to absorb what had by then become traditional genres and forms. By the mid-70s Stax studio was a burned out, bombed out carcass of a movie house. When real money started to be made really fast, and Memphis banks and record company executives exploited and abused the still ascendant popularity of soul music, failing to properly cultivate the phenomena and its artists, the scene deteriorated and went down fast. All record companies of any significance pulled out of Memphis. Burned as badly as they were, the major labels and record companies still have not returned.

Anyway that scene was for rich bond daddies and fancy pimps driving canary yellow Cadillacs and wearing Stetson hats. *Who cares?* Those sorts of bubbles always blow themselves out. What is important is that the music survives. There will always be blues in Memphis. There will always be a Saturday night in Memphis for some nigger or dago – for white or black – to go out and shake a tail feather, or to court his good gal on the front porch with a steel stringed guitar. That is indigenous music. This is the fountainhead, the lodestone, the Mojo Hand, the High John the Conqueroo *root* of black inspired music, and that is the music of America which distinguishes our music from all others. It is a wild root that cannot be weeded out. It is the swamp root from which grows all forms of American popular music that travels upriver to commercial centers and then gets packaged and re-sold and pretty soon Madame LaZonga is doing the Conga on Broadway, and it all comes back down river again. The long silver thread of the blues is unbroken and always connected, yet to most it remains invisible. So the Cramps or the Sex Pistols can come to Memphis and consciously re-fry a fine-cooked Southern meal in a way that no one down home has ever quite seen before. Point is: blues, jazz, rock 'n' roll have become universally recognizable and like any great and genuine genre, it lends itself to universal interpretation and re-invention. It is natural then that Memphis musicians connected with the rest of the world, and vice versa. Inspiration is where you find it: in traditions, in trends, in extremes, in multi-cultures.

BOMB: I read that you had not met Alex Chilton before and was not aware of his previous work. True?

TAV: Well, "The Letter" I had heard on the radio, but I had little awareness of a group called the Box Tops. The woods were full of hit records in Memphis and rock 'n' roll stars on every corner.

BOMB: With all the revisionist chatter that surrounds Big Star nowadays, it's difficult to gauge their impact in Memphis at the time. How did you view the Big Star/Ardent Studio influence in your early days? Was it a bit too poppy and jangly for your tastes or did it really open up a new 'sound' to rival Stax/Volt in the 70s?

TAV: Apologies, but I had no knowledge of the band Big Star at that time, and still don't know much about them. During the 60s & 70s, I was listening to cotton patch blues, to psychedelia, and to Karl Heinz Stockhausen.

BOMB: How important do you think Panther Burns was in resurrecting Alex's career and all of the critical attention surrounding his work?

TAV: If Panther Burns were responsible for anything concerning this gifted artist, surely it was nothing more than personal diversion and a few kicks.

BOMB: Similarly James Luther Dickinson was a kind of one-man institution stretching back to his inclusion on The Rolling Stones' Sticky Fingers and his production on Sun Record's finale "Cadillac Man". What was your introduction to him musically and how did he fit into the philosophy of Panther Burns?

TAV: Jim Dickinson in my mind is hardly a one-man institution, rather he is representative of a community of artists and their audiences, and he is a spokesperson for those artists and for the aficionados attached to them. Jim understands the axiom that for there are to be great poets, there must be great audiences. In that sense, Jim Dickinson is characteristic of the 'people' in the most poetic and robustly independent and American sense. From the beginning Jim Dickinson was fully cognizant of the realm of the theatre of Utopian Anarchy from which Panther Burns sprang... and as our mentor he showed Panther Burns how to sing and dance the songs and shuffles of electric medicine show minstrels. As Piano Red before him, Jim – like Panther Burns – was and is still running on Train Time.

BOMB: Many of your records, particularly the early material like Behind the Magnolia Curtain, were infamous for their very minimal production, where songs were performed 'live' and often in one take. You had said in an interview that, "Most of the tracks are one-take. We didn't do any real mixing, and of course, there were no overdubs. We went into Ardent and we recorded all the tracks in two afternoons of three-hour sessions. A couple of the tunes we did two takes of, but usually there was just no stopping." Although this was the norm for most traditional blues and country records of the bygone era, it's almost unheard of in the age of big studios and multi-track players. I believe around the same time you and Alex Chilton were working on these recordings in Memphis, he was also producing The Cramps' early material, much of which had a similar production value. Do you recall how much of Panther Burns' stripped-down approach was a collaborative effort and how much of an influence Alex had in mimicking the sounds of early Sun records?

TAV: *Behind the Magnolia Curtain* was in fact recorded in one and two-takes within about 6-hours. There was the presence of the Tate County, Mississippi, marching drum band, members of which were stalwarts in Napoleon Stricklin's Cane Fife & Drum band. The Drum Corps appeared on four tracks marching around Studio B of Ardent and were recorded simultaneously with Panther Burns – all of us playing and thrashing at once. We were *bon vivants* of the swamps living it up on ample doses of fried chicken and short pints of bourbon whiskey. The ensuing threshold of noise was so far overreached that the engineer of the session gave up entirely on observing any recognized parameters of recording standards in a desperate attempt to just get the mess on tape. The battle cry raised by Alex as we waded into each new number was, "I'm *right* behind you, man." There was no real mixing... there was a modicum of EQing during the dumping of the 16-track material onto 1/2-track reels for engraving onto an acetate master disc. Nor was there any er, production... or anyone in charge of production as I remember. As always in those early days of Panther Burns, it was every man for himself.

When the mastering engineer began the task of cutting the acetate production disc from the 1/2 track material, the level of uncontrollable noise that saturated every frequency appalled him. The resulting grooves cut into the soft acetate master disc were so shallow and so close together due to the density of noise present, that fidelity was compromised and the acceptable industry standard for total program length of a vinyl album was exceeded by over three minutes per side. The Cramps' early recordings as produced by Alex and by Jim Dickinson had consciously achieved a level of sonic excellence and dynamic presence, whereas the first Panther Burns album just sort of 'happened' by a process of spontaneous generation.

BOMB: Can you remember what kind of relationship you and Alex had in the studio and what your working dynamic was like? Were you more of the 'idea' and 'music' man while he was the guy behind the controls or was it more of an equal writing/playing relationship?

TAV: Sure we had our recording idols as reference and the studio sounds of SUN Records and the inimitable Joe Meeks productions that we idolized, but we found it impossible to even begin to emulate such sonic wizardry. The equipment and techniques used in those innovative recordings had long disappeared... except for the acoustic, walk-in echo chambers, which we used extensively in our maniacal quest for the lush sounding echo. As for our roles in these ventures, the concepts were generally of my instigation, but it was Alex who was the musical alchemist... me never, because I was not and still am hardly a musician. I am simply a performer, a provocateur... and only play *upon* musical instruments, rather than approach such devices with any degree of musical understanding other than intuitive. On later recordings Alex twirled the knobs more or less 'fixing' everything in the mix as was his extraordinary talent to do... such talent matched only by his astonishing gifts as one of the few towering guitarists and singers of our age, among whom there is no finer. What song writing that has been done in Panther Burns came much later and was by my own hand.

BOMB: You've made mention of theorists/poets Antonin Artaud and Louis Aragon as lyrical and 'stylistic' influences on Panther Burns as well as practitioners of 'art brut' who much like the forgotten Southern musicians toil on the margins of culture – I agree with you whole-heartedly on this. In fact (quick aside) I dedicated the introductory section of the Spacemen book to a kind of alternative history of radiation and music that flows through the 20th century demimonde of Georges Bataille, Jean Genet, etc. but centering on the electronic experiments of Artaud contemporaneous with the invention and use of the Atomic Bomb.

TAV: These are exciting considerations and connections you are evoking. Certainly Artaud and Aragon were influential, but more than lyrical and stylistic, it was the overriding import of their MANIFESTOS that inspired me to action and their unbridled flaying of thought from the bone meat of existence that moved me. How far their influence may have extended, outside of France and Spain, and the narrow strata of those who explore the extremes of theatre and poetry, to equally marginal Southern musicians and bluesmen is difficult to imagine. Perhaps one can relate the rants of Hasil Adkins in some sort of Artaudian context, but the derivative nature of most of these Southern musicians and bluesmen was essentially agrarian. However disenfranchised they were, however mistreated they became, however much their tolerances warped, and once transplanted to the cities, whatever complexities, anxieties, and uncertainties they underwent, they all possessed an understanding of, a thread to, an inner peace, an inner clear spot or memory of it: a pastoral numinous beatific oneness that infused the lives of those who lived or had once lived in the country.

The poetry they wrote, however dark or opining, was always composed as a measure of their inherent connection to universal mysteries, but expressed in compelling everyday, barnyard terms and metaphors. Whereas the awareness of Bataille, Genet, Artaud was self-conscious, erudite, spewing, disassociated, psychoanalytic, subversive – involving a perception of the so called natural order of things from an inverted, convoluted, and irrationally angular view... as Bataille's vision of his syphilitic father's sightless eyes transforming into chicken eyes as he was straining to piss. Even though the radiophonic experiments of Artaud were suppressed toward the end of his life as was his theatre before then, it is interesting to think that aspects of his fractured and frenzied incantations were already taking root, even in the constellated thoughts of country people. With the advent of the Bomb and the Atomic Age, for the first time men began to live with the threat of total annihilation resulting from development and deployment of their own technologies. The mandate to confront the resulting absurdity of existence, the universal fragility of life, as we know it, and the thought of life having less significance than a smear of slime mold, came into startling focus.

BOMB: Experiments with electrical noise seem to share an historical and procedural similarity with Southern musicians of the post-War era. For example, in another interview on your influences you explained, "In the '50s when these white cats were taking up electric guitars for the first time and black cats were taking them up, this was all new. Audiences weren't educated to this kind of music. You walked out with a tiny Fender amplifier with one 12-inch speaker and one microphone on stage and it was revolutionary. And it was loud, too. They got an incredibly fine mix – an awfully hot sound."

TAV: As referenced earlier in our discourse, the use of a cracked guitar speaker in Memphis by the incendiary electric country blues guitarist, Pat Hare, thus producing the first fuzz tone guitar sound may have been simply accidental... like many innovative discoveries. The velvet noise that floated on the razor's edge of Pat Hare's guitar sound became his signature when he played with James Cotton or whomever else. The discontent, the urgency, the RAGE heard on the recordings of his guitar are more poignant, more powerful, and more meaningful in its country blues phrasing and lyricism than a freight train load of all the million selling faux-revolutionary, ghetto hate-music one hears everywhere today. Pat Hare's origins were traced in a lineage from Robert Johnson, but instead of poisoning by a jealous female, he died in prison convicted of murdering his woman.

Personally, I have come full circle in my proclivities for aesthetic expression that I choose to wrap around myself tipping down this lonesome road. I now seek harmonious tones infused with noises... harmony in extremes, in contrasts of blacks and whites and its delicate gradations in between. I crave dissonance in its most discordant elegance; movement in its most dynamic and erotic transports and postures; body movement of the most subtle and dimensional form like two people walking through each other. Light and Shadow... and shadow *lifted* from its object. Bombardment of Noises and its attendant silence. TOUCH and the UNtouchable. THRILL and the ENthralled. Wherever I go I am searching the *doppelganger*... Mirror and reflected Image. Sound and the VOID.

BOMB: What kind of connections did you find between the mid-century French poets and the Appalachian and Delta musicians that drew you to both? Was it purely lyrical? Or was it a connection made between these two embattled groups taking up electric equipment to incite a kind of musical violence?

TAV: Regarding mid-century French poets, I was not particularity drawn to any as I was drawn to mid-19th century French Symbolists, until these last three and a half years spent in Paris when I discovered the actions, provocations, and antics of the Situationists and their *Führer*, Guy DeBord. With this movement, I feel kinship... as I do with the era of Happenings that occurred in New York in the 60s, and later in the 80s with such saintly art-actions as Chris Burden nailing himself to a Volkswagen. Here again I must reiterate the fact that Panther Burns do not engender or mitigate toward evocations of violence. Although once backed into a corner, we have incited to *riot*... as in the case of being retained by the Clash and their manager Cosmo Vinyl to open the first two dates on their last and abortive US tour, wherein Panther Burns were denounced on the Vanderbilt University stage and greeted with howls of derision by an audience of benighted college students.

Onstage next night in Knoxville, the band was greeted by 6000 inebriated rednecks at the University of Tennessee, whereupon fistfights were breaking out everywhere as Panther Burns attempted to entertain this assemblage of unruly music lovers, only to finally throw up our arms in pale and ashen futility, and launch into a 20-minute fuzz-toned rendition of the "Bourgeois Blues", which even *they* understood the true significance of, and which inflamed an already volatile situation beyond the threshold of riotous invective. If they'd had beer bottles, they would have killed us.

When Panther Burns at last acquitted themselves, heroic only as victims of pure desperation, and left the enormous stage with its ponderous PA monitors the size of a Ford Focus, we had departed in the defeated glory of knowing that we had been *heard* and heard well before an auditorium overstuffed with rattling puppet heads. When the Clash came out with their massive amplification stacked high and with the redundancy of three tuneless electric guitars blaring and myriad electronic processing devices running, the grinding wad of indecipherable and uncalculated *white* noise they produced had the untoward effect of *assuaging!* the lusts of the assembled. The same army of Clash fans who, when Panther Burns were onstage, had been panting and clawing the air for something even more hot and nasty, were now transformed from riotous celebrants into an appalling host of docile troglodytes.

BOMB: I'm also curious how much of an effect the French and Beat poets had on you as a 'stylized' performance artist?

TAV: When I first saw the Cramps on stage, I was sure then that I recognized a significant and contemporary manifestation of Artaud's *Theatre of Cruelty*... for this is a multi-faceted dramaturgy beyond hardcore. There must be lyricism, eroticism, Dionysian thrashing, masks, and the forked tongues of vipers. Groups such as Throbbing Gristle and Furo del Baus in Spain further embody this theatre in our era. Panther Burns, however, are not consciously or unconsciously adherents of the *Theatre of Cruelty*. Rather, Panther Burns are an iteration of the Orphic Vision... as celebrated by symbolist poets, and as opposed to mystical vision. Thusly it is the mission of Panther Burns to stir up the dark waters of the unconscious.

BOMB: I also really enjoyed your explanation of Panther Burns' perspective on celebrity that you espoused on the Marge Thrasher Show on WHBQ-TV: "We create an anti-environment to make visible that part of Memphis and of life that is normally overlooked...the Panther Burns are anti-stars. They're black holes where a star should be. The purpose of the Panther Burns is to forge an anti-environment to make authentic music that's all around us more visible, especially in Memphis." How much of Panther Burns' mythology do you think comes from your very definitive image and style?

TAV: It is impossible to separate Panther Burns from its mystique.

BOMB: Once again, it seems you've surrounded yourself with an admixture of classical Gothic elegance and the American hillbilly aesthetic—

TAV: Panther Burns is a Southern Gothic, backwoods ballroom musical troupe – purveyors of *Antler del Arte*. We are, however, as Eggleston would say, *gentlemen*... not farmers.

BOMB: Is this an intentional tribute to past idols or do you see it as a 'postmodern' reinterpretation of these influences?

TAV: Both, in fact. Jerry Lee Lewis has referred to himself as an interpreter of styles. Likewise in the case of Panther Burns, yet in terms of post-postmodern positioning, we would be considered as *re-* interpreters.

BOMB: In another interesting quote from the 80s, you were explaining the relationship between blues-based groups like Panther Burns and atonal musicians like Arto Lindsay on the New York scene. You said, "Groups like DNA became our friends. Whereas Arto Lindsay works from a radically different point of view, this atonal 'beyond free jazz' music, is hardly without emotional content in the conventional sense of the term and at a point in its trajectory, converges with that of Panther Burns."

TAV: Certainly Arto Lindsay impressed me as an artist and as an individual, as did Tim Wright, the bass player of DNA who in fact introduced me around New York and to Chris Stein/Glenn O'Brien's TV *Party* cable show in particular. The terse, 45-second musical implosions delivered on stage by DNA as 'songs' at Hilly Crystal's (himself a 60s icon) joint called CBGBs were the kind of extreme atonal primitivism that appealed directly to my sensibilities. Yet inherent in the yowling vocals and the fearsome electric instrumentation of DNA lurked an intellectual gradient that had sardonically turned in upon itself. Something like the image from antiquity of the snake biting its tail – the ouroboros. There was a completeness of expression in DNA that brought rampant atonal chaos around full circle with an enthralling cataclysmic dissonance… resulting in a totally luxurious sonic abstraction.

BOMB: You were quoted: "The no-wave ethos was mainly the ideas of people who turned up at the Mudd Club: the notion of a detached relationship, bloodless, under narcosis. And groups like The Cramps or Panther Burns had the kind of flame, which seemed ideal to give an antithetical direction to this type of empty engagement. There was a demand for what we did; the scene needed groups like ours, and we could work elbow to elbow with bands which, on the surface, appeared completely different."

TAV: Panther Burns originated in Memphis as an Anti-Environment affronting prevailing conditions. Arriving in New York we quickly found ourselves likewise positioned in the sense that we represented unbridled emotional frenzy and sentiment – tribal, anti-intellectual, provocative, and by any standard, reckless as only renegades from the heathen swamps can be. In New York it was not our progenitors whom we set in relief, but our esteemed, ultra-chilled, and in most cases quasi-professional colleagues. Panther Burns were not and still are not professional anything. However, we did bring with us the flourish of a suave and stylish urbanity that only certain southern cities possess. For these attributes Panther Burns were accepted on the fringes of the downtown scene, and at times celebrated by the cognoscenti. Yet for most New Yorkers we would probably be looked upon with curious condescension as hicks from Arkansas and Memphis... expressive of a lingering northern attitude toward Southerners in general, which in itself is revelatory of a benighted projection of themselves.

BOMB: Can you explain how/why Panther Burns decided to migrate to NYC at the time? How would you compare the Memphis scene surrounding Ardent and Jim Dickinson with the New York scene of the late 1970s/early 80s? How exactly did you ingratiate yourself into the Mudd Club and the Downtown '81 scene?

TAV: Well, despite the unfortunate term, 'ingratiate', Panther Burns were actually invited to play in New York. Before Steve Mass had even thought of the name, *Mudd Club*, he was traveling through the South, and he, in fact, dropped by my pad with Anya Phillips, later a cohort of James Chance. It was on this trip south, that the concept of the Mudd Club befell Steve Mass. This joint on White Street in NoHo with a uni-gender, no-doors bathroom evolved into a kind of social club, a *demi-monde* for puerile exuberants from all five boroughs who were responsible for its ever-mutating, artful décor and downtown philosophies. It was a democratic room like CBGBs. I mean there was a doorman, but not too discerning. A relaxed crowd, usually stoned, but ready for anything. Part of its success was owing to the eclectic nature of Steve's booking. Even Johnny Thunders went there one night to catch a doubleheader with Panther Burns and Beatster poet John Giorno holding forth on the same bill.

In Memphis, Ardent is a state-of-the-art commercial recording studio. Panther Burns were tolerated at Ardent. Once the owner, John Fry, brought us a box of cookies while we were mixing. Reckon that's righteous treatment for a group that never sold any records. Jim Dickinson is not only a formidable musician and a sensitive artist, but he is also an erudite closet gentleman. Jim made a living in the recording studios in Memphis, he has fronted the raucous and provocative Mudboy and the Neutrons, and he has been supportive of alternative and underground groups and artists... to the point of personal sacrifice. One miserable day in Midtown Memphis, Mudboy grunted and gave birth to a critter called Panther Burns.

BOMB: How did you view the electronic/dance sub-culture that was also brewing at the time? Did you ever go to the Danceteria or the SoHo loft parties that hosted these various events? Did you see any particularly outrageous 'noise' shows around that time, like Glenn Branca's guitar orchestra, or early hip-hop shows? If so, do you think this kind of foray into experimental sound affected your own work?

TAV: The first gig Panther Burns played in New York was organized by Jim Fouratt at Danceteria, who was in charge of booking the club during the heady, incipient phase of its existence. Maybe it was a Mafia joint, like Peppermint Lounge, but who cares. On this auspicious event at Danceteria,

Panther Burns hit the stage around 2:30 in the morning as the headliner usually came on around 4:00 a.m. in New York in those days. We came out six-strong including a fellow Arkansan, Bob Palmer – then Pop & Jazz critic for the *NY Times* – wailing on a savagely dissonant clarinet. Panther Burns sawed through a brutal forty-five minute set of such cacophony that the audience seemed riveted in some swaying, yet petrified trance. Afterward, Fouratt came backstage to our dressing room and proclaimed, "That was the worst sounding crock of unadulterated *NOISE* I have ever heard... *in my life!* But there is someone outside from London who wants to talk to you about recording a record. Geoff Travis from some company called Rough Trade. Shall I let him in...?"

By the time Travis had left the room, Jim Fouratt was still undergoing a verbal flogging from Alex Chilton on the topic of Panther Burns' tone-science versus Fouratt's unsolicited opinions. Some months later when the album was released, a half page review in *Melody Maker* appeared under a block letters subheader entitled, "PURE SICK NOISE", thus corroborating the prophetic nature of Fouratt's remarks. In a subsequent show at Danceteria, Panther Burns invited performance artist and actress, the exquisite Anne Magnuson, to share the bill with us, and later I joined her onstage in one of her performances at Life Cafe on Avenue B. Diagonally across Tomkins Sq. Park from there was a tasty underground pit called the Pyramid Club where Panther Burns also delivered more than one darkly luminous concert on a bill with house favorite, John Sex.

Further uptown at Peppermint Lounge, Panther Burns shared an Anti-Nuclear Rally bill with Allen Ginsberg during the period when he was playing the harmonium and backed by Parisian street musicians on electric guitars. I presented the bard with our first album entitled, *Behind the Magnolia Curtain*. Some years later when Panther Burns were in town, we dropped by Allen's pad on East 12th Street announcing our arrival by tossing a pebble up to what we suspected to be his apartment window. Miraculously, the poet appeared at the windowsill and invited us up. As we sat around his table, I asked if he'd remembered ever listening to the album I'd once given him. Allen gave some sort of ambiguous reply. A few minutes later I was astonished when I happened to notice our very album was actually sitting on the turntable of his phonograph!

As for the Glenn Branca guitar orchestra, I did not see it. I can, however, say that I witnessed an all girls orchestra named Pullsalama, who often played Danceteria and who were outrageously noisy. The only hip-hop events that moved me were those of Afrika Bambaataa, whom I met and grooved on, along with Fab Five Freddy on Avenue D. Still, the one orchestra delivering arias of melodic atonality, which had a formative influence on my own aesthetic, was Sun Ra & the Solar Myth Arkestra who enthralled me at the Squatt Theatre.

BOMB: When discussing Panther Burns' contribution to the New York No Wave scene, you had said that the rebirth of great music in the early eighties was a product of the sixties. How did you see the interrelationship between these two different eras of music? No Wave had a reputation for 'killing the idols' of music's past, whether it be in the traditional punk sound of The Ramones and The Sex Pistols or the monolithic histories of the 60s and 70s. That said, how do you connect the sounds of No Wave with the 60s? Was it more a spiritual kinship than a musical connection?

TAV: As for the No Wave ferment that emerged in New York during the 80s, what you had for example were musical groups such as the Lounge Lizards or James Chance and the Contortions working out of an often atonal bag blatantly inspired by 60s jazz titans and pioneers ranging from early Paul Bley to a spread of 'cool jazz' artists like Eric Dolphy. DNA and Arto Lindsay were perhaps the closest to outright celebration of pure noise in the sublimely exalted moments of their performance... connected, in my mind, to such experimenters from the 60s as LaMonte Young. We can distinguish No Wave in degree from its musical antecedents in terms of spirituality or absence thereof, by its supreme lack of emotion and by its bloodless attempts to adopt a posture of narcotized cool, contrasting with transports of emotional frenzy produced by thrashing instrumentation and extreme vocalization as in the case of Arto and Chance.

No Wave was iconoclastic. I have not read any manifestos of No Wave, but its attempt to wipe the slate clean, to hatch an original genre, and to explore a completely original direction was, as always, practically impossible. Under this mandate, what artists often do is to emulate their mentors, and then once having absorbed what techniques, attributes, styles, and innovations they can manage to acquire, they destroy or try to expurgate traces of their masters' influence. The residue of what is left, combined with the contemporaneous psychology of the moment, is the kernel of that which will emerge and be heralded as a new direction.

The essential connection between the fertile scene of the early 80s in New York and San Francisco, and the era of the 60s was a sense of experimentation. The notion of the errant individual; the idea that anything is possible with or without training, resources, money; the job of breaking down barriers between art forms and between social strata were the driving forces that connected these periods. Out of this experimental scene in New York surfaced performers as diverse and supremely inventive as Ann Magnuson, Klaus Noami, Suicide, and later Antony and the Johnsons; there were artists as iconic as David McDermott and Peter McGough, Keith Haring, Kenny Scharf; visionary publishers such as Betsy Sussler and Diego Cortez, and filmmakers like Amos Poe and Eric Mitchell. All of them were experimental, individual, and defying strict categorization. As in the 60s, personalities emerged who were products of an experimental and explosive art scene and cultural movements that sprang from the underground.

The magazines got their interviews, the labels got their records, the band got its audiences, and as the end of the second decade of Panther Burns approached, and as assorted Memphis hussies were closing in on me, I had the idea to split from the Bluff City to another river town, way, way down south – to Buenos Aires on the Rio del Plata. Tav Falco had more or less matured to the point where he could handle himself onstage in the usual unreliable scenes and places. I passed some luxurious months in the Argentine capitol hanging out at *milongas* and dancing tango every night. Alas, it was the call of the Panther Burns that brought me back to the States to New York to orchestrate the formation of a traveling line-up of young turks from Gotham for an upcoming six-weeks tour of the European continent.

Memphis musicians never proved hardy enough for such protracted ventures, so their crusty Yankee brethren had to be cajoled into coming aboard. After the exit of Ron Miller from the group, an East Village gentleman scholar, humanitarian, and Avenue D wit named Kai Eric took over the bottom frequencies. He played a lavender electric bass that the Gibson office in Hamburg had soon bestowed upon him as a core member of Panther Burns. Kai was the son of a ranking official at the United Nations in New York. He seemed to know everybody on the downtown scene, and everybody knew him as a Rod Serling spin-off, down to the same Twilight Zone dark suit and banter for which Sterling was famous. He was a roommate with John Michel Basquiat before the untoward OD of the Warhol protégé. The presence of Kai Eric was invariably stimulating, stylish, and amusing, and I pushed for his inclusion in the group. Nevertheless his tolerance for the vicissitudes of the road was limited. After a few weeks of hardship on the road, his entertaining personality morphed into that of a mutinous conspirator that almost wrecked the tour. Yet, to his credit, Kai Eric was no quitter, and inevitably he rode out the tours to the bitter end. As my high school Go-Devils football coach insisted, *a quitter never wins, and a winner never quits.*

After the last Euro tour the band decided to establish a beachhead in Paris and try to land a new record deal in the City of Light. Initially conceived by me as a memoir of sorts under the title of *The Argentine Diaries*, from the notes I'd kept in Buenos Aires, I had transformed the poems and scribbles into songs while in New York. As Falco was not such a prolific songwriter, I gave this folio of songs to the band and in a rehearsal studio in Saint Vincennes, the group constructed a roughly hewn skeleton of album demos. We solicited the demo – the first demo ever made in the career of the Panther Burns – to independent labels throughout America, Europe and Japan. Alas, the answer by A&R execs was a resounding NO. Instead, they offered up any number of "suggestions" of how to change the Panther Burns concept to make it more popular and more profitable. And the answer from Falco – ever the stubborn Calabrese – was an equally intransigent NO. Falco, in the grandiose vision he had of Panther Burns, actually thought he had something rarefied in those recordings. He informed me, *what a critic doesn't understand, he despises, and despite the rhetoric, what a label finds strange and new, it discards as rubbish.* OK, who was I to argue with hotheaded, road weary singer who'd drifted into Memphis from some nameless place in Arkansas. Eventually Falco retreated back to the Bluff City to chill, and left me in Paris to flog the demo. After a couple of years it became apparent that the demo was doing more harm than good, but at least the demo had the beneficial effect of weeding out the men from the boys on the indie record scene.

Left in Paris to my own devices was not so bad, I came to realize. I could dance tango any night of the week, and I started spending many happy hours viewing obscure films in the Cinémathèque Française on Boulevard Bonne Nouvelle, and I hung out at Café Zimmer at Place Chatelet – a café that reminded me of my days in the coffeehouses of merry and sinister Vienna when we were recording the *Shadow Dancer* album with Panther Burns, and making the short film, *Masque of Hotel Orient*, with Kenneth Anger. Soon I was attending to soirées in galleries and in private salons with artists, musicians, and photographers.

Introduced to the best musicians of the city, I persuaded a promising guitarist to join the band, Grégoire Garrigues, who'd started his career at seventeen in the band of leather clad French idol, Vince Taylor. Laurent Lanouzière, a young bass player and fanatic for Panther Burns, came on board. The saucy Italian girl from Rome, whom we had met eons before in New York and brought to Memphis to play with the Hellcats, rejoined the fold on drums. Falco flew over when we booked mini-tours for the group here and there around the continent, then he'd shuttle back to Cox St. where he continued to live as a kind of stranger in his own hometown.

One evening roaming around Saint Germain-des-Prés, I ran into Julien Hohenberg and Bibi Ford in front of La Closerie des Lilas. We went inside and had a few rounds of drinks. They were newlyweds! They had gotten together when Julien had hired Bibi as legal counsel during the litigation of his estate. It became obvious that she was trying to resurrect him, but Julien was severely depressed, drooping his head at the table in La Closerie. He ended up losing all his money, basically, like he'd told Connie, *what if he lost his money*. Had only his children and stockholders had faith in Julien's speculation, his business acumen would've been vindicated and all concerned would be sitting on easy street. Julien and Bibi seemed to be in love and celebrated their union with élan, still he was a walking advertisement for solemnity of trust that's been broken. A year or so after our encounter on the *trotoir*, I heard that the droll couple had divorced, and Julien was hanging with a bevy of black girls in north Memphis who were taking him for a ride.

Then, out of nowhere, against the grain, and despite the all apparent odds, the new album, CONJURATIONS: *Séance for Deranged Lovers*, was picked up by Stag-O-Lee records in Germany. Falco caught the next plane, smoking, and came sailing in on the wing to the fatherland. Concert agencies put the French/Italian version of the band out on another six-weeks tour of all the equivocal clubs, canal barges, and RnR festivals on the continent east and west. Last I heard, Tav Falco and the Unapproachable Panther Burns are still out there... touring in some god-forsaken place in the Orient.

III.

god sits over the picture ways and let him sit quietly

words are also swords a forgotten

man, the poet

does not believe

┘(•°•┘)♪ └(★o★)┐ ┌(☆o★)┘ ／(v˙v)〉 ゞ(*‿ᓚ‿*)ゞ ／
(、—,)ヽ (ゞ A。)ゞ (ゞvv)ゞ /(•O•/) ／(。O。／) ／(。◇。)ヽ ／(。◇。)
ヽ〃/(*ㅁ*)ゞ ⊂(•¯•,O) /(*、ㅁ,*)ヽ /(ₒ- ₒ*/) /(* ₒ-ₒ*)ヽ (ヽ* ₒ-)ヽ
/(ₒ△ₒ/)(\vmv)\ /(≋A≋/) ／(@v△v@)ゞ ゞ(‾-)ゞ ／(vOv／)
(∨vOv)∨ ／(__m__／) (∨__m__)∨ (∨__—__)∨ ／(__—__／)
┌(‿0‿)┘ └(‿0‿)┐ ┌(,—、)┘ └(,—、)┐ ~(__▽__~)
(~__▽__)~ ~(v△v~) (~v△v)~ ~(__△__~) (~__△__)~
°(‿△‿°) (°‿△‿)° /(、□,/*) /(*•m•)ゞ /(、△,*)ゞ。/(vmv/)
／(··／) ゞv v)ゞ ／(、ς‾‾,／) O(vvO) (Ovv)O ／(v‾v／) (∨v‾v)∨
┘(•°•┘)♪ └(★o★)┐ ┌(☆o★)┘ ／(v˙v)〉 ゞ(*‿ᓚ‿*)ゞ ／
(、—,)ヽ (ゞ A。)ゞ (ゞvv)ゞ /(•O•/) ／(。O。／) ／(。◇。)ヽ ／(。◇。)
ヽ〃/(*ㅁ*)ゞ ⊂(•¯•,O) /(*、ㅁ,*)ヽ /(ₒ- ₒ*/) /(* ₒ-ₒ*)ヽ (ヽ* ₒ-)ヽ
/(ₒ△ₒ/)(\vmv)\ /(≋A≋/) ／(@v△v@)ゞ ゞ(‾-)ゞ ／(vOv／)
(∨vOv)∨ ／(__m__／) (∨__m__)∨ (∨__—__)∨ ／(__—__／)
┌(‿0‿)┘ └(‿0‿)┐ ┌(,—、)┘ └(,—、)┐ ~(__▽__~)
(~__▽__)~ ~(v△v~) (~v△v)~ ~(__△__~) (~__△__)~
°(‿△‿°) (°‿△‿)° /(、□,/*) /(*•m•)ゞ /(、△,*)ゞ。/(vmv/)
／(··／) ゞv v)ゞ ／(、ς‾‾,／) O(vvO) (Ovv)O ／(v‾v／) (∨v‾v)∨
┘(•°•┘)♪ └(★o★)┐ ┌(☆o★)┘ ／(v˙v)〉 ゞ(*‿ᓚ‿*)ゞ ／
(、—,)ヽ (ゞ A。)ゞ (ゞvv)ゞ /(•O•/) ／(。O。／) ／(。◇。)ヽ ／(。◇。)
ヽ〃/(*ㅁ*)ゞ ⊂(•¯•,O) /(*、ㅁ,*)ヽ /(ₒ- ₒ*/) /(* ₒ-ₒ*)ヽ (ヽ* ₒ-)ヽ
/(ₒ△ₒ/)(\vmv)\ /(≋A≋/) ／(@v△v@)ゞ ゞ(‾-)ゞ ／(vOv／)
(∨vOv)∨ ／(__m__／) (∨__m__)∨ (∨__—__)∨ ／(__—__／)
┌(‿0‿)┘ └(‿0‿)┐ ┌(,—、)┘ └(,—、)┐ ~(__▽__~)
(~__▽__)~ ~(v△v~) (~v△v)~ ~(__△__~) (~__△__)~
°(‿△‿°) (°‿△‿)° /(、□,/*) /(*•m•)ゞ /(、△,*)ゞ。/(vmv/)
／(··／) ゞv v)ゞ ／(、ς‾‾,／) O(vvO) (Ovv)O ／(v‾v／) (∨v‾v)∨
┘(•°•┘)♪ └(★o★)┐ ┌(☆o★)┘ ／(v˙v)〉 ゞ(*‿ᓚ‿*)ゞ ／
(、—,)ヽ (ゞ A。)ゞ (ゞvv)ゞ /(•O•/) ／(。O。／) ／(。◇。)ヽ ／(。◇。)
ヽ〃/(*ㅁ*)ゞ ⊂(•¯•,O) /(*、ㅁ,*)ヽ /(ₒ- ₒ*/) /(* ₒ-ₒ*)ヽ (ヽ* ₒ-)ヽ
/(ₒ△ₒ/)(\vmv)\ /(≋A≋/) ／(@v△v@)ゞ ゞ(‾-)ゞ ／(vOv／)
(∨vOv)∨ ／(__m__／) (∨__m__)∨ (∨__—__)∨ ／(__—__／)
┌(‿0‿)┘ └(‿0‿)┐ ┌(,—、)┘ └(,—、)┐ ~(__▽__~)
(~__▽__)~ ~(v△v~) (~v△v)~ ~(__△__~) (~__△__)~
°(‿△‿°) (°‿△‿)° /(、□,/*) /(*•m•)ゞ /(、△,*)ゞ。/(vmv/)
／(··／) ゞv v)ゞ ／(、ς‾‾,／) O(vvO) (Ovv)O ／(v‾v／) (∨v‾v)∨
┘(•°•┘)♪ └(★o★)┐ ┌(☆o★)┘ ／(v˙v)〉 ゞ(*‿ᓚ‿*)ゞ ／
(、—,)ヽ (ゞ A。)ゞ (ゞvv)ゞ /(•O•/) ／(。O。／) ／(。◇。)ヽ ／(。◇。)
ヽ〃/(*ㅁ*)ゞ ⊂(•¯•,O) /(*、ㅁ,*)ヽ /(ₒ- ₒ*/) /(* ₒ-ₒ*)ヽ (ヽ* ₒ-)ヽ
/(ₒ△ₒ/)(\vmv)\ /(≋A≋/) ／(@v△v@)ゞ ゞ(‾-)ゞ ／(vOv／)
(∨vOv)∨ ／(__m__／) (∨__m__)∨ (∨__—__)∨ ／(__—__／)
┌(‿0‿)┘ └(‿0‿)┐ ┌(,—、)┘ └(,—、)┐ ~(__▽__~)
(~__▽__)~ ~(v△v~) (~v△v)~ ~(__△__~) (~__△__)~
°(‿△‿°) (°‿△‿)° /(、□,/*) /(*•m•)ゞ /(、△,*)ゞ。/(vmv/)
／(··／) ゞv v)ゞ ／(、ς‾‾,／) O(vvO) (Ovv)O ／(v‾v／) (∨v‾v)∨

┘(•°•┘)♪ └(★o★)┐ ┌(☆o★)┘ ／(v˙v)〉 ゞ(*‿ᓚ‿*)ゞ ／
(、—,)ヽ (ゞ A。)ゞ (ゞvv)ゞ /(•O•/) ／(。O。／) ／(。◇。)ヽ ／(。◇。)
ヽ〃/(*ㅁ*)ゞ ⊂(•¯•,O) /(*、ㅁ,*)ヽ /(ₒ- ₒ*/) /(* ₒ-ₒ*)ヽ (ヽ* ₒ-)ヽ
/(ₒ△ₒ/)(\vmv)\ /(≋A≋/) ／(@v△v@)ゞ ゞ(‾-)ゞ ／(vOv／)
(∨vOv)∨ ／(__m__／) (∨__m__)∨ (∨__—__)∨ ／(__—__／)
┌(‿0‿)┘ └(‿0‿)┐ ┌(,—、)┘ └(,—、)┐ ~(__▽__~)
(~__▽__)~ ~(v△v~) (~v△v)~ ~(__△__~) (~__△__)~
°(‿△‿°) (°‿△‿)° /(、□,/*) /(*•m•)ゞ /(、△,*)ゞ。/(vmv/)
／(··／) ゞv v)ゞ ／(、ς‾‾,／) O(vvO) (Ovv)O ／(v‾v／) (∨v‾v)∨
┘(•°•┘)♪ └(★o★)┐ ┌(☆o★)┘ ／(v˙v)〉 ゞ(*‿ᓚ‿*)ゞ ／
(、—,)ヽ (ゞ A。)ゞ (ゞvv)ゞ /(•O•/) ／(。O。／) ／(。◇。)ヽ ／(。◇。)
ヽ〃/(*ㅁ*)ゞ ⊂(•¯•,O) /(*、ㅁ,*)ヽ /(ₒ- ₒ*/) /(* ₒ-ₒ*)ヽ (ヽ* ₒ-)ヽ
/(ₒ△ₒ/)(\vmv)\ /(≋A≋/) ／(@v△v@)ゞ ゞ(‾-)ゞ ／(vOv／)
(∨vOv)∨ ／(__m__／) (∨__m__)∨ (∨__—__)∨ ／(__—__／)
┌(‿0‿)┘ └(‿0‿)┐ ┌(,—、)┘ └(,—、)┐ ~(__▽__~)
(~__▽__)~ ~(v△v~) (~v△v)~ ~(__△__~) (~__△__)~
°(‿△‿°) (°‿△‿)° /(、□,/*) /(*•m•)ゞ /(、△,*)ゞ。/(vmv/)
／(··／) ゞv v)ゞ ／(、ς‾‾,／) O(vvO) (Ovv)O ／(v‾v／) (∨v‾v)∨
┘(•°•┘)♪ └(★o★)┐ ┌(☆o★)┘ ／(v˙v)〉 ゞ(*‿ᓚ‿*)ゞ ／
(、—,)ヽ (ゞ A。)ゞ (ゞvv)ゞ /(•O•/) ／(。O。／) ／(。◇。)ヽ ／(。◇。)
ヽ〃/(*ㅁ*)ゞ ⊂(•¯•,O) /(*、ㅁ,*)ヽ /(ₒ- ₒ*/) /(* ₒ-ₒ*)ヽ (ヽ* ₒ-)ヽ
/(ₒ△ₒ/)(\vmv)\ /(≋A≋/) ／(@v△v@)ゞ ゞ(‾-)ゞ ／(vOv／)
(∨vOv)∨ ／(__m__／) (∨__m__)∨ (∨__—__)∨ ／(__—__／)
┌(‿0‿)┘ └(‿0‿)┐ ┌(,—、)┘ └(,—、)┐ ~(__▽__~)
(~__▽__)~ ~(v△v~) (~v△v)~ ~(__△__~) (~__△__)~
°(‿△‿°) (°‿△‿)° /(、□,/*) /(*•m•)ゞ /(、△,*)ゞ。/(vmv/)
／(··／) ゞv v)ゞ ／(、ς‾‾,／) O(vvO) (Ovv)O ／(v‾v／) (∨v‾v)∨
┘(•°•┘)♪ └(★o★)┐ ┌(☆o★)┘ ／(v˙v)〉 ゞ(*‿ᓚ‿*)ゞ ／
(、—,)ヽ (ゞ A。)ゞ (ゞvv)ゞ /(•O•/) ／(。O。／) ／(。◇。)ヽ ／(。◇。)
ヽ〃/(*ㅁ*)ゞ ⊂(•¯•,O) /(*、ㅁ,*)ヽ /(ₒ- ₒ*/) /(* ₒ-ₒ*)ヽ (ヽ* ₒ-)ヽ
/(ₒ△ₒ/)(\vmv)\ /(≋A≋/) ／(@v△v@)ゞ ゞ(‾-)ゞ ／(vOv／)
(∨vOv)∨ ／(__m__／) (∨__m__)∨ (∨__—__)∨ ／(__—__／)
┌(‿0‿)┘ └(‿0‿)┐ ┌(,—、)┘ └(,—、)┐ ~(__▽__~)
(~__▽__)~ ~(v△v~) (~v△v)~ ~(__△__~) (~__△__)~
°(‿△‿°) (°‿△‿)° /(、□,/*) /(*•m•)ゞ /(、△,*)ゞ。/(vmv/)
／(··／) ゞv v)ゞ ／(、ς‾‾,／) O(vvO) (Ovv)O ／(v‾v／) (∨v‾v)∨
┘(•°•┘)♪ └(★o★)┐ ┌(☆o★)┘ ／(v˙v)〉 ゞ(*‿ᓚ‿*)ゞ ／
(、—,)ヽ (ゞ A。)ゞ (ゞvv)ゞ /(•O•/) ／(。O。／) ／(。◇。)ヽ ／(。◇。)
ヽ〃/(*ㅁ*)ゞ ⊂(•¯•,O) /(*、ㅁ,*)ヽ /(ₒ- ₒ*/) /(* ₒ-ₒ*)ヽ (ヽ* ₒ-)ヽ
/(ₒ△ₒ/)(\vmv)\ /(≋A≋/) ／(@v△v@)ゞ ゞ(‾-)ゞ ／(vOv／)
(∨vOv)∨ ／(__m__／) (∨__m__)∨ (∨__—__)∨ ／(__—__／)
┌(‿0‿)┘ └(‿0‿)┐ ┌(,—、)┘ └(,—、)┐ ~(__▽__~)
(~__▽__)~ ~(v△v~) (~v△v)~ ~(__△__~) (~__△__)~
°(‿△‿°) (°‿△‿)° /(、□,/*) /(*•m•)ゞ /(、△,*)ゞ。/(vmv/)
／(··／) ゞv v)ゞ ／(、ς‾‾,／) O(vvO) (Ovv)O ／(v‾v／) (∨v‾v)∨

hello
why
does
the
earth
not
fall
down
b/c
it
can
fly
what
else
can
fly
women
with
kites
dogs
in
mesh
carriers
birds
of
course
and
the
time

they
told
me
i
could
be
anything
so
i
became
feels

for
awhile
i
wanted
to
be
a
ninja
but
to
be
a
ninja
one
must
work
hard
be
silent
kill
i
like
people
paying
attention
to
me
i
like
noise

poets
all
they
want
to
be
given
something
picked
by
the
wanks
and
gimme
some
tenure
look
dude
punk
is
dad

poetry
now
with
more
crying

make
up
for
it
by
being
fucking
awesome

i
like
to
think
that
at
least
once
in
each
of
our
lives
weve
been
the
nude
coming
down
the
staircase

texas
is
this
crazy
fuckers
dream
someone
forgot
to
turn
off
it
gets
good
at
the
3:33
mark
where
static
meets
the
sky
clouds
crumble
i
wish

this
world
is
mad
warm
coffee
i
joined
a
teenaged
gang
our
base
was
a
bucky
ball
com-
pound
no
girls
allowed
no
just
kidding
girls
are
awesome

some
known
knowns
art
is
hard
(sort
of a
joke)
do it
every-
day
(sure)
get
a job
(done)
keep
doing
things
that
makes
them
insane
do
it

want
to
grow
up
to
be
mick
jaggars
daughter

when
words
get
made
every-
thing
gets
clear
around
life
gets
all
crystal
and
imma
not
even
afraid
of
dying
not
even
worried
about
the
next
car

haiku
where
the
kigo
is
all
my
pets
are
dead

gesture
of
moral
support

clicked
through
all
my
troubles
were
sucked
into
the
sky

remember
kids
music
be
trap
fashion
be
trap
words
be
trap
religion
be
trap
remem-
brance
be
trap
nostalgia
be
trap
sports
be
trap
tennis
4
eva

color
of
home
work
picked
berries
on-
blacked
canvas
of
all
the
art
project
youve
done
which
made
eyes
roll
the
hardest
puke
and
rally
tru
luv

those
poems
based
on tons
of
wiki
research
then
suck
really
bad
my
friends
husband
with
unspella-
ble
name
we
call
wiki
and
he
rules
so
hard

evil
eye
sees
lilied
pipe
fogs
literally
the
place
where
image
sup-
posed
to
happen
instead
this
misused
word
we
have
a
rival
gang
i
hate
them

quick
!!!
to
the
yolo
mobile
!!!

i love
tell
off
songs
they
just
like
f u
im
awesome
you
not
awesome
im
better
off
without
u
hope
you
feel
love
again
but
not
really
see
f u

banging
into
further
reaches
yer
scene
yer
war
call
up
with
yer
outsized
prob-
lems
crew
wrecked
exs
what
should
you
do
leave
and
dont
say
why

YOU
DO
THIS
4 LIVING
I DO
THIS
FOR
NOT
DYING

give
me
all
crush
all
rooftop
party
mouthful
tube
steak
easy
on
the
catsup
save
the
clock
tower
corn
eyes
endless
summer
deep
throat
moebius

can
we
start
calling
day
drinking
aperitiffing

talking
flarf
with
fanny
howe

heres
to
feeling
good
all
the
time

were
calling
tacos
squawkos
imma
call
you
up
and
say
squawkos
depend-
ing
on
time
of
day
or
yer
mood
you
just
say
yes
migas
barbacoa
or
shrimp

come
up
with
almost
everything
if we
could
write
the
story
where
we
live
forever
then
we
write
the
people
they
live
long
enough
to
read
it

did
you
give
did
you
give
your
self
did
you
give
did
you
give
your
best
did
you
give
did
you
give
up
did
you
win
will
you
win
can
you
win

hope
it
works
or
fails
beautifully

not
to
self
yes
said
not
not
note
but
you
get
it
not
to
self
sell
custom
poems
on
craigslist
thinking
ten
dollar
minimum
good
ones
be
twenty

woman
sees
snake
burns
down
home
you
okay
there
fox
spirit
tails
unbent
and
working
that
nose
skyward
in
the
sunlight
working
for
the
living

do
poetry
do
lyrics
do
internet
do
stealing
do
sports
do
monies
do
cars
do
ladies
do
boys
do
holies
do
unholies
do
spoilers
love
spoilers
do

hi
there
cosmos
watching
aurora
with
cocktail
in
hand
an
experi-
ence
you
dont
lego
easily
but
dont
believe
what
atoms
say
they
make
it
all
up

put
a
shirt
on
like
person
go
see
the
rain
run
the
buildings
and
the
cars
if
you
want
to
know
what
to
give
me
for
my
birthday
close
yer
eyes

im
okay
with
this
ending
guys

First Person Plural, First Person Singular

"A woman's voice is naked."
Babylonian fragment

"A single line, at the bottom of the page, leaves too much space."
Printer's Handbook

I. *Oui*

I was never interested in falling, as you
Told me you had fallen, *head over heels*;

I was interested in *heels over head*,
My legs straight up, twin columns against your

Shoulders and you like Samson between them.
Veux-tu m'epouser, you'd ask, and that

Seventh time, I answered, smiling, open-
Mouthed. Oh, I remember the chill of that

April day, the heat from your body caught
In your black cashmere sweater as you draped it

Over my shivering shoulders, and I
Remember that looking blinded me, that

Talking deafened me, that kissing muted
Me. I remember gesture, remember intent,

Remember intensity, remember mornings
When the tables were turned, when we over-

Turned the table, each day all lattice for
Us to twine upon like morning glories, open,
Closed and open according to the light.

II. *Non*

I see the light gone from your green eyes, I
Feel the cold of your hand, much colder, I
Think, than the chill of the anodized table I

Find you lying on; I'm aware that I
Am thinking *this is not you, this is not, I*
Don't believe it. (Beloved, once I

Waited for you in the lake, breathless, I
Opened there in the water for you, I
Was origami unfolding, oh I

Was a paper flower dissolving, I
Felt your legs scissor me, heard you gasp I
Was so warm, and I was the lake and I

Was the water and then I was, oh, I
Was, wasn't I, anything—wasn't I
Something, and I was flesh of your flesh, I

Was bone of your bone, I was one of two, I
Was singular, wasn't single). As I
Linger here, no arms to hold me as I

Shiver, except my own; I am tower, I
Am *obelisk, obituary,* I
Am *survived* by, I am *loving wife*, I

Am *beloved*, first person singular, I
Am poor typography, *widow*, I, I

I.

Triage

"Nothing is ever lost." *All the King's Men*

A cut into your eyebrow from a fall
Onto my bedpost, seven stitches so small
They were set in with a loupe. Cat's-claw nicks
On your left fourth finger—a cicatrix
Hidden under your class ring—trying to
Trap that tabby. Stigmata on your palms—you
On top of me in a flash in gravel,
Some muscle car backfired, and then you travel
Back to Khe Sanh. (I landed on green glass,
Heineken. The shards like floaters rise).
That caterpillar-shaped scar on your ass
From shrapnel. The scratches by your eyes
The mortician couldn't cover when you drowned.
Wounds I never sutured, closure I never found.

It Pays To Increase Your Word Power: Diminuendo

clover
cover or lover
over

Bee respondent above *clover*, clover as ground *cover*, bee as *lover* who leaves the clover, the finality of *over*, not as in bee from clover but the causality of cleaving.

cleave
leave
eave
Eve

The infinitive is Janus—*to cling to* or *to sever*, to clasp as the girl drowning holds to the mast; to split along a natural fault line. This is how we cleaved—I no longer aligned myself against your back; at 3 a.m. you no longer turned to cup my breast. The whole seismography of home has cracked to house, and I am left useless as gingerbread trim rick-racking the eaves, of the period but peripheral; I am left with fundament, with pediment, with other architectural salvage; I pick up what I can and preserve it but whatever leaves, leaves. I am in this garden with statuary and salvia, but there is no tree of knowledge I can find, no apple beckoning among the leaves, although certainly there are any numbers of copperheads.

cloven
coven
oven

The devil has left his mark in the earth outside my window—too big for a deer, and only one hoof print next to a boot sole mired in mud. We could take a perfect cast of it, if we had plaster of Paris, and if we were still a *we* and not just an *I*. Sometimes I feel like an evil eye, I do I do. I could call out for others like me; I could convene a coven with the dozen bees caught in the trapdoors of the foxglove. The sun bakes these tracks to a brick, and I dig it up and put it in a pot. I wonder how long I'll have this mark of Old Nick on my porch. I wonder what I have unearthed.

clove
love

I remember the sizzle and hiss of your clove cigarettes—*Kretek*—and the taste of them on my tongue as your tongue eased into my mouth. After you, kissing is for nieces and weddings and is just a parenthetical move for dates. I understand kisses now that they no longer act as anodyne, now that my life is no longer studded with them.

lover
over
over
over

I look at *pomander* differently, too, an apple embossed with cloves, a scent I love. How we'd lie together at the lake, your curls against my breasts. The carapaces of cicadas, the segmented bodies of cryanoids embedded in limestone; lawn chairs blue-green as lichen, our Song of Songs translation over coffee and sugar cookies. Cleavage, how you loved it when my locket slipped. *I'd be happy in there forever*, you laughed. Your photo's embedded in its frame; it still slithers between my breasts, and that sterling heart won't stay shut. I snap the frame, lock up the locket, and the reliquary opens again to show us both sequestered. What's left of my heart is a sprung gear. Like the artificial nightingale, music is just not quite right these days, although the tune still plays if I wind it up.

In Ictu Oculi

"Sorrow is my own yard."
William Carlos Williams, "The Widow's Lament in Springtime"

My irises are blue,

Last November when weather was balmy,
Unexpected, sabres slashed up through
A scrim of gold gingko leaves; in early

milky with cataracts; still

December the last iris unfurled
Its frills, sinuous scallops bisected
Central from ciliary—blue ink pearled

I should have seen

From your fountain pen, blue lines crisscrossing
Your atlas, blue veins traversing your wrist.
An unseasonal gift that Christmas morning:

the cyanotic nails, looked

Blossom on the white wicker tray—the vase
That held the last iris was delicate,
A milky blue. "There'll be more," you said, "next

closely at your hands,

Spring. We'll have iris for years and years." Blades
Of green slice through the earth this autumn,
Your ashes in winter's bedded gardens.

not what they held.

(for Harvey, 1964-2010)

Some Yellow Tulips

Old Mrs. Sonnenkratz, there in her yard
Bent over like a bulb herself, works hard

To edge her sidewalks, salt the slugs, and spray
The aphids from her roses. Every day

She's pruning, pulling, plucking, culling out
The strays that might be festering. No doubt

She loves her lawn, loves order, symmetry
Of seedlings, herbal borders; she would be

Ruthless to seeds gone volunteer, to Queen
Anne's livid bruise, half-hidden in its green-

White froth of lace. Today, her turban slants
Askew over her blue-rinsed hair; her plants,

Once straight as soldiers on her patio,
Are *blitzkrieged* out of order, the yellow

Tulips (three days blossoming in a vase
Atop her wrought-iron table) don't erase

Her frown, her sloppy slippers, or the brown
Age spots (about the size of dimes around)

She often hides with gloves. A jagged scar
Runs up her forearm, where the numbers are.

The tulips, like her, blowsy, need to go;
Eine Kleine Nacht Musik's on her radio.

She thinks, *Acht nicht, acht nicht, nacht musik*...
Their leaves are lances, and they slant, oblique.

The tulips stems outlast their showy flowers;
For years she plants by day and, at night, cowers.

The yellow of the petals starts to burn;
Perhaps the worst of absence is return.

She smokes and shakes and smokes. Each flowerbed's
As neat as graves. She stubs out ash. The heads

Of these tulips wore bright turbans, tight-wrapped
And now unwrapping. In Berlin, she was slapped:

Sie ist ein Jude. Dry-eyed in Dachau, how
She's crying over bulbs bloomed too far now.

In a world of absence, presence leaves a scar.
Each tulip ravels to a six-point star.

Teachers, Masters in Their Places, and this is a spirit world

i
My parents made a house
a nest not like birds make, the non—
migrators—drifting back to nest. stayed
in ways of field,
steady as rats, mice under piles of
wood. we brought a colony here from a torn-down
barn; under the long beards and beams
                big field rats, others their young in
pieces of quilt and cotton willow. in the winter
they dig under roots

in that still town
           i had few friends,
yet a child. one little girl, her brothers.
we ran to the swings together
a mad whirl; hands to thrown rods we raced
and plunged our bodies into
the desperate gyrations. mindless as children are.
         a poor family and she came to my house;
family of children. my mother
stood on the long front porch and sent them home—
she did not know how lonely I was
she did not know what she was teaching me

         Taking us to what she thought was rich houses
we sat in a soft rug room and closed our eyes
while a man hid the glistening globes,
painted eggs. i was afraid. i cried spending a night
in that place
they taught us virtue, and love, and success, and
how to get along with people; with words
they taught us
and their own shapes made shapes on us
giants—riding the horses of all evil
(of pain, of hunger, of poor, of race and
wealth) and
at last shut the gates to a school of religion;

great heavy protesting angels, the Protestants.
their flames were swords
their burning flames became the action of their bodies

the seeds of war are in us
            we have long training for
destruction

oh my mother
you, could lose a son. you have lost all
your sons; as family
saving our souls you have lost our
lives. you never look at us. the sorrow

of the girl-lost years (that we could not
know)
past exhilaration—
you celebrate in pain with gladness.   believing
the dead speak. the dead.
and you speak of war

ii
When the leader wanted to find the rock-bottom young
people of America
he did not go to the universities;
he went to see William Monday. when will the churches
teach peace. a baptist church in Waco, through the
war, War II, prayed for their boys, every hour
perpetual prayer, like
rain, rain going upward, turned around, falling down
on heaven
and the pastor stood on his porch after.
they kept off the bombs
they kept off the rifle shots
not one of theirs 'got it' he forgot
my brother. but of course my brother didn't put in his
        letter of passage. though my mother did
salvation is singular

we are all singular as god

let us see their faces, over
the TV the faces tell us something. they tell us
silence. what the words can't say, what a man has become
at liberty not to tell. suddenly, the shadows
make an illusion. the police army-man stands at attention,
our attention, all are wearing

glasses that darken their eyes
the shadow of emptiness comes over the air waves;
the mouths on the questioning board are all straight
slits of lines that open in their faces. the lips
are gone
they speak through lips of enforced silence
nobody trusts us

Nobody expects us to act as men, as women, in passion
of discernment. even the Christ hangs
forgotten, an emblem of
our legends that are not valid
anymore. the Holy Grail has absorbed back into only an
inapplicable line of verse, learned long ago in past
school rooms. and that is well
we give up our illusions. the passionate, discerning

come also to us over the hot tube box and my neighbor
says: 'now there's a communist' what is it
we cannot teach in our schools—'i ain't got
nothing against the niggers' big shot says and is
elected. we are trapped by the box, reactions to
the box

god sits over the picture ways and let him sit quietly
words are also swords a forgotten
man, the poet
does not believe. to work in the form, from the form, the
ideal . . . becomes now our diversion; from truth to see
the areas of truth, a man

can be purer than any ideal
we must make our way henceforth

in division

The Song

the little girl kept singing

the king is fallen in Cambodia—tonight
a TV Special *where* we stand, where do we
stand—
outside the palace the people are clamoring
for rice
'i love arkansas' the little girl said

her dog was killed this afternoon, run over by
a car, buried in the orchard
everywhere are bloody hands, bloodless hands, bleeding
on the TV
my father, old man
quarreling for war, lost a son
and it taught him nothing

driving home at night
too old to fight, and i am still a child
it was the first time we defied him, not the last

'she is now wicked', i said, evil
shaping the little girl's mind with dreams. what is
a little girl
singing
'heaven—guide her', and i remember
my own stories, my own time, before
the blood came
menstrual flow, the mental fear
covered the earth. heaven has burst
i feel it

along the road tonight we passed a truck parked
        waiting for hounds. a big white slob out
with a flashlight
running hounds. the wolves are all dead. the young
rabbits race from the lights

but the little girl singing . .

calling down the gods calling down the saints

Flood Rain (Wind

washing the plowed earth raw
you ran from it
at last
still as animals
sat in the dark confusion of water

plants wouldn't grow

against the lightning cuts
a red sun
(ball of fire
hurled up from what we thought was
night
hung there
caught in a mesh of lightning

in back of us
a cleared reflection
ran deep over trees (tops
bent holding the wind thrown
hard with color

we traced in our hands
where the bow fell

roof of the earth echoing with thunder

I REMEMBER THE LIBRARIAN THROWING AWAY A MAGAZINE BECAUSE IT HAD THE PICTURE OF A BLACK MAN ON THE COVER

i worked for her
she had defended me

sitting in the office, the mail had come
violently, she looked at the picture
and my black heart looked at it

a leading Southern man (it was long ago)
his face
lay folded, not to be seen, in the waste basket

and i went back
straightening the files

straightening the files of the mind, how
religion, or race, or prejudice
could so desecrate her White face (could
it ever derange mine) could it?

and the black Choctaw of my heritage
who had denied me, stood
his fierce face above the stacks, higher
than i. he stood, his steady feet
that had touched the earth

watching. (before the intention was clear
what my life was)
his face
became the man in the picture. his face
drew in to my face
a recognition of consequence

his eyes—
(but i had to stay and serve my
    bondage) 'education' came
by opposites. a life had to learn vicariously
where its own movement

at last, held him. tight as a rope of blood
he held me

THE SIGN READ: LOS HOMBRES /TRABAJANDO

heaving a great stone bent over the stone the eyes curving slits the pit of eyes the mouth open a little in quick agony looking in pity and appeal the head down the face turned up sudden the white of the eyes and the dark black in the upper portion a mask of pain of intent freak pity and labor

they are chopping a road out through the wall rock mountains

Though the End Be No Mystery

Scent unmistakably sweet and otherwise
marked out the territory
of something dead;
the taste of death marked it too,
the way you can taste river bottom,
tobacco barn, clay pit.
A prize bovine, it was, days dead—
he'd gone stiff-legged and splay;
he'd gone gas-fat,
hide stretched to a fare-thee-well
in noonday sun;
and over such bloat and gurgle,
noise of blueflies,
dizzy by the hundreds,
alphas and omegas of flies,
an iridescent cape of them
in a continuous wheeling away,
then back into a rippling shimmer
above and along his length
as if the impending combustion of guts
made him hot to the touch.
Like most creatures,
the flies were delirious with need
for corruption as it beckoned,
fear tracing the outline of want,
want taking the measure of fear,
all that drawing nigh
and drawing back,
making the way to the feast familiar.

Conspiracy in White

Consider the snowy owl making a pass
and another and another over snow;

the bolus,
a tough-luck egg of mouse bones.

How wave by wave
confused water breaks up on a point;

how ring by ring the reservoir
descends into another drought year.

As water at the whim of temperature is
now ice, now steam,

so the heart is also:
here's the crucible paled past pouring

into anything,
here's the current wedded and arcing.

Ever before us the grief of raw materials
become Styrofoam cups,

starched collars, virgin cuffs
begging for a drag through gravy;

nurses' shoes, their continual traffic
in the service of removal,

as in the sugarcoated gallstones
of agonized innards,

as in biopsies.
Consider cholesterol built up

and building rumor by rumor into
the worst possible news come sweeping

its little ice storm through the brain.
(That epiphany is so much less

like our headlights' brief but titillating
affairs with fog

than their double-barreled wedding
to the head-on collision.)

Consider the bones—yours, your armature,
your underpinning—

undermining all that is you,
ready to lay the hell down.

Consider the grub
unearthed at the gravesite

where marble figures may at any moment
begin losing their poker faces.

In the Temple of the Bulrushes

It's as if all the man-parts of this world
were suddenly standing up for Jesus
and holding against whatever
impulse of stream flow.

Heaven knows, what I love there at hand
and velvet, the miracle of seed-swell
holding on by some invisible patina
for a kind touch that might mean business.

The man I love leans out long-armed
for the ones I can't reach otherwise—
so I won't go getting my feet wet,
he says, though there are times he risks more,

whole body sideways out from one hand
in my two for an anchor.
He'll do one himself once in a while,
but I'm not fooled—

it's for more than that innocent joy
he claims he sees in my face
that has him scanning for one more—
fuzz from the last still lifting

to our lips and eyelashes—
and again leaning impossibly further out.
He likes to watch, of course, sees
something in this act of what, all seized up

himself, he misses of me in another.
Ever my hero, he grins and hands it over.
And so he can see what comes natural,
I get beyond the idea of birdwatchers

scanning various and sundry winter geese
from off the flyway, beyond great blues
pinning these murky waters to the ground
with their bamboo legs for the shyest

of wood ducks, and beyond even them
to what of the world is in my care,
my hand curled to meet the integrity
of the whole swollen length

where on the rougher side of caress
is a spring just short of a cure for grief
where the patina breaks also from the stem
into a holy-redeemer dream orgy

of coming out—a blond unfurling
fluff from hidden reserves that
for a moment graces the whole of my hand
to the wrist like a nothing of ash

before gathering up one and all
into the very air for a next life, hallelujah,
joining together with the mind of wind
amen.

Stormdraining

That summer we grew tired of fishing for the mammoth carp
of Richland Creek—those freshwater airships who lulled in the deep,

warm runoff and who rose, open-mouthed and wide-eyed, toward
our lures like the souls of the forgiven we were told to believe in

before turning mockingly back over to flash their brilliant bellies in the sun.
When Tim learned from his preacher that carp

didn't eat worms, *only duckweed*, that bioluminescent cloud cover
that couldn't be strung on *even God's tiniest hook*, he and Sam

started talking all the more about the stormdrain that fed the creek
with its perfect rectangular mouth half-mile upstream, the stormdrain said

to reach *as far as Niggertown*. So we built a raft out of scrapwood
and old tires, filled the gaps with off-white beads of caulk, and stockpiled

flashlights and rubber waders and canvassed the neighborhood
for the empty gallon milk jugs that served as pontoons when strapped

to the keel of our marauder. One day, my father must have overheard our talk
when he emerged from his work to tell me, "Son, nigger's not a word

you use in my house," but when I tried convincing Tim of this, Tim only
looked up from hammering yet another roofing nail and said, "Andy,

Niggertown is Niggertown," and that was that. All summer we searched
those viaducts of night, like spelunkers in God's most perfect cave,

grave robbers tunneling toward the unknown dead, each excursion venturing
us further beyond the point where the pearled tubes of our flashlights faded

as Tim and Sam recounted tales they'd heard their fathers tell of Niggers
and Blacks and "Aunt Jemimas" to pass the time while I kept quiet

about my father who'd marched in Little Rock, my father
who still had the death threat rubber-banded to the brick pitched

through his dorm window in 1966. Yet I went with them: I the spotter,
   Tim the gunner, and Sam the navigator, our journey measured

every quarter-mile by the bars of sunlight that rayed
   through the street grates and my companions who waded out

into the still, flat water to form a makeshift ladder of hands to boost me
   to the steel I gripped, searching for names on street signs or addresses

on mailboxes—any indication of where beneath our world we were.
   Eventually, Tim and Sam grew tired of those days of undiscovery,

of the decision left, right, or straight at the junctures, our voices echoing
   as they descended into the unlit fathoms: *Hello, hello, hello…Where are we,*

where are we, where are we… Who, who, who, who… And it was all I could do
   but listen to the mad splashes of abandonment the day Tim and Sam

boosted me up to a high street grate, then took off with the raft as I hung there,
   slatted by bars of daylight, the echo of their cackling slowly receding.

I have no idea how long I hung there, gripping the steel bars of the grate,
   but I know it was long enough for night to descend and for the stars

the night owns to appear as though they'd always burned in the black walnut limbs
   in which they beamed. And there was the calm that came with letting go—

a flash of weightlessness and the drop of all pressure.
   Then the waiting that followed. And the night. And the dark.

The Year Hyakatuke was Said

> Comet Hyakutake, formally designated C/1996 B2,
> was discovered on January 31, 1996. It was dubbed
> The Great Comet of 1996, its passage near the Earth
> one of the closest cometary approaches in recorded history.

The year Hyakatuke was said
to strike the earth, I was in love
with Lauren Orr, the girl I watched crosscourt
at the homecoming game—her school
our rival—and who I believed watched me despite
the close contest—a foul, a free throw,
a buzzer beater—Lauren
a dancer with short, even blond hair
and who wore that night
a blue, floral-print blouse I still like to imagine
she slept in, thinking of me
as the delicately stenciled violets
branched up from her sleep,
their heart-shaped foliage spreading wild, Venus
unfolding from the crests of curtains
like waves with the wind through the windows
of her small white bedroom
in her small white house with its sloped
green roof and cool, yellow glow.

I first heard of Hyakatuke a week later
as I walked the wide hallways between German
and Trigonometry, mouthing the words
Ich liebe dich, I love you, Ich liebe dich,
in love with a girl for the first time
and suddenly vision of that halo-winged coma
of white-hot gas, the core a pupil widening
on the horizon, that angry eye of iridium and ice
streaking in on its fuzzed spectrum of light
having swung by for so long on its innocent
elliptical through the solar system.

I wanted to run, make something
of that orbit I wore in the brick-red track
of recycled tractor trailer tires—

fifty seconds per loop, four-and-a-quarter minutes
per mile—track meet after track meet
my name pressed in thin columns of print
on the last of the Sports pages on Sundays,
her school named after the man who wrote *Letter*
From Birmingham Jail
three miles uphill past barrel fires
and men circled around them,
the bits of glass I picked from the soles
of my Nikes turning my fingers red
before I turned back in a sprint downhill,
calves saddled to my legs and I riding them
wherever they would take me.

Since, I've not known such heat.
Have not been pressed beneath such extinguishing
fire: landlocked by hall monitors, "College Application:
Pending," conjugating German modals: *Ich* liebe,
du liebst, *er*, *sie*, *es* liebt, in one mind,
and in the other, the mountain
I often dreamed of: a perfect green isosceles,
blue veins of rivulets swiveling down to the foothills,
woodsmoke in wisps from the stovepipes
of a few cottages as, above it all,
Hyakatuke draws a bead, its bright white iris
widened to the polished skull of a ghost hare
returned for blood, Lauren and I atop that apogee
as the seas boil over and the earth's core retracts,
great steamed jetties blasting solarward
from the evaporated poles,
our bodies spiraling upward to the heavens,
light of our cells *flash flash flash*, vaporized,
great plumes of smoke rising,
the American elms that lined my street
bursting into bright red asters, the wobbly
machinery of the moon dropping
toward the bleary square of light that shone
from the basement window, its splashglow
articulating the laces of our sneakers
as we listened to the sound of her father
between notes. The piano. All that sound.
The chords drifting upward and out
into nowhere.

When Was Early

The arc of the bumblebee curdled at the change

In temperatures is speed. The photons spin
Counterclockwise some times.

Some times. Emphatic facts.
What's safe to eat when

Attached to a body

By a chord. Play it like before. Like before,
When before was understood to be imaginary.

When the Cause is Lost

Hold the mess
in one hand.
Your webbed palm

grasps in an Anti-Gravity refrigerator;

someone unscrewed all the lids.

Deaths on Other Planets

Vacuum seal burst.
Uncontrolled cellular mutation.
Cancer presumably caused by radiation overdose.
Multiple stab wounds from metal claws.
Drowning.
Starvation.
Dehydration.
Oxygen poisoning.
Overgrown with mold.
Hiccups.
Eyestalk hemorrhage after hovercraft accident.
Narrative necessity.
Influenza.
Robot rebellion.
Strangled with own tentacles.
Crushed by weight of own cranium.
Beaten to pulp by human children at play;
sun-dried and washed out to sea.

Presque Vu

I can't be held responsible for my subconscious. These dreams are like,
what do you call it, and you're in them all, so familiar. Last night we put out
a burning building with a, a, thing, starts with an ex, and it's shaped like
a spring. I can't recall the dream I had the night before, something about
birds, I remember thinking I could have been saved if I could have found the
words among the wings. A few nights ago we clung to each other and I kept
hitting snooze before waking to my empty bed. The world seems intensely
new and young after these dreams, and like you're right there,
right on the tip of my tongue.

HOT COP AT IHOP (W4M) -

There's no closure.
You were my first everything.

The last time i seen you, I was pregnant
early 30's, sexy grin
the same aisle at toys r us
the victim of wishful thinking

couldn't help but overhear your broken Spanish

flirty banter
a little
handful of seeds
a flock of pigeons
in my apartment

I was in there taking a drug test for a job

I have nothing to offer you but me
the nights we where together i could not sleep i was afraid you would
go poof, and yes you did go poof,

There is so much I want to tell you that you may never hear.
I felt your presence across the park.

Still have you r voice mails on my phone.

Life is good I bartend and love it (m4w) -

Anyone know anything about the girl that dresses like a boy at the fairview McDonalds?

She's got a tattoo on her arm that says 'believe'.

I go speachless when our eyes lock.

if this is you please own up

I just realized how cool you are

I say hi but what I want to say is good morning.

you got me to my Mothers house by driving through deep water

I thought we would be washed away.

and you were yelling out your truck window at a school bus.

I think I blushed for the first time in a decade.

Can't stop thinking of you in your fluorescent shirt

You winked bye at me, not sure if that was flirty or just friendly.

I gave you my skype info but not sure if you wrote it down.

whatever, hope your blog is lucrative

Our daughters are on the same soccer team. (w4m) -

Hot tattooed firefighter in the grey Chevy truck
Met years ago at Hooters.

I glanced over at you because I heard you blaring Slipknot.
you had blue eyes..and two zip codes

You grabbed my arm and started reading my tattoo while I was in line.
We heated up the dance floor at the bar.
Group hug turned into kissing.

I was scared and trying to protect my ridiculous little heart.
i noticed Tears in Your Eyes, but i was shied to ask you why? and then a taxi came up ;-).
so much to remember and talk about

I think about you all the time
headed east bound on i24
even during sex and during church lol
unmistakable crystal eyes.

Rose colored lenses

Thank you for making me believe that rainbows and unicorns do exist at a time when being a hot mess is all I know.

i believe you think you are clever
this is the first time ive been proud of myeyebrows ever

put your favorite pizza topping in the subject to prove you arent a robot

Arbys cowboy (w4m) -

fair skin, and light freckles
so very afraid of life
but you were pretty as a sunset
on a cliff overlooking lake Huron.

billy joe I have been searching for you
I miss being able to email you.

i bought that 55 acres of rolling hills with a pond.
my phone's playlist set to shuffle

a baby won't change anything

TO THE GIRL IN THE BLACK SHORTS AT KMART (M4W) -

Never tryed this b4,
I'm the guy who pulls up in a green truck up front look like I just got done painting.
I couldn't stop staring at you.....I think you bought freon, and we both drive volvos.

I had just purchased arrows for my son.
You had Georgia plates.
tattoos on your face i was overwhelmed
entering as I was exiting
Camo pants that fit you like a glove, tan wedge heels that moved you into all
the right places,

I was lost for words.

I have thought about that a thousand times.
beauty looked into my green eyes with tears

you had a six pack in your bag
and
the avocados
startled me

I hope you have nice teeth and breath
So I could kiss you for an eternity

I am single, sexy, hard-worker, good job, new car, my own place, romantic man.
This is a small town
i sit in a room full of clutter Here

I know you will never see this
You had Georgia plates.

I don't understand why this bothers me so bad.

I figured out what you were going to say about the hot air balloon.
Tickets have been on sales since August so we have to do this soon.

Hint...... streetfighter

IV.

but what mattered was the tone—

not a drive-by spondee and never the fricative

connotation as verb, but from her mouth

voweled, often preceded by "well," with the "u" low

as if dipping up homemade ice cream

I.

The Erection of Another Paschal Mystery, Nocturnal Emissions, and Immaculate Lady (Slight Return)

from *Grave Matters, Doctor Lamb*

(For Toughie)

Doctor Patton Stonewall Lamb Jr. derived a sickly sort of pleasure from defiling holy institutions. Accompanying propensities for cruelty had manifested in early childhood when he'd been compelled to heave a knotted pillowcase—taut with broken bricks, sharp shards of limestone, and a litter of inbred barn cats—into teeny-tiny Mason Lake (where the riffraff of outlying Calloway County citizenries had once baptized their children in murky shallows alongside watering livestock). The snuffed sack of meows had bubbled only a bit before giving way to water. Patton was convinced that he'd inherited the blasphemous and violent compulsions that marked his fledgling years from a wicked kindred—a suggestive cacophony of disembodied and spiritless whispers calling upon him from the nothingness, slowly building in both volume and intensity, finally becoming a painful buzzing in his head, like a discordant mass of chain saws taking it to a thousand bothered honey hives—and he truly believed that these inherently heterodoxical urges formed the bulk of his twisted birthright.

The Lambs of western Kentucky hailed from a hard and horny stock of grifting frontier folk who'd descended into the sacred hunting ground by way of armed stagecoaches and covered wagons bearing *Ambrose Lamb's Wandering Wax Gallery*. According to Patton's grandfather, the Major, who spoke often—and highly—of the family's "well-hung" patriarch, Ambrose's collection boasted upwards of 20 staged reconfigurations of highly sensationalized moments in the history of mankind. For a small fee—always accepted in trade—wigged and hatted wax mannequins and castaway theater props helped isolated settlers to fully "reimagine" momentous instances passed. The gallery spoke explicitly to the wholly American trinity: violence, virtue, and vice.

Among the life-size dioramas were Hernando de Soto, dead on a nondescript bank of the Mississippi, facedown, surrounded by weeping and recently deflowered Casqui daughters of the river's valley; the Plymouth Rock Pilgrims' first Thanksgiving spread—anachronistically replete with pork chops, bejeweled goblets brimming with wine, and a feverish orgy of wife-swapping Mayflower men and their Wampanoag counterparts' "guest gifts"; an early Puritan strapped to a tree and receiving an impassioned deliverance of 39 stripes by way of a nine-tailed scourge—a half-eaten stolen pie at his feet; Jonathan Edwards beckoning the fiery wonders of imminent holy wrath from a whitewashed pulpit, as from below, a kneeling toothless widow stoked his flame with equally inspired servitude; a cadre of drunken and nightgown-clad founding fathers (bespectacled Franklin, Jefferson, and the like) entertaining a merry band of well-fucked—and stark-naked—strumpets while framing an emboldenedly godless but scrapped draft of the Declaration of Independence; George Washington orating an artillery sermon for a ragtag gaggle of shoeless but willing warriors wintering in Valley Forge, men literally gnawing at their bits in all-encompassing fits of hungry soldier-love; soul-thirsty Shawnees scalping a pregnant mother and her two children—all contorted faces, bulging eyes, and gaping mouths—their pained lights forever soon to be dimmed to darkness; the biggie Boone brothers, Squire and Danny, naked but for their coonskin caps, sleeping on a bed of crumbling Cherokee skulls, sucking thumbs beneath a death quilt fashioned from nearly fifty stitched-together-scalps; a frumpy Martin Luther—indulgently commando beneath his writing cloak and sporting massive early-morning wood—nailing his 95 theses to a latched door; tomb-raiding disciples ransoming the body of Christ from Roman sentries with shares of stolen silver; a gory representation of the Crucifixion on Golgotha; a confusing Mary and Joseph-less Nativity scene—no wise men, no shepherds, no gifts, no star to guide them—only a stuffed parrot perched on a mangered baby; and a shockingly graphic portrayal of the Immaculate Conception that attributed the divine impregnation to an impromptu threesome consisting of a phallus-bearing/phallus-burying sheeted ghost, its receptacle, the not-so-Virgin Mary, and her hard-bitten husband, Joseph, gazing with wide-eyed longing on the improbable coupling he'd stumbled upon—cock-in-hand and passionately awaiting his eternally yet-to-come turn.

As the Major's legend had it, while wintering in the Beech Woods, near what had once been Camp Knox, Ambrose (bastard son of Maryland, forger of documents, unlearned surveyor of land, shepherd, failed diviner of water and women, sideshow barker, sculptor of wax, renouncer of the Catholic faith, and above all these things, denouncer of Christ Our Lord) wedded one April Dickins (then pregnant with their first child, Woody). Blue-eyed April was the firstborn daughter of Ennis, a homesteading minstrel cook who had trekked with the Long Hunters, and Chick, his converted Cherokee bride. The Lambs led Ambrose's nomadic gypsy life for a stretch, but April's melancholic nature was ill-suited for such travels. After a summer of restless wandering, Ambrose buried his root deep in the westernmost reaches of the desolate realm, passed even the lunatic fringes of outliers in the farthest regions of what had once been the Transylvania Purchase, vanishing into the dense woods beyond cleared stretches of timber and toil that offered his blossoming family a brief respite from the second sons of Virginia, land-warranted veterans of the American Revolution, the Presbyterians, the Methodists, the Baptists' "Travelling Church," and the postmillennial ramblings of a Great Revival.

Ambrose felled lumber there for the construction of three crude cabins: one for himself and his; one for his favorite brother, Enoch, and his; and one to house the grounded wax gallery. The following spring, Ambrose and April and Enoch and his wife, Sara, tilled earth and planted plush gardens and row crops of corn and smoking tobacco. Far-flung brothers followed, just clippety-clopping from the Northeast (families, mistresses, and livestock in tow), this pack of exiled miscreants and outlaws yoked as one by blood, sex, taboo fetishes, syphilitically-sown seeds of love, and clannish tendencies. All together, the motley crew constructed an additional 12 cabins, along with a fortified structure meant for weathering Indian raids, protecting the Lambs and their heirlooms and valuables: books, china, silver, sketched and painted portraits, cameos, stained chamber pots traced back to British royalty, wigs and dentures of wealthy forbearers, powdered merkins of favored

Baltimore whores, and whatnot. The castle-like keep had also been equipped with a store of rifles and provisions: salt-pork, hard biscuits, and such. Invoking early squatter's rights, the brothers Lamb established their unnamed fort without charter. Roaming Indian hunting factions—mostly Chickasaw—came to revere the Lambs' violent dispositions and their isolationist principality of darkness, and for the most part, respected the established boundaries of the stolen settlement.

Horror rightfully followed: plagues of fevers, coughs, and dysentery, crop blights, blights of souls, starvation, eaten horses, mistresses, and dogs. At the age of 27, April Lamb was struck dead by an errant lightning bolt while picnicking with Ambrose and their upstart family on a gorgeous limestone bluff overlooking a communal watering hole. The strike seemed to come from below and branched from her head in a brief flickering of heaven-bound roots, and as April rode the lightning back to the house of God, her charred body smoldered to ash. Ambrose spent the rest of his days in relative peace: lackadaisically raising a motherless brood of impishly cruel children, tending to gardens and fields, seeing to his flock of stolen sheep, pigs, horses, and a pair of retired sideshow cougars well into twilight years. When Ambrose exited earth proper by firing a flintlock revolver pressed to his temple, he was in a decrepit barn, surrounded by resting heaps of half-melted, graven wax figures (with whom he was well pleased) and their moth-eaten costumes and props; the godless sexton and his reliquary smelled of death and the lustful friction of adultery and brothers' wives.

Multitudes of sins defined the Lamb bloodline in the years that followed: from land squabbles to rapes and murders, from bearing false witness to bearing no witness, incest, necrophilia, bestiality, be it stolen pigs or stolen pies, court dockets in Richmond, Kentucky County, Superior Court, and later scattered county seats narrated the early Lambs' "festoons of fancy" and spoke to their hardscrabble existences in the Kentucky wilds. Upon hearing his grandfather's apocryphal poetic waxings regarding the deviant and lawless exploits that had birthed family lore, Patton developed his own insatiable urge to test the jurisdiction and temperament of the Lord, distinguishing himself Lamb-worthy in his thirteenth year while assisting in the administration of the Blessed Sacrament at a rest home in Benton.

Before partaking in the consecrated body, young Patton (substituting for a no-show altar boy) had slipped away to the lavatory with a fistful of consecrated Eucharist wafers. In a diabolical attempt to trigger an ass-to-mouth outbreak of E.coli and to invoke biblical wrath, Patton had further sanctified the bodies of Christ by stamping each one between clenched butt cheeks. He'd returned to the Bingo room, bowled the tainted Host for the silver and white coiffed senior citizenry, and waited for the bacterium to work its black magic—one quickened by a hyper-accelerated satanic gestation—and to in turn be struck down by lightning himself: suicide by supplicating the swift hands of an angry God.

But none had fallen ill (then or later), and there was neither lightning nor thunder. Patton linked the disheartening inconsequence to either Divine Indifference or Absolute Absentia. From then on, he was wholeheartedly contained in a fervent state of limbo—somewhere between disbelief and disrespect. (Patton's short-lived tenure as apprentice acolyte at St. Mary's had ended with a fake seizure, followed by an impassioned sequence of feigned stigmata that many attributed to an attempted suicide.) Though his ill-fated communion hex was indeed psychopathic (and altogether heavy-handed), it was not inconceivable behavior for an orphaned child who had come to his grandparents' stead through a succession of tragic happenstances that included, but was by no means limited to, the baptismal drowning of his mother, Lidio Ladythings Famosa de Lamb (a former Santeria priestess and the only daughter of Alejandro and Lola Famosa, Cuban exiles who'd settled in New Orleans), and a fatal deer-hunting "accident" that claimed the life of his father, a troubled mime and Protestant zealot who had stumbled across Ladythings—the lost santera—while silently proselytizing in the heart of voodoo country. Crier-like whispers in Benton attributed the "accidental discharges of buckshot" to shotgun rites of code duello born from an oedipally heated dispute between Big Patton and his father, the Major, Christie E. Lamb.

Despite Patton's seemingly genetic proclivities for extreme acts of sacrilege, he'd always gone to great lengths to see that his paternal grandmother, Margery, never attended church alone. He and his grandfather—who refused to step foot inside any establishment of organized religion—considered Patton's visits to the house of God as stolen opportunities for reconnaissance and referred to them as "spy missions." Margery, who was raised by staunch Catholic parents in Old Louisville, had always considered it uncivilized to enter church without the aid of a gentleman's arm, and while Patton's beliefs—or lack thereof—were antithetical to almost any doctrine or dogma, as a distinguished southern gentlemen, he sought to appease the old woman's convictions when he was able and willing. The most unlikely of traits—a mysterious regard for mannerly gestures—is what found Patton, on this Palm Sunday morning, accompanying Margery to Oh, Immaculate Lady! for early Mass/Reflection (which had been dubbed "Christ Comes to Town") with the Major's loaded Colt .45 tucked in the waistband of his trousers: He'd desired a preordained exit strategy for this particular visit. Pressing matters were at hand. Bizarre circumstances had rendered the pair markedly late.

The car had announced itself with a screeching halt at the foot of an enormous yellow cross, a looming McDonald's-ish beacon that—when funding permitted—glowed in the nighttime sky. Cloaked in a rapidly dissipating fog, the emblematic construct twittered errant flutters of electrical static in the remnant dusk, a flickering of light towering above the vehicle and its two occupants (both of whom were dressed to the nines): a hefty elderly woman clad in a light blue dress and a plastic rain-bonnet and a young man with a colossal, oblong head. Patton, the top-heavy oddity in the shotgun seat, was in a state of dishevelment. He was wearing an outdated suit—much too large for such a slender physique—and his face wore the remnants of a leisurely morning spent in semi-drag: ghastly dregs of foundation, eyeliner, and lipstick.

The engine shuttered to rest, and the muffler offered forth a bang akin to a celebratory 12- gauge blast. "Already too much, presumptuous and unfortunate," Patton thought. The automobile, a shit-brown '77 Impala coupe—with a frayed vinyl landau that had succumbed to dark patches of mildew—was a relic in and of itself. Hard rains had passed through some hours before, and strong winds still carried an ominous mist that speckled the windshield with faint pitter-patters. Patton and Margery remained in the car, silent, waiting. Thoughts of Ambrose's shattered skull and splattered brains coating the walls of his barn ("in an abstractly expressionistic slop of teeth and skull and purpled crimson gore") entertained the distinguished gentleman. For a long stretch of time, there were no words at all. This was fine by Patton. He could handle the nothingness. He'd learned all he'd wanted of its grim business that autumn when he'd been reborn unto the night. It sometimes seemed that that his family's only shared existence lay in the brief moments of haunting silence that preceded escapist fancies of grace.

As if to cleanse the moment of all trappings of doom, Margery leaned over Patton and fetched her massive leather purse from the floorboard. He resisted the urge to step on her dainty white gloves with spit-shined penny loafers. After rummaging through the cosmetics, paper-clipped coupon rolls, and peppermint disks that filled the handbag, she withdrew a handkerchief and placed it on her lap. She then pulled a plastic bottle of rubbing alcohol from beneath the driver's seat, unscrewed its pink cap, placed the bunched rag to the bottle, and shook. The fumes struck Patton's nostrils nicely; they burned acrid, like a plug of snuff. The scent reminded him of beauty parlor forays with the old woman. In fact, it made him wish that he still donned the made-up face in all the splendors of its entirety.

Margery glared at him, lips pursed. "Tilt your head back, little missy." And Patton's grandmother went at his face. After a brief rest to catch her breath, she spat in the cloth and returned to work, scrubbing around his mouth and eyes with surprisingly reserved force. Breathing heavily and satisfied with her cleansing, she said, "I certainly hope that you haven't burned any bridges with this shocking nonsense. You worked so hard for your doctorate."

"No, ma'am, I'm sitting on the declaratory papers. I'll always be a goddamned doctor. They can't take that away." The degree in Southern literature had been conferred by the Longbush Institute of Cleveland, Ohio. Patton had written his doctoral thesis ("Wrathful Whirlwinds and Slivers of Manufactured Grace Bequeathed to a Parade of Zealots, Freaks, and Soulless Meats: a Revelation") on the canon of his beloved, Miss Mary Flannery O'Connor. The Longbush Institute was neither prestigious nor respectable, but the diploma was in fact legitimate. Unfortunately, proclamations of intellectual distinction granted by the establishment held little—if any—value in the hallowed realms of genuine scholars. This was of no consequence to the young man bearing Longbush's valediction. His business was with the woman herself; the authoress' concerns guided his unsung labors in the field of dead letters.

In the waning moments of his thesis defense, one of the committee members had inquired about the Lamb of God in O'Connor's work. Patton had ignored the question, instead speaking at length about the woman's futile submersion in the sacred waters of Lourdes; then he'd wondered aloud about the papal blessing she'd received from Pope Pius XII in Vatican City. With a raised, accusatory voice, Patton had directed questions of his own towards the sorry lot of academics: "Had there been a glow about her, or was she just another speck propped up on crutches in a swell of desperation, maimed bodies, and sick souls? Had she closed her eyes, clinging to Pius' vestments, weeping? Had she later traced the callused forefinger of her writing hand over the scars that mapped her precious body? An upturned kidney? A calcified hip? The poisoned womb? Did she ever curse the name of God? She was writing with death rapping on her bedroom window, cloaked in the darkness of a gallows' hood. Hers are cautionary tales, parable-esque in manner and form, sublime propaganda encrypted with divine symbology. The character-driven stories are carefully plotted and anchored by manufactured epiphanies, catharses, and forward progress. Apart from 'Parker's Back' and 'Judgment Day,' her final tales, and the ones in which she found her legs, narratively speaking, many of the works are dizzying, especially the 'Goods,' 'Good Country People' and 'A Good Man Is Hard to Find.' Her brevity is fucking golden. This much is true. She built cathedrals. It would be wonderful, though, to have more of that lovely voice gracing the pages. I so want her to let her hair down and often find myself yearning for ample sections of spliced regresses akin to the Faulknerian lay-back stretches, those wondrous wormholes of exposition and narration that swallow us whole and plod along like jazz funeral dirges, their grand marshal marching us gladly into lands that transcend the constraints of time. Friends, soon-to-be confidants and confidantes, I am going to be very frank with you. I, Patton Stonewall Lamb Jr., am madly in love with this woman, and my devotion outshines any vacuous exploration of the literal and figurative constructs and conceits of language and narrative. I won't allow foolhardy forays into literary criticism to taint the purity of my obsession and love for her.

The committee had gazed blankly at Patton, who'd grown flushed and manically animated. The thesis defense was an uncomfortable and disconcerting affair. No more questions. Every member had avoided eye contact, save for Dr. Julius Peckinpah, who had always gone out of his way to engage the strange young man. Fearing a lunatic outburst or mental breakdown, all present parties had bestowed their signatures on the title page. After the council scattered, Peckinpah approached Patton, nodding his head in approval. As he got closer, the smile faded. "Christ, Lamb, you smell like death. Have you been sleeping in a funeral parlor?" Patton had worn the Major's Army service uniform to the defense—along with a vintage powdered wig. The dress greens reeked of mothballs and Aqua Velva. The newly-minted Doctor Lamb had embraced Julius and whispered into his ear, "I am deeply honored to be indoctrinated into this distinguished company of upright scholars. Now I am truly worthy to tread on these hallowed grounds."

The group's concerns regarding Dr. Lamb's mental health were not unfounded. A mere three hours after the thesis had been signed by all present parties, Patton found himself on an involuntary 72-hour hold in the psychiatric wing of Cleveland Memorial Hospital. He'd been severely beaten by the patrons of Boony's, a bar in the industrial district. Just before he'd been pummeled (and after many vodka tonics), Patton had stood on a tabletop and pontificated to a brood of blue-collar barflies. "I am a doctor of letters and demand to be addressed as such." His limp body—bleeding from both ears, face mangled by fists, boots, and pool cues—had been found on a sidewalk. A passing streetwalker had urinated on Patton's battered face in front of a gathered crowd.

"Poor son of a bitch is speaking in tongues."

"That crazy whore just pissed on the Holy Ghost."

Somewhere between midnight's chimes and the witching hour, Mary Flannery had come to Patton in the psychiatric ward, summoning him from a wet nightmare. His lady was awash in a heavenly green glow, and the horns of a bull jutted from her skull, parting her freshly shampooed hair. Patton could hear the fluttering of her moth-like wings from within. Suspended in the air, she'd rapped on the barred window of his room; then her glorious hands had passed through rusted iron and glass. La Santa Muerte had brought him a moonlit Twinkie, an ice-cold bottle of Dr. Pepper, and six Luminal tablets.

"Don't furrow your brow over such silly matters, Doctor Lamb. Everything's been done before, and no one remembers any of it. Not a whit. It's for the birds, love, just a bunch of derivative goddamned gobbledygook, merely stands of risen sand," Mary Flannery whispered in the cottony tongue of rebel angels.

Like sacrilege, the Impala, too, was part of Patton's inheritance. He was to receive the remaining portion by signed check in an afternoon meeting with the Major. (Nobody called him Christie; even Margery addressed and referred to her husband as the Major or just plain Major. The old man loathed the feminine implications of his given name.) Major Lamb was—among other things—former Army medic, would-be painter, fraudulent rural veterinarian, raconteur, and confessed mass murderer. The Major boasted of taking twenty-odd lives while touring Belgium with the 526th Armored Infantry Battalion during the Battle of the Bulge, along with three stateside killings. (The Major included his only son among the counted coup.) The old man claimed to have received a discreet battlefield citation for euthanizing an ambulance crew and the handful of wounded GIs they were transporting to a triage station; the ambulance, a WC-54 Dodge, had been lit up by German Panzerfausts and nearly 1,200 MG-42 rounds on the outskirts of Malmedy. "A fucking mess, this holy chorus of screams, moans, and refined gore. Some were merely bug-eyed torsos and gnashing teeth." The Major put them down one at a time—under sporadic MG-42 fire from German pillboxes. "After I delivered them their 'night, night' doses of morphine, their eyes swelled up all big and beautiful with vibrant colors that faded only as their pupils became pinpricks, and they tumbled back into the depths of themselves, bound for the only nothing that is." One had been salvageable. Out of morphine, the Major had gladly smothered him with a cupped hand. By cozy firelight in their sitting room—tongue loosened by hearty mugs of stout eggnog—the Major offered his confession to Patton every Christmas Eve, hours after Margery had retired for bed. The Major had never been a major. The self-proclaimed title was honorary.

The same collective Bentonite voice that spoke in speculative hushed tones of Patton's father's murder at the hands of his grandfather also doubted the self-anointed codger's accounts of wartime valor; in fact, many suggested that the bulk of the Major's 31-day stint in the Ardennes Forest had been devoted to identifying dehumanized corpses, assembling piles of parts ("like rebuilding disassembled G.I. Joes"), assigning lots, and digging graves in the frozen Belgian earth by moonlight on pilfered, dead men's shares of morphine, giggling to himself until the very moment he was shipped home. He'd received a Dishonorable Discharge from the United States Army after pushing a psychiatric ward nurse down a flight of steps at the Carlisle Barracks in Pennsylvania, where he'd been recuperating from his brief visit to the Bulge while taking courses in forage inspection, meat and dairy hygiene, and animal husbandry.

Dark times had lately befallen the Lamb Empire. The Major had suffered a series of strokes in the early spring that had paralyzed the better part of the left quadrant of his frail body. He spent most of his waking hours propped up on a stack of sweat-stained pillows in the upstairs bedroom of his scaled-down Jeffersonian mansion on Mockingbird-Creek-Mill Road. The Major had designed and built the home himself, just past the shaded stretch of peeling sycamores lining the dead-end road, their slouching branches resembling a canopy of conjoined skeleton hands. The roof hadn't been properly reinforced, and portions of it had collapsed into the attic space. Blue tarps were draped over the exposed boxes of family heirlooms and bric-a-brac—mostly the possessions of Patton's dead father. The columns on the porch (steel rods sheathed in misshaped plaster moldings) bowed beneath the weight of the hallmark extended roof. The entire frame slouched leftward. None of the oddly narrowed windows aligned. (Passersby often noted the few discernable right angles of the bizarre construct.) The proverbial "They" of Benton called the lilliputian madness "Monticello's Little Bastard."

The old man was certain that the afternoon deathbed address ("goddamned Dickensian nonsense") would appeal to the sordid romance that had consumed him and his only grandson, and he was not wrong in this assumption. The Major regarded his own encroaching end with genuine but subdued excitement. Manic dispositions were ill-suited for properly retying the loosened threads of one's life. Margery had told Patton that the Major had taken to drooling through mid-morning sponge baths, and how she'd recently caught him attempting to masturbate while watching a re-run of *Three's Company*. "A crooked grin had spread across his face, and he said, 'If I'm not masturbating, I'm procrasturbating.' My disgust made him giddy, and he'd bellowed a sad song. 'Come and knock on our door… We've been waiting for you…' Your grandfather kept right on with the futile and pathetic dirty business, too, and I left him to it. What else was I to do?"

Although Patton was intrigued by the formal morbidity of the afternoon's agenda, he was not altogether unafraid. The old man drew his stories from a darkened well and spewed them forth with froths of spittle, but none of the yarns disturbed Patton; in fact, they made him feel less alone in the peculiar shadows of his overwrought world. His ripened noggin brimmed with the Major's imparted darkness. And he stole. As the vessel, all he need do was remember. (Such is the way with tales. There is no truth in retelling—if any tales are ever true at all.) Sometimes, while alone, Patton would speak the stories aloud, mimicking the Major's untamed tongue, repeating them over and over until he conjured them at will. In the months following the strokes, after Patton had been called home from the depths of his own crack-up to help care for the old man, the Major had begun crafting the fitting ends for his beloved evolved macabres: "Honeymoon Burning," "Merry Christmas, Clay Henry," "The World According to Mr. Watson," and "Tombstoned Babies" among the better of the lot. From his throne of yellowed pillows and bedding, each ending was delivered with reverence—in a soft grumble that was half spoken and half slurred. Patton took dictation, reading the cathartic finales back to the Major. He'd looked in on his grandfather that morning, a bit after the drag incident. Patton had been wearing the Major's suit, a wool Norfolk pinstripe number from the 1960s. The Major was a broad-shouldered son of a bitch in those days, and the jacket slouched on Patton's bony frame like armor. The old man had been reading through the Bible, redacting sections he didn't like with a marker held in his good hand. It was Patton who had mentioned to the Major that Thomas Jefferson had edited his own draft of the Holy Book. The elder Lamb had set about his project with haste. "I don't have time for bullshit," he'd said. (He stored a stack of stolen Bibles beneath his bed.) The Major was a hack editor; he kept the narrative skeleton of his Pentateuch—the Creation myth, the flood, Abraham (progenitor of the 12 Tribes), Moses' travails—minus dictations of Mosaic Law, genealogical ramblings, judges, and prophets. (Moses—foundling, murderer, savior, penultimate antihero—was close to the old man's dark heart. "He was the vessel.") The Book of Job was included, too, but the rest of the Old Testament had been scrapped. The New Testament fared better, but it was still under the gun. The Major had left the canonical Gospels mostly intact. The four chosen disciples' dueling accounts of the Messiah's mystical inception, prodigious childhood, the telling gaps of his lost years, later life miracles and teachings, the Crucifixion, Resurrection, and Ascension. "Grave robbers in a heated tale-telling contest, by God, that's what it's all about: tampered tombs, ransomed bodies, and the falsified yarns of the risen dead ascending into the clouds." Old man Lamb had negated the apostles' acts and letters, though, along with the madcap cryptology of Revelation. There was no day of Pentecost in the Major Lamb's Good Book, "no tongues of fire, no Holy Spook." When Patton had entered the Major's bedroom that morning to read him their story, "Go-Cart Donny," the old man was having at the Beatitudes with a black Sharpie. "I'm partial to my own Sermon on the Mount."

The Major had spun Donny's narrative hundreds of times. It was standard grim fare: During the post-TVA boom, Donny West had opened a go-cart track—along with accompanying batting cages. In 1977, he had been shot in the face with a .357 magnum during an armed robbery at the track's garage—all for 27 dollars in quarters. Some said it was over unpaid gambling debts. The deviants had desecrated the nearly headless corpse. After cutting him from his mechanic's onesie, they'd tethered go-cart Donny's spindly arms and legs to four souped-up go-carts with stretches of towing chain. When the evil fuckers pegged the opened-up engines, they'd quartered his soulless body at track's center. Patton had delivered his stock reply: "Donny deserved better than that." It was a good one: funny, bleak, ultra-violent, and bestowed with a faint sliver of its own redemptive grace: A go-cart parade/funeral had been held in his honor on "Donny Day." A Homeric allusion concluded the miniature grotesque: *And so we buried Donny, renter of go-carts.*

Margery reached over and parted Patton's shock of oily black hair and placed a clean monogrammed handkerchief in the front right pocket of his coat. "I'm grateful that your grandfather has finally seen enough of this car. I hope it lasts you a year or two." She pressed a gloved hand to the ceiling's drooping liner. They both studied the vinyl seats in the flickering light of the cross. Time had robbed the synthetic upholstery of its sheen, but it was not without character. The car's interior was covered in tell-tale black and red ink, cryptic messages penned during house and farm calls. The old man had kept ballpoint pens in a Styrofoam cup wedged into the narrow gap between seats. Among tiny, meticulous printed script were a few notes dictated in the too-large handwriting of a child—red and black chicken scratches: *Test Goats./ Kill box of puppies./Buy Medicine for cows./Pay Gilbert./ Save the good doggies?/Stillborn foal at Greer's place./ Vaccinate./ Give Treadwell to the nothingness./Fetch him the killing bag.* The backseat was a myriad of Patton's doodles: stick men and women in coffins, hanging from gallows, nailed to crosses. Margery's light blue dress—which Patton thought beautiful—obscured the work in its entirety, but Patton could still decipher some of the Major's encoded shorthand:

Brewer's cow, Birddogbeaver, Anthrax? Foot-and-mouth? Isolate and call Gilbert in Gilbertsville ASAFP—have motherfucker call Frankfort./ Leyland's lab, Old Man River, stroke—no legs, no bladder, no colon, no nada—take phenobarb. and sodium pent. Scare up some booze and Dexedrine. Pack the Colt and Gideon's Bible.

Patton ran probing fingers over familiar Majorisms: *Gut-shot dogs must scrap, fuck, and kill their way through moonshine into the dimly-lit Promised Land./Tents stand pitched till camp breaks down.* He picked up the warped cup from between them, pocketed the emptied ballpoints, and chucked it over his shoulder into the backseat of the car. "It's a good vehicle, Grandmother. I'm happy to have it. The old fucker can tote a load. Who knows? The thing may last forever."

"We've been running around in this god-forsaken thing since '77. Good riddance, I say. The writing is unsettling."

“Well, you’ll most certainly be picking the next car alone. Find comfort in that.” Patton gazed at the familiar stains of dried animal blood in the floorboard’s tan carpeting. He’d plotted and dug his share of graves over the years. After the Major euthanized family pets, Patton would bury the newly departed in grieving families’ backyard pet cemeteries. It was his job. He’d burned his share of passed animals, too, stoking the pyres of the Major’s incinerator in the uptown office. Patton was death’s willing underling.

The woman studied her handiwork on Patton’s face, tilting her head slightly as if trying to fashion a painful narrative to the strange business that had transpired that morning. The violent pre-church whore’s bath had given his eyes and mouth clownish red rims. “You’re of mine, Patton Lamb, and you know that I love you, but you’ve wandered into a place that I want no part of.”

“Oddness is in my blood, woman. I had no hand in that.” He looked into his grandmother’s eyes; a hollow cheerleader’s grin consumed his face, and he drew deeply from a Benzedrex inhaler procured from the inside pocket of his sport coat. Then he chuckled, rapped his knuckles along the dashboard, and said, “On a much lighter note, Christ Jesus, one hell of a morning we have on our hands here. Hardly enough light to properly illuminate the memory of the man’s ballyhooed donkey ride down Palm Branch Road through Holy Town. Crowds will turn on you, snapping like half-mad, car-clipped dogs. That’s the walk away from the gig. But considering what’s coming down the pike—the dying, the short-sheeted limbo, and the rising. Hell, a crucified dead man emerging from the bowels of a borrowed tomb transcends all the harbingers of gloomy weather. Kind of leaves you marveling at the wondrous simplicities of existence. I’m talking creature comforts. Let’s remember him with a meal of saltines and grape juice.”

All at once the sun cut through the clouds—a plump blood orange sandwiched between a stand of scrawny slash pines behind the church. The sunlight made the trees look like giant spears thrust into the ground at their hilts, almost pleading to be adorned with heads of the devout. Patton envisioned his own decapitated gourd resting on a steel pike, eyes fixed open, tiny black marbles set against the ruddy red maps of burst capillaries. He felt blood rushing to his groin. Biting reddish lips, Patton willed the erection away with steely resolve. The instantaneous transformation of the sky quieted them. It was a manufactured moment of gravity. Patton knew how he would spin it to the Major: "Sorry, man, called one in on Palm Sunday, resorted to stock footage."

The church before them was bastardization of Roman Catholicism, a hodgepodge: partly Episcopalian, partly Presbyterian, and partly Church of Christ (a chorus of deathly nasal twangs unaided by musical accompaniment). It was a strange amalgamation indeed. Marshall County lay on the outskirts of a feeble diocese. The closest respectable parish was in Paducah, so Margery had settled for the limited salvation at hand. The church and congregation was led and founded by Father Edmund Diddle, a defrocked Episcopalian priest and eunuch. Father Edmund had lost his testicles in a St. Mary's sanctioned event: "The Great Backwards Bicycle Race to Reverse Karmic Wrath." (St. Mary's had been Diddle's first church.) Upon crossing the finish line, the then priest had collided with Miss Martha Hargis, the portly organist of St. Mary's. Miss Martha was competing in the cosmically insignificant charitable event high on a crazy-train pharmacopeia of phentermine, Librium, and top-shelf marijuana. Though Diddle was later declared to be the race's victor through a VHS recording replay, he'd also racked himself into eunuch-dom; Father Edmund had been neutered and fractured his pelvis. The spectacle had shamed the church. Some months later, as news of his impending defrocking trickled down from the top, the sad-sack priest had turned to drink: Jungle Juice and Barton's Vodka. He wore a perpetual reddish Kool-Aid mustache for a number of months.

Edmund had risen from the proverbial ashes, though, swore off the booze and started his own church. He'd christened it Oh, Immaculate Lady! (And it was, in fact, a direct address to Mary, mother of Jesus.) Diddle had even plugged his fledgling church on television. WKBS-7 had produced a moving account of the eunuch's prosthetic implants surgery in a series of nightly segments entitled "Edmund Diddle Gets His Groove Back, Again a Doting Father." Representatives from the Vatican—or any other church governing body, for that matter—failed to sanction the existence of Oh, Immaculate Lady! Diddle and his flock were a vanguard movement.

Patton ran a slender finger along the window, leaving a vanishing trace of fog along the glass. He dreaded his grandmother's return to cross-dressing matters and hoped the woman would suddenly regard their untimely arrival with a sense of embarrassment, restart the car, and head on back home, so Patton could fulfill his obligated conference with the Major and be gone. After a stop in Louisville for some much-needed entertainment and to attend an O'Connor conference, Patton would be making a pilgrimage to Milledgeville, Georgia, where he would visit the woman's home, Andalusia, and—most importantly—her modest gravesite on Memory Hill. Patton had packed that morning in the pre-dawn hours and hoped to arrive in Louisville later that night. He'd failed to mention that he was to meet a pal from his Longbush days there, one Percival Pepperfield, for a night of wilding that would most certainly end in tragedy. Margery loathed the bush-league novelist of ill repute. Percy, a whale of a man, was no stranger to sexual deviancy. His turn-ons included—among other things—bathroom smells, antique furniture, and confined spaces. Patton had happened upon Percy at Hook's XXX Shop, a hidden gem in Cleveland's unappreciated red-light district. Patton's former professor had given him directions to a downtown bar known to be frequented by hookers and johns. He was to present Patton with his graduation gift there: "The Gals of Southern literature" sex doll collection. (Percy had suggested that Patton work his way through them chronologically, starting with Miss Eudora. "But I do hope you'll enjoy the whole sloppy gamut.")The pair's meeting in Louisville was to coincide with Percy's newfound freedom. He'd been serving a three-month stretch on house arrest.

Dr. Pepperfield's cabin fever dance stemmed from an Indecent Exposure charge in Virginia. Percy had revealed himself to an audience at a Civil War reenactment while playing Ulysses Grant. Old Percival had stumbled drunkenly from his tent and proceeded to unfasten the gold-painted buttons of his authentic general's trousers, playing a little game of show-and-tell for a blonde mother-daughter duo swilling hot dogs and huggied beers. Doing a little side-to-side shimmy with his wide hips, he'd slurred, "Feast your thwarted eyes on the schlong that slew the South, the carpet-bagging tally-whacker that brought old Robert E.

Lee to his rug-burned knees here in this blessed city of Appomattox. This here Yankee's doodle is a noodle dandy." Pepperfield took great delight in bedding Southern belles in full Yankee regalia. "You haven't truly lived until you've had a Daughter of the Confederacy in the bed of a pickup truck, dawn breaking behind you—the gal riding the old pommel horse like a northbound money train."

Patton had secretly visited Pepperfield at his vacation home on the Dismal River—where he was serving the stretch. The debased getaway consisted of three double-wide trailers stacked end to end. He'd chain sawed connecting passageways between the trio of abodes. Percy had been serving the time in Caligula-esque fashion—drinking, drugging, and degrading. He'd deemed the innermost lair of his catacombed resting digs "the nest." Patton had helped Percy weld together a human-hamster's wheel with scrap metal and the frames of two miniature merry-go-rounds—using a torch pilfered from Longbush's shop. Percy had worn oversized Bill Dance-style sunglasses while manning the torch. "I can't lose my eyesight over the manifestation of a hamster cage fetish. Goddamn it, I'm a writer." The novice torch man and his apprentice had been welding indoors. Illuminated splinter-shards of orange and blue light had cascaded into the dark room. (Percy had draped a myriad of blankets and quilts over every window in the burrowed dwelling's cozy den.) A spark had met the trailer's blue shag carpet and set it ablaze; overlapping flames had careened over one another, spreading across the room and up the wall like a million forked devil tongues ascending towards the gates of heaven. Patton and Percy had smothered the fire with wet towels and a gorgeous tapestry decorated with the woven visage of "Gambler-era" Kenny Rogers. ("I prefer to remember the crooner as he was—in all his white-maned glory.") The wheel was stationed in the trailers' nest. The entire night that Patton was there, a postmenopausal gas station clerk with sagging breasts ran on the squeaking wheel, stark naked. Occasionally, Pepperfield, wearing a silk half-robe, would direct her to nip from oversized "hamster bottles" (which Percy had cobbled together with empty, gallon-sized milk jugs, syphoning hose, and duct tape) along the nest's walls. In the early morning hours, the party had moved to the porch. Percy's cat, a fat tabby named Ignatius, had drowned in the hot tub at some point. The novelist was unconcerned, saying only that the "whiskered fellow had led a full nine lives." As Patton was leaving the following morning, the hamster's wheel was empty. Below the perverse construction—and resting on a bed of freshly chipped cedar—was the scatological coupe de grâce: a solitary human-hamster turd.

Patton checked his watch, hoping to steer Margery from the realm of psychosexual intervention. His grandmother expected eloquent Freudian explanations for his foray into donning woman's underclothes and makeup. He shifted in his seat, avoiding his grandmother's gaze. Perhaps the thought of him wanting to look like a lot lizard on Palm Sunday had been too much for her to endure.

Margery broke the silence. "The not-so-lady mess left on your face this morning leads me to presume that you're a late bloomer in the shifteroo business. I suggest keeping this ritual in the darkness it's accustomed to."

"It's complicated, Grandmother."

"I'd imagine so."

Patton tipped his head. Perhaps he'd oversimplified. He could have told the old woman that shape-shifting had been the culmination of something grander than the perverse nature that she'd grown accustomed to over the years. He could tell her that he often fancied the notion that he was a displaced character ambling through a half-imagined O'Connor-scape, and that his were pages preordained as lining for the authoress' celestial chicken coops and peafowl aviaries. Patton had long feared that his tragicomic, cartoonish world was mostly a nightmarish work of fraudulent fiction. He could tell his grandmother that his charade—Flannery-Patton's charade—concerned the grave matters of love. He imagined telling her many things but said nothing at all.

Margery leaned over Patton and started for the glove box before shifting her hands back to the wheel. She gripped the worn steering column. Patton envisioned the whiter knuckles beneath her white gloves and took great pleasure in his silence's unsettling of the woman's heart. He ached to sense the pained pitter-patter buried in her ample chest. Perhaps he'd wanted her to find him there. The shower was running. Patton had been standing in front of an oval mirror—clad in his grandmother's underclothes (loose-fitting cotton panties gathered in bunches beneath dark pantyhose) and wearing a shockingly inept made-up face. The odd academic had been mimicking a pre-lupus Flan, on his tiptoes, face nearly pressed against the mirror, hot breath rendered white against the glass. He'd been whispering his own name in a lazy Georgian drawl. "Patton Lamb, Patton Lamb, where are you, my little heathen boy?" He'd been speaking for the woman, repeatedly forming his hooker-red lips into O-shaped kisses, each one punctuated by an audible smack. When his grandmother made her entrance, Patton was unfastening one of her best bras and speaking to a laminated paper doll propped up in the corner of the sink. The doll's head was that of Flannery O'Connor, black and white print: The torso and appendages were in glossy color; at the convergence of legs—the oracle's orifice—was a swelled *Cheri*-page beaver airbrushed to wanton perfection and glistening like a Thanksgiving coupon-turkey.

Truth be told, he loved O'Connor before he loved her words. Patton had discovered Mary Flannery in his grandfather's attic, a nook the Lambs called the "midget room." Its entryway, a small half-door, was hidden behind a large oak chest of drawers. Patton had come across a slew of pictures Big Patton had clipped from paperbacks, anthologies, and articles in a stack of dusty books he'd left behind. They were all of Miss Flannery. The frayed stack had been sandwiched in a 25¢ paperback edition of her first novel, *Wise Blood*. The book's title and blurb ("A Searching Novel of Sin and Redemption") intrigued the already morbid youngster, and while her dust-jacket life (writing, raising peafowl and other pheasants, dying from lupus at 39) was almost erotically tragic, it was one of the pictures that set the hooks in his odd little heart. The photo was of her seated on a couch below the painted self-portrait, her misshapen head surrounded by a haze of halo-like light, a sinister pheasant standing guard beside her. Brimming with black and white want, O'Connor's gut-sickly lonesome eyes sang a muted siren's song from an uncharted realm beyond the River Styx. Patton would sit in the steaming hot midget room, seduced, spellbound, and hornily mesmerized—his hair slick with sweat, a translucent beaded mustache covering his upper lip. Willingly haunted, he'd gaze into the woman's eyes and often would imagine himself walking into the photo, naked and ready for a roll. Beneath flickering daylight emanating from the aerator vent, he'd study the patterns of the woman's homely dress until it vanished. Her body was not altogether beautiful to him, and Patton felt shamed by this. The miniature conjurer conceived strange things done. Eventually, Patton took the picture from the book, taped it to one of the cardboard liners from the Major's laundered dress shirts, and tucked the paper doll between the box spring and mattress of his bed.

And he tended to his fetish like a wet-nurse. Courtly love's end was swift. With years, Patton developed a fantastical nutscape to accompany the doll—and it was there that he stretched his legs. He would envision his way into O'Connor's bedroom in Andalusia. And she is always waiting there, wearing only a necklace of heirloom pearls, her cat's eye glasses, and a mustache of heavy cream. The pearls are knotted loosely around her slender neck like an unslipped noose. After brief pleasantries regarding works in progress, Patton has her fast and hard on the old mattress of her bed. As they become one, a large peacock struts back and forth, roosting on a tree branch and watching them angrily from the bedroom window. Flannery-Patton's panting and moaning intensify as the squeaking box spring struggles to sustain the blessed tryst. Shrieks of near-ecstasy fill the room—from beyond, a muffled staccato chorus of hinnies' neighs, roosters' crows, and peacocks' cries weigh in on the sacrilege that is transpiring within. And the star-crossed fuckers ride one another, switching things up, just going at it like a pair of moonlit dumpster dogs well into the thick of the night, where the stars and moon choreograph their circus of spirited bones and skin. As a misty dawn breaks, the bed rocks like a distressed fishing vessel navigating frigid Atlantic waters. And young Patton is still bearing Winslow Homer wood. With deep-thrusted fog warnings, he rocks the bed-boat harder and harder, cresting with such velocity that even the dusty hardwood floors quake and tremble. The bedposts crash against the wall, loud bangs joining the wondrous music of clapping flesh on figurative flesh. Flannery-Patton is a tangled mess of moans and burning bushes. Finally, the bed—and Flannery-Patton—give way, and the lovers crash through the wall of the farmhouse, coming down on top of the congregation of hot-and-bothered peafowl and chickens on the front porch. In a heap of splintered lumber, their bodies glisten with cortisone-fumed sweat, covered in bits of straw, broken eggshells, and yolk. Dust and feathers cling to the glimmering skin of their flushed, naked bodies, Flannery's tell-tale butterfly rash a passionate crimson on her face and chest. They cling to each other tightly in the rubble, each holding the other's stare until their eyes conjoin. Flannery's desk and typewriter are in shambles; her aluminum crutches are bent and twisted; and revised manuscript sheets—black typeface slashed with red ink—are carried away by the wind, page by page. The warm sun is upon them, and they drift off into dreamless sleep, oblivious to the ruins surrounding them.

Such romantic daydreams are rarely enough, though, and at the brink of 17, Patton had altered the doll by gently snipping the base of the woman's neck with scissors and gingerly pasting her head atop the body of a spread-legged porno vixen from *Cheri Magazine*. Patton had also included the *Cheri* gal's teased bangs in place of O'Connor's understated Joan of Arc clip. He'd taken a box-cutter to the stenciled collage on top of the cardboard liner and sealed it in plastic. The Venus de Milledgeville's neck was perfectly aligned with the X-rated torso. Patton christened the juxtaposed beast PornO'Connor. Just between PornO'Connor's legs (mere inches from the sanctum sanctorum) and printed in bright yellow bubble letters was a caption that read *It's not your clit that makes you come: It's your heart*. And though he'd later come to discern that O'Connor did not care at all for the Protestant heathens that littered her fiction (and in fact took great delight in the violent wrath that rained down upon their empty heads), Flannery was, to Patton then, all heart; and he'd come to his own understanding of the phrase's essence over the years, as PornO'Connor was shuffled to and from the bathroom in the folds of a shower towel, and during their late-night rendezvous when the doll was carefully laid out on starched bed sheets, Creator and Creation having at it beneath a glowing blanket tent illuminating a darkened room by flashlight, and the essence of the phrase was this: One must wholly surrender to their beloved—surrender all— revealing frailties and darkness that must then be transcended—and their want must resonate after the fluids of lust have been spewed, swapped, and comingled. This—and only this—is salvation. Mind and body, heart, head, spirited cock, and soul: Such is the way with said matters of love. The most fruitful lovelusts are frailty-born. Subconsciously, Patton had attributed the crude phrase to O'Connor herself, as if it had been pulled from the pages of some unpublished manuscript—and not from the pen of a wunderkind intern at *Cheri Magazine.* While completing his undergraduate studies at Longbush, guilt and shame had driven Patton to add a handwritten postscript to the metamorphic beast conceived from holiness and smut, a sentence from Mr. Shiflet's prayer in "The Life You Save May Be Your Own."

It's not your clit that makes you come: It's your heart.

Oh Lord! Break forth and wash the slime from this earth!

Patton Lamb was unable—or unwilling—to apply such romantic daydream-drivel to souls encountered in the living world. He couldn't summon a drop of slime without Mary Flannery's unblinking eyes upon him, and to do so would be an unpardonable act of unfaithfulness. The woman conducted the ebb and flow of Patton's ejaculations from the land of the dead.

Our young man felt the cold heft of the .45 in his waistband. It was an Army-issued M1911A1 (single stack clip, a coven of seven bullets, plus the chambered round). Patton had stolen it the night before—along with some tools from the shed (which he'd wrapped in blankets and placed in the Impala's trunk). The Colt's stock was a darkened grey, and its walnut grip had been chipped—but it could still work magic. Patton had always been taken by implements of passage. As a child, he'd gaze for hours at the syringes and vials in the Major's black leather death bag. He'd never forget the pleased look on his grandfather's face as he ended animals' stays in this world. The firearm's metal felt uneasy against his stomach. Gooseflesh spread over his body in a quick wave, and he offered forth a horny ball-sack-begotten shiver. The car had grown hot. Beads of sweat fell from Patton's face onto the bulges in his lap. His testicles hurt. They'd retreated into the bowels of his gut. There was a three-part remedy for such matters: PornO'Connor, copious squirts of baby oil in the palm of his hand, and friction. The holy relic needed to coax his balls back into the land of scrotum and Norfolks was in the Impala's trunk—at the bottom of a duffle bag, tucked away in a copy of *North American*

Grave Architecture: The Post-Civil War Years, along with an assortment of spades, shovels, and a crowbar. Patton was hungry and horny—both natural yearnings, he assured himself; he wanted his pound cake. The head of little Patton snaked out of his boxer shorts' pee-hole. The shaft swelled past the steel until its tip met the coarse wool fabric. He need only refrain from coating his trousers with ample spurts of his own agape love. Wise to the variety of his excitement and completely disgusted, Margery looked at him, wincing. Patton eyed himself in the rearview mirror. His grandmother had worked a number on him. The skin around his eyes and mouth was still red. All that remained of his morning misadventure were dregs of foundation caked where earlobe met face.

Margery worked out the wrinkles in her dress with slight hand strokes. In the distance, the blood-red sun had risen over the stand of trees. Warmth spilled into the Impala in felt waves. The light found the woman in a strange manner, covering only the right section of her body, forming a vertical line that sliced her into halves. She tugged at the base of her gloves until fingertips met fabric. Then she lightly brought both hands together with a muffled clap. "You need to get out more, Patton, interact with some people besides the Major. Your trip to Louisville sounds exciting. You're bound to have some admirers after giving your speech."

Patton had told his grandparents that he'd been invited to give the keynote address at the O'Connor conference. It had been a palatable distortion of the truth. The gender-bending incident that morning had been a dry run. Patton had been practicing for a cocktail party that was to kick off the third annual gathering of the Kentucky chapter of The Disciples of Our Lady of Milledgeville. The event was to take place in the grand ballroom of the Galt House in Louisville—past attendees had deemed the three-day extravaganza "the passover." All of the disciples had been encouraged to attend the booze-fueled commencement dressed—and personifying—a character from the landscape of O'Connor's fiction.

Fully aware that fellow disciples would view the gesture as one of impiety, Patton planned to attend the soiree as the woman herself, crutches and all. It would cause a stir, but Patton's desire to embody the authoress in public transcended any imaginable scenario of consequence. He foolishly envisioned this convergence of two like souls (so cruelly parted by unbridgeable distances of time and space) to be a pious act that would testify—in dramatic fashion—to the singularity of their intimacy. He'd write Flannery-Patton on the sticker nametag they'd hand him at the registration table: *Hello, Our name is Flannery-Patton*. He was taken by the marriage of names. The juxtaposition was kind on the ear—and had always begged for hyphenation. He hoped the gesture wouldn't deny him entry. What kind of looks would meet him as he navigated the cliques mottling the grand ballroom on crutches? Would they cast stones? Persecution would only strengthen his faith. Patton did not fear scorn—or excommunication, for that matter. Why waste time in futile speculation when one had access to the dame's mouth? The young man had been sanctified by the authoress. He'd only be at the gathering for the first night, long enough to enjoy the cocktail party (and an allotment of twelve drinks), confront a few individuals, and to attend a post-party reading of "Beautifully Martyred Freaks: A Crucifixion of O'Connor's Metaphoric Godhead," which was to be given by semi-renowned O'Connor scholar Gregor Mann. Clutching manuscripts, Patton would take the stage midway through Mann's reading—by force, if necessary. Microphone in hand, captive audience beguiled before him, he would read from the unabridged version of his doctoral thesis, which he'd re-titled "O'Connor on O'Connor: Conversations with the Woman Herself." (Perhaps he'd call the woman forth, speak her into existence.) Patton—little shepherd of kingdom come and author of sin—would consummate the emotional evening by orating a teaser snippet from an undone yarn he'd penned in the booby hatch. The tale was tentatively titled: "Cured Meats, Rise and Walk Again." It was most certainly far-fetched and irreverent, but he hoped it wasn't completely void of verisimilitude and that there was a bit of magic in the heretic dinosaur act. In the piece Patton had selected for oration, Allister Finkhaven—would-be faith healer or minion of the Prince of Darkness—is summoned from Chicago to Carbondale, Illinois, by John and Abigail Marcher, a grieving couple—both devout Christian Scientists. Finkhaven arrives by train, wearing a straw gardening hat and holding a black doctor's bag. The healer, a morbidly obese midget, moves with a portly side-to-side hobble that is *not particularly without grace*. The Marchers had called upon his services in the hopes that he could resurrect and rejoin the mutilated legs of their daughter, Li'l Ally, who'd been pinned under a lightening-felled oak tree: *Awaiting the arrival of the man of God, the Marcher's had been storing Ally's mangled and battered limbs inside the old refrigerator out in the garage. They'd been reverently covered with plastic wrap, placed in a grocery sack filled with ice-cubes, and bound tightly with butcher's twine. The legs were in deep-freeze, resting on a mess of frozen crappie—between a bag of Green Giant Vegetable Medley and a Butterball turkey.* The unfinished story was an O'Connor knockoff, both a lovesong and an exorcism of influence, but who knew? Perhaps its legs— so quickly pulped by loud bouts of longwinded exposition and since given to stink, worms, and maggoty rot—could also be resurrected, reanimated, and infused with strength enough to carry the weight of a darkly broken gothic tale to a silent place of rest.

Fuck

is what she said, but what mattered was the tone—
not a drive-by spondee and never the fricative
connotation as verb, but from her mouth
voweled, often preceded by *well,* with the "u" low
as if dipping up homemade ice cream, waiting to be served
last so she'd scoop from the bottom
where all the good stuff had settled down.

Imagine: not a word cold-cocked or screwed to the wall
but something almost resigned, a sigh, an *oh, well,*
the f-word made so fat and slow it was basset hound,
chunky with an extra syllable, just enough weight
to make a jab to the ribs more of a shoulder shrug.
Think of what's done to "shit" in the South; this is
sheeee-aaatt but flicked with a whip, made a little more
tart. *Well, fuck, Betty Sue, I never did see that coming.*
Can you believe?

Or my favorite, not as explicative but noun—*fucker,*
she said, but what she meant was *darlin, sugar pie, sweet beets,*
a curse word made into a term of endearment, as in
Come here, you little fucker, and give your grandma a kiss.
If the child was young enough for diapers, he'd still be a *shitass,*
but big enough to lift his arms and touch his hands together
over his toddling tow head, he was *so big,* all grown, *a cute little*
fucker, watch him go.

Fuck is what she said, but what she needed was a drum,
a percussion to beat story into song, a chisel tapping
to crack the honey from the meanest rock,
not just *fuck if I know* or *fuck me running* or *fuck me*
sideways or *beats the fuck out of me* but said tender,
knowing there was only one thing in this whole world
you needed to hear most: *You fucker you, don't you know*
there wasn't a day when you weren't loved?

If you still don't understand, try this: a woman
up from poor soil, bad dirt, pure clay. A woman as
succulent, something used to precious little
water, hard sun. Rock crop maybe, threading roots
able to suck nutrients from the nothing
of gravel, the nothing of stone, a thriving thing
sturdy, thorned, green out of mere
spite and, because you least expect it,
laughing, cussing up a storm—my grandmother
who didn't ask for power but took it
in bright, full, fuck-it-all bloom.

Go Put on Your Face

is what she said, and what she meant was
a little somethin-somethin, a little dunka-dunk,
a little mascara and blush, gloss and perfume,
and *better conceal that stork bite,* that hot *V* that flared
between my brows, that red check pointing down
to my pink gum-flavored gum, chewed and blown and popped
with a flirt, me pulling it to string and twirling it with the tip,
just like a dumb blonde should.

Spit that gum out now, and hurry, go put on your face, we got to go,
she said because who knows who might see me eyeing

glossies at the checkout, studying women on the cover
who don't let their self go, no, not for a second,
they keep their pretty selves up, they know how to contour,
how to highlight, how to erase their face into a foundation
to build new, how to shadow deep-crease shadows
in their *come-sit-your-handsome-ass-down-here* gaze.

I was taught: without your face put on
your face is a turnip jerked round and pale from mud,
that your face without your face put on is flat-footed,
a gal fanning herself with her own apron, a daughter
with eyes too far apart that don't know no better,
bless her heart. And what girl don't need a little color?
What girl don't need those tiny boxes of pressed powder to catch
sparks, those applicators and brushes and wands to change
her, saying you came from something even though you ain't from
nothing, saying a good man, he's gonna find you,
gonna keep you, and someday, yes, someday, even a kitchen
all your own.

You see, child? You listen to your grandmama.
Someday a kitchen all your own, the air so high
the cool will crank through the vents like money, your husband
coming home any minute now cause he works hard for you and he's
coming home to sheets hot from the dryer and all that cool inside. He's
honey-I'm-home through the door and you're there, feet up,
cared for as a hothouse orchid,

pedicured and manicured and foil-bleached bright,
and if you want to keep him, best put on that face, every damn night.

After Forty Days, Go Marry Again

—for Vova Tumayev
Beslan School No. 1, September 1, 2004

She was only just here. That's her,
that's her in the red dress, that's
her, too, fists full of balloons as if
she would fly away. That's her at the
bottom of the hill. She ran as fast as she
could toward the top, arms wide,
cheeks flushed. She reached me
breathless and toppled both of us.
That's her, and her again,
her black hair in pigtails held
in yellow ball-stay barrettes.
Girls of that age are particular about
such things. I sleep in her room
some nights with all the lights on,
everything as she left it.

There she is in Rostov, there she is
and there she is and there she is.
There she is: bits of black hair
and the earrings. They say: *maybe*
that's not her. Look. There.
The ball-stay barrettes. Yellow,
flowers stretched around. There she
is at Christmas. There she is that
summer she grew three inches. They say:
after forty days, go marry again. But
there she is, and there she is again with
her friend from class. That girl is dead too.
There she is at the carnival. There she is
with her mother, her fists
clenched on the balloons. There
she is at the door, lunchbox in one hand,
waving with the other. At night,
I pretend to sleep; there she is
standing over me as if there are words
left to say. There she is. There
she is in the dark.

A River Returns Emmitt Till to the Earth, 1955

The time for secrets has long passed us.
The morning after they thought the lumber

had fallen into the river before you realized
I refused concealment. Understand, you need

to ask a river to take from your hands.
You must ask permission and then I will open

my sparkling robes and take in whatever
offering. Or I must give the bodies back,

wedge them where my borders meet
the earth. Keep secrets if you must,

but I am older, your hands so bloody,
your secrets too pedestrian to bear away.

Meridian, MS 1978: I Asked Her Late to Remember

Don't you know I have asked,
that I have asked, how I have asked?
When it was time for bed, I would

ask her in the dark because I was a child,
because I was new to this earth, and the world
should withstand scrutiny. I asked

because her answer meant she would stay
a while longer with me in that dark.
Some nights, when the moon was new,

I could not see her face. I would interrogate the air
in her general direction: *What was it like?*
She told me of the ice man, how he would lift

the block of ice off the truck and bear it inside,
biceps big as hams. How she carried out
the linens to dry, and the snapping sound they made

resisting wind. *Grandmamma, was it like Mama said?*
Was it dogs and fire engines and were we very, very sad?
She was quiet so long I thought she disappeared.

Then her voice in the dark: *Yes, there were dogs. Fire,*
and worse than fire. But how could she forget? There was joy.
The moonlight lingered like song among the pines.

Late at Night, I Go Hunting

After I've been drinking. Some say,
I've been drinking a lot or more than

I used to. But who's to quantify or
know how much I'm to carry? At

night, I reach into the icebox. All
that is left are condiments, rotten fruit

and olives. Olives, olives of every
kind from back after the miscarriage

when the scars were healing in
a way that was killing me. The

doctor told me something in olives
built iron, which I lacked and want

of it was the reason for the mess
I was in. After I've been drinking.

Late. When the dark is almost
tender, I take two or three jars

of olives and take one or two
out of each one and think about

how close I got to dying and how
it's all a matter of velocity and

momentum. There are so many
reasons for the mess I always

find myself. I just want to slow
down, slow down and die at

the same leisurely pace as everyone
else. After I've been drinking.

Gaslight

It was the raft, it was the sea.

It was the starlit voyage to some god's country south, the disorienting whispers of the reeds along its shore, the war-sized wings of thunderbirds overhead, the serene overlords you could only imagine for yourselves and the lack you suspect in every world you inhabit.

It was the prayer against want you could never unlearn. The fire demons who followed you who demand sacrifice in blood and smoke. It was you. You brought this to us. It was you and it's
been you all along.

Independence Day Afternoon

A wash of light,
and the particulars
before Bottle Rockets,
Roman Candles,
Whistling Petes,
a twirling pinwheel
nailed high
on a stout tree's trunk,
shooting streams
of sparks. Remember
the year that tree
caught on fire?
Small flames
doused quickly,
a few low branches
wept and smoldered.
But I was going
to tell a before-sunset-story:
the grown people
clutching chilled bottles,
a graceful flick
of cigarette cinder
to concrete patio,
music and voices
raising their timbre. Plunged
into a cooler, numb,
my fingers diving for
the very last
root beer.

New Year's Day at Whatcom Creek, Far from the War

Feeling human is a useful form of political subversion.
-Robert Hass

By 3 p.m. I'm no longer struggling to feel
something specific about the ducks' ease of movement
through their maze of pilings, their bodies' split-second
Pinball Wizard decisions
to dash this way or that in the too-early evening light
as the creek's current pushes them always out
toward the railroad bridge that divides us
from the bay.

Not far away a grebe submerges strangely,
its neck convulsing
like a snake in the water. I remember how my father
says the word 'grebe,' with a smile
at the edges. How he says 'grebe' more often
than necessary, how he must love
the word 'grebe.' But I'm no longer certain
that's the bird I mean. Still, I name it
like we do with most things, when we can.
Like today.

Anti-Aubade

For DM

A crow gouges the lead sky
now smeared pewter and tungsten
with new rips and drags of aluminum
every passing second,
all alloy and amalgam and fusion,
then spit-shined—your shine,
my spit—the crow's eye and caw
cut back to us after it lights on that limb
broken free at the elbow, nubbed
like a gray-veined bust,
how nature might suppose
Balzac caught in his fury
if nature could suppose
or how I now knot Rodin's Balzac
folding into himself with inspiration
with the dead white oak's
overlapping bark, its chippings
and leavings, a slow shed, spread legs,
thick arms, necks, our branchings,
knuckles, cusps and curls and braids,
our inward foldings, our eyes cut away
from one another because they must,
our clothes shed on the shore.

Years from today, this white oak trunk
will fill with worms and woodpeckers,
maybe with this owl whom we hear
in the distance, the one I am flirting with
as my father's father taught me,
(you have heard this before)
or its progeny or progeny's progeny
in a stolen hole, its head unwound.
And with the mourning doves'
swollen breasts and whinnying
on wires we cannot see
but know are there, we devolve—
because, again, we must—from human
to amphibian, our desires now simplified
to the dead-still water in which we submerge
to our noses, to the great rock beneath us
we shimmy and scuttle along, hands
and feet indistinguishable until ours
meet by chance, and we move closer.

River Politics

I spit my smack,
Jim slugs his Jack,
Rob stews his lack,
Carey prepares his rack,
herons hunker on blowdowns,
deer wait on high moon for their rounds,
and the campfire
might as well be an empire
we all
watch dissolve
(in the slough, a carp roll, a splash)
into ash.

The Golden Years

I said, "The jasmine blooms along the fence."
You set the cuckoo clocks to different times.
The bird in the hall is thirteen minutes slow.
You devil some eggs, spread out the greens to dry.

You set the cuckoo clocks to different times.
"It's Sunday; the mailman doesn't come today."
You devil some eggs, spread out the greens to dry.
You dress your childhood dolls in faded clothes.

"It's Sunday; the mailman doesn't come today,"
you said. "Tomorrow, we'll have chicken and rice."
You dress your childhood dolls in faded clothes.
You brush your hair, push back your cuticles.

You said, "Tomorrow, we'll have chicken and rice.
Your sister called again. Your hands are filthy."
You brush your hair, push back your cuticles,
take out your book, ready yourself for bed.

"Your sister called again. Your hands are filthy."
The bird in the hall is thirteen minutes slow.
"Take out your book, ready yourself for bed,"
I said. The jasmine blooms along the fence.

After Warhol's *Rorschach*, 1984

Too easy
to say Shiva

or Janus
or butterfly
effect or tree

of life or
Christmas

wreath because
it is December
or hood ornament

or Pompeii
or ball mask

or Burgundy
masque or drop
zone or topo map

or gilded intestines,
Barneys, Wall Street.

Instead, please see
a honey *P*
inscribed inside

a Wonder
Bread fold-over.

After Tom Wesselmann's *Great American Nude #57*, 1964

Daffodil demi-bob,
satsuma bedpost,

pouty curtains—
and he dipped
from the same arch

of his palette
for her vulcanized

nipples that he did
for the crevice
of her mouth.

The beach and ocean
nuzzle one another
out the window.

Black stars behave
within the angle iron

of her *Oh-My* arm.
The cheetah chaise longue
beneath her

ripples its pattern
of runes, vertebrae,

knuckles, shark teeth.
A parched veldt
of public hair erupts.

Post-Elegy

After the plane went down,
the cars sat for weeks in long-term parking.

Then, one by one, they began to disappear
from among the cars of the living.

———

When we went to retrieve his,

you drove the rows of the lot
while I pushed the panic button on the fob.

———

Inside, a takeout coffee cup
sat in its cradle,

a skim of decay
floating beneath the lid.

I'd ridden in his car
many times, but never driven it.

———

When I turned the key,
the radio
opened unexpectedly,
like an eye.

———

I was conscious of the ground
passing just beneath the floor—

and the trapped air in the tires
lifting my weight. I realized

I was steering homeward
the down payment

of some house we might live in
for the rest of our lives.

The People's History

The People moved up the street in a long column—
like a machine boring a tunnel. They sang
the People's songs, they chanted the People's slogans:
We are the People, not the engines of the city;
we, the People, will not be denied.
                                                        Then the People
descended upon the People, swinging hardwood batons
heavy with the weight of the People's intent.

And the People surged, then, into the rows before them,
pushing the People against the blurred arcs
of truncheons, the People throwing rocks
into the plastic shields and visors,
                                                        behind which
the People blinked when the rocks hit, then pushed back
so the mass of People before them compressed.

In the windows above the street, the People looked down
and thought, Thank god we're not the People
trapped, now, inside the confines of those bodies.

And soon the People on rooftops loaded their rifles
with wax bullets—which looked like earplugs—

which the People had produced in factories
full of People flanking machines designed by the People.

When the bullets buried themselves in the People,
the People cried, Those shooters are not the People,
some piece of them has been removed—
like a fuse—the true People are a surface
that floats on the sea of our fathers—
How they buoy us! the People shouted.

But the People had grown tired of the afternoon
and released dogs into the crowd, dogs
that could not tell the People from the People;
and the People fled in all directions, back into the city,
singing with pain.

—And now, children,
when we meet the People in the market
how will we know them? *Their clubs and their bruises,*
their language of power.
What about concepts?
Yes, they fill them with bodies.
And weapons?
They spend hours in fluorescence piecing them together.

What else? *They open their mouths.*

And what else? *Nothing—they open their mouths.*
Is that wrong?
—Excuse me, sir,
what gives us the right to define them?
That's not what I'm saying.
Excuse me, sir,
aren't we, too, the People? Yes, but wiser.

But sir, how can the surface be different from the sea?

Some Notes on Human Relations

We pulled the rope around the neck
to squeeze the mind

Then we had no mind

We turned the faucet of the garrote
to stanch the air

Then we had no air

We pulled the handle
so the blade's weight split the breath

Our breath was split

We lit ourselves on fire in the square

The fire couldn't last forever

We stood across the field
and pulled the row of triggers

The burlap target covered our heart

We knew we were hiding
somewhere in the trees

We watched helplessly from the trees

We tied two bodies together in the river
and shot just one of them

We pulled each other under

We used a thousand cuts

We were quaint—and merciless

We said repeatedly:
This is what the Father wants

In the end we said:
This is what the Father wants

We tipped the body upside down
and sawed from crotch to jaw

Our head kept filling with blood

We threw the body from the plane
into the flat ocean

We became the ocean

We covered the body with earth

We became the earth

In the still house
we listened to our favorite record

The chorus always killed us

The music made an ocean around the table

We sat on both sides of the table

A Bit about the Soul

Little fuse. Little blip. Little ball of snow.
Little packet of heroin
egged inside him
(though how could he know?).

And when it burst on the airport shuttle—
like a timer going off—
well, that was his moment
next to the jumble

of suitcases. How little it had to do with you
who'd sat beside him—
though now the story
of his dying breaks through

its capsule, leaking
suddenly outward. Little trigger
pulled—and you feel it
inside you, speaking.

Allegory of the House

When it was clear there was nothing left
between us and the valley's flooding—
that even nature had come to live
inside the body of the State—

we built our raft of logs and plastic barrels
around the house, cut the pipes
that bound us to the stone foundation,
and waited. On the second day

the river came over the flood bank
like an endless, unraveling cloth
and slid down into the family grove.
At first, the house just sat there,

water climbing its side. Then
we could feel the structure loosen,
and the scene that had filled my window
all my life began to tilt. Those ancient,

familiar elms drifted to the right
and disappeared—but soon
the house caught hard against them,
and for three days more we rose

precariously up their side, Sis and I
pushing back with an oar
to keep the spreading branches
from swamping us. The next morning,

we found the house triumphant
atop the water. We'd become
the tallest thing, sailing softly
over the space in which we'd lived.

Each night I lie in bed and watch
my window hold the moving world—
all of it unlocked and turning. I know
our ancestors are heavy seeds

buried in that fiction below the surface,
but the distant shoreline slides around
and past as though we're a compass—
and how can the earth beneath us,

the liquid air rolling over and around
our presence, ever be still again?

An American Prayer for the Second Coming

Before my brother murdered the sea, I thought he acted like a gentleman.
Before I saw birds drown, I never listened to women reading bibles.

A police officer found the 30-06 rifle wrapped inside a blanket.

Combing the blood of the sea from our scalps, we saw him on the news.

People cried like televisions left on all day.

After that, who could ask why the Harpeth river
jumped its banks or if we deserved the rain
filling Nashville's ditches.

Dirt and nails on the floor of our house, children in the street
playing in the water,

a blues LP turns inside my rib cage,
clicks on its turntable; they still shovel
birds into bags.

There is shame today in every thing—
I have a rib inside of her, but I can
not protect my wife.

Our house no longer dreams. A cop clicks the button:
Please evacuate your homes immediately. His voice
follows his car.

There is no escape: all airplanes are booked.
Even the neighbor's dog has been abandoned, scared, choking.
Brown water swirls with sickly colors.

Please God, come back and this time,
breathe fire.

HTIAF

Th s ound
 dnuos ehT
of ba ckward ma sking
 gninrom eht ni
t he so und of v cto r y
 !e m p l e H !e m p l e H !p l e H
p l he ease me!

!n a t a S l i a H !n a t a S l i a H !n a t a S n a t a S !n a t a S l i a H[1]

t urn m eon de d ma n t urn me on d ed m a n tu rn meon
n a m d e d n o e m n r u t
 t urn meo n[2]

ded man
t
h er e
w as
 a lit toll s hed
w
here
he m ade us

s uf or[3]
 bo rn t o

dy l if e i s b orn t od y i s e f i l is
pai n dre am
 eve ry day h ow d I

h w do I
 d o i t d o i t d o i t it doit doit doit[4]
p e e l s
with the lights
turned off

---

[1] "When Electricity Came to Arkansas" by Black Oak Arkansas
[2] "Revolution 9" by The Beatles
[3] "Stairway to Heaven" by Led Zeppelin
[4] "Better by You, Better than Me" by Judas Priest

In the Pines

We ran in the pines,
Arkansas night wet our cheeks.
Shared stolen cigarettes.
Watched the smoke curl
from each other's lips. Every July
on the lake—campers, parents, coolers, barbecue.
Once, we cut our hands with a razor

dragging the knife across our palms,
gripping tight to make it count,
turned leaves red at our feet,
the cutting louder than our breaths—

imagine shivering and answering *nothing*,
when your lover asks what's wrong, and meaning it.

The Killing Trees

There is one tree for every person, and the trees have all started falling on the person they've grown tall to fall on, crushing their people's skulls into the ground. I take a train to the forest and stand before the tallest tree. It's *time* I tell it, but it keeps standing. When I try chopping it down, a cloud falls on me, and then a burning airplane, and then my mother and father, and then more burning airplanes.

Death Letter

I get a letter in the morning that said the woman I love is dead, that she has been trampled by elephants. I haven't seen her in years, but I think about her every time I make the bed, every time I set the table. I think about how perfect we would have been together. When I arrive at her house to pay my respects, to deliver flowers to her front door, I see her in the window, dusting the sill. She isn't dead at all. She shows no signs of being trampled—even her clothes are starched and pressed. *You're not dead* I say. *Who are you?* she says? *What do you mean?* I say. *It's me.* But her eyes just squint at me as if I were microscopic. *Weren't you trampled by elephants?* I say. *No* she says. *There aren't even any elephants around here.* When I walk away, flowers in my fist, I think about all the different kinds of death. I wish she would have been dead just like the letter said. There is more truth in that kind of death, and I felt so much closer to her then.

The Reckoner

I am walking through a series of doors. On the other side of most doors is the same empty red room, but one door opens up to a room that is actually a field of heather, and another to the same room that is actually a field of heather full of dying dried-out swans. One room is loud with the baby versions of all the people I've ever loved and one room is silent with their ghosts. A dark hallway leads me to the last door. On the other side is a mountain town. The air is clean and cold. I can hear the ice breaking in the distance. There is a woman in a long black dress and a black scarf over her face. *Welcome to Spitzbergen* she says. Then she lifts up her dress. Nothing happens next.

V.

teachers stealing gum
from under shipwrecked desks
offices full of missals and T.V.'s

Creole

The only date I had the entire year of 1980 was with a Creole prostitute. Much happened that year: the Iranian hostage crisis; worrisome, long lines at the gas pumps; the beginning of the Reagan years, but I couldn't get laid. I lived in a three-room tenant farmer's shack (rent was twenty-five bucks) with a soybean field as a front lawn, full of doves I poached to feed myself and a one-eyed, semi-feral cat that snuck in mornings through an unknown hole to scatter rat hearts and livers around my shucked clothes. A watershed moment with my father—I'd confronted him with my knowledge of his mistress—had sent me to the country with some hush cash and an out-of-the-nest lecture. My one college ex-girlfriend visited once but wouldn't leave her car, remarking she had little use for a man determined to romance such squalor. I'd thought my little home improvements—thick plastic to winterize the windows, a crooked screen door and a HOWDY! mat—had manufactured that homey look.

"I'll not live like a poverty queen, even for one night," she'd said. I didn't even have enough cash left for a cheap motel.

For one whole summer, I was a dangling man. Determined to improve my lot, I signed on with Thomas Paint and Paper and landed a spot on their out-of-town crew. The company had contracted to spray those industrial gas storage tanks outside the Charlotte airport, and one of my jobs was to hang from a rope lowered by a Lumbee Indian named Saul who claimed chief status when drunk. Hanging in what felt like heaven fall, I dabbed at the missed spots called holidays which the guys in the cherry picker had missed or couldn't reach. Little men like me got such jobs. On my first two-hour ride to Charlotte, the crew boss tried to pick up a battered woman with birthmark-like bruises at a mini-mart where we filled up on gas and quart beer. She peered inside, calculating gains and losses. An angry driver in a station wagon, not Providence, kept her from joining us.

"I told you this ain't no goddamned TV movie, so quit acting up," he screamed. This meant something to her, and she got into the back seat like a resigned, church-bound child.

Each week, we stayed in the same shabby hotel, Traveler's Rest Motor Court, which had an enchanted forest motif. The office's lawn was filled with concrete dwarfs and gnomes and mushroom cottages—all for sale—that Saul thought so cute he lugged one home to his third wife but which reminded me of circus escapees turned to stone. The rooms were a hybrid of most any grandmother's bedroom and an office; a group of wingchairs with potholed naugahyde cushions and doily frou-frous sat beside an officious desk that doubled as a chest-of-drawers and a TV stand. The lampshades had bead fringes but the overhead light was flourescent and brokenly flickered. The wallpaper's hunting motif depicted bucks with trophy racks in pawing poses or in bounding midflight, while clumped does frozen in grazing postures nibbled at nothing. I half expected a caveman's handprint to appear in a hidden corner.

Traveler's Rest's parade of prostitutes began Thursdays at dusk. Past the concrete barriers, the interstate whooshed with the collapsed wave sound of lives in motion and tire whine and beyond that, night hung like a drop cloth spackled with so many stars the Charlotte skyline seemed a constellation that had run, sagged. The electrical company crew lodging across the courtyard's pinto bean shaped pool and hobbit land knew how to bump the poles into blackout. From this blank page of starry darkness the demimondes wandered, college-boy-me thought. These were women who lived loud lives in projects and shanty towns with houses like mine or who'd been field hands and stropped. They appeared utterly without context, like the wallpapered deer, separate from the civilized skyline and divorced from the world of routine danger, where a misstep on a ladder or any unbalanced moment could become a lost time accident.

"Last call for love," Saul called through the megaphone of his fist. "Hubba hubba, hoochie coochie." I'd heard stranger love songs at college, where I learned to disappear when a roommate entertained. While Saul called out and grunted in our room, I wandered to a phone booth. Whenever the ex-girlfriend would accept my collect call, I'd tug on the metal cord and study the numbers written everywhere in desperate haste. Had the needed Western Union plea materialized; was momma still comatose; did the right directions save the lost? The glass box of light cast my reflection on all sides— drunk me times four—and often I'd wave at a car crammed with family to ease the last man alive feeling.

My last week on the job, I broke down and purchased. She was pint-sized like me and wore a crocheted halter which showed walnut breasts without a tan line that screamed YES. Her Easter bonnet had plastic cherry sprigs and cloth violets, and her skin was the color of worn wooden handles. When we went inside and I bolted the door, she grabbed the remote, found her show, stripped off everything but her hat, and stretched out on the frilly comforter.

"Name's Tina. That's short for Eugenia, which I don't answer to anymore." She upped the volume and said, "Have at it." That constituted foreplay. When I tried to kiss her, she said she didn't go in for that smooch stuff and my lips shouldn't stray past her bellybutton. "Are you crazy" was her answer to my fellatio request.

"There." I'd ask her to fondle me but I got a quick pecker pet. Things weren't erecting correctly. The whole time I couldn't do it, she lay under me watching *Dallas* and humming the theme music. She addressed my flaccid willy during the commercial break. Off came the hat. She'd curled her hair with cotton rags and left the ties in so her hair looked like a field of daises.

"Some white guys like a pickaninny look." When nothing kept happening, she patted beside her. "Get over it." Over fetched drinks, we chatted like a couple with a thousand nights to kill while soap opera concerns played themselves out. Years later, the woman I'd marry who'd claim fixer-up rights over my heart would have Tina-Eugenia's same blue eyes. We'd rocket past the real Dallas skyline as newlyweds headed towards the horizon and our brief purchase on happiness.

"How was Pee Wee?" Saul would use the room too that night, while I waved from the phone booth; his scrubbed raw look seemed a cross between *The Waltons* and *Happy Days*.

"He was wonderful," she lied. With festive backslaps and cheered beers, I was accepted without courtship into the floating world of rough men while Tina blended into the darkness of other lives.

Yellow Fingers

One hundred and forty three
pounds would be
the best guess I could give
of my weight
when only judging
by the pressure on my feet.

Shoes make a big difference
when trying the science:
density of the sole,
the surface I stand on,
the socks I choose.

All of these things come into play
in the algorithm I have created.

God hides from me now.

The streets are filled with men smoking
pipes in white t-shirts, but my eggshell
room only looks at the tree
cradling its fallen lover in
between yellow fingers.

Woman in the Shower

A doorknob
twisting
shows
smoke and fog
churning the
greedy lungs
of speech-

lessness
and beginnings
slowing, breaking
the scent
of time that moves
like the pianist

playing nocturnes
on a Steinway
or the piano tuner
alone
on a stage for days.

FROM FRIEND

Isn't it wasn't it isn't it so
strange to invite anyone
into our lives? Isn't it wasn't it
isn't it so strange to love
the same people? Isn't it
wasn't it isn't it so strange
to be a girl when you are
a boy? Roth Rose. Cindy.
Lawn Bite. Andy. Melissa
and her astounding name
Wickramasekera that taught
me Ceylon, Tamils, Veddas,
we were the age she was
when she bore the daughter
she named the same name
as she, Melissa. The daughter's
name, the same, but more
gorgeous for this reason.
To be in the presence of this
act, this love, the same name!
How defiant, because so
patriarchal. Isn't it wasn't it
isn't it mitosis? Isn't it
wasn't it isn't it sharing
the fear of death and so
easing it? Isn't it wasn't it
isn't it none of this, but
something solitary, some-
thing stark, something like
solemnity and vice, the moon
and our pants around our ankles.

The Whistler

Here I am so selfish I can only remember my reaction. Each fact loosening falling away like icicles along the eaves. I once saw one so large & the earth so soft that it pierced the ground below it. I once walked through a spider web so vast, I felt its tug as I pulled through it. I once drove 30 miles at night through pitch black counties without headlights, using only my cellphone light to guide me. I was once so high I thought I wrote a paper backwards. Once I got a fifth wind during a swim meet. As the fish grows increasingly long, life accumulates like a US Ironworks slag heap. Once my date dropped me off at the front door and I ran through the house out the back into my boyfriend's waiting car in the alley. Once I lost control in the middle of northbound 95 and somehow spun across the median, arriving in the shoulder of the southbound lanes, and I just kept driving, nothing mattered. I once bought an $80 cab ride because I couldn't remember where I was. Simultaneously building a bed in a refrigerator box stealing gas from the Racetrack flying to Denver to marry a stranger. I once strangled my boyfriend at 65 mph on the freeway until I started laughing so much my grip loosened. Once I wrote the most erotic sex fantasy I could dream got paranoid that someone would read it, chose a password to protect the document, promptly forgot the password and let that define my sex life for years. The only secrets are forgotten ones. I once sang Swing Low in a cop car and felt like a coward. I once told a man I didn't want a boyfriend and a week later admitted to him I had gotten married. Who said, biography is a story true enough to believe? Who told me they once ate a joint before getting pulled over, but at the last minute the cop car flew past them, worked in a gas station and stole all the money, painted a donkey with zebra stripes, danced on stage with Bootsy Collins, who told me that for one day he was the best whistler on the planet, could whistle any song in the world perfectly, rivaled the skylarks and finches, invented gorgeous sonatas whistling them into the sunset, into the blushing dusk and by morning forgot how to do it?

Federal Holiday

Everyone strolling
through the Native Plants Garden
works for the government.
Everyone ordering hamburgers
with a napkin in his or her lap
works for the government.
Through glass, I witness
the world's loneliest actor
working for the government.
This morning, I promised myself
a new city and saw
how the trembling light
works for the government.
My friend the poet
is dying of cystic fibrosis
for the government
and everyone is scared
to come home because the web
across the door reads
Some Government.
I call my mother's broken pelvis
driving to the emergency room,
but in the end, really
working for the government.
I write to my friend my sister
who will marry her boyfriend
the day after the apocalypse
for the government.
I sleep next to my friend
the poet my husband
whose heart is a library
lace machine whose roots
sailed the only boat lonely
in the sopping world
for the government, and I wake.
I visit my father whose children
are Quakers at war since birth
who point at helicopters
allergic to air who write novels

at bath time for the government,
and on the bench the sun
slicing through the coreopsis,
the zinnias, the coxcomb—
after the flowers blazed
and died, I learned every name
working for the government.
Door with no wreath
sabotaging holy days.
Sunset hinged to the sky.
You smell like chrysanthemums
working for the repairman
who fixed the leak, how it
used to snow on you
when you peed, now tarred
over skylight sealing out
the government.
The exact moment I decided
to charge your phone, you
applied to work for the government.
We're all out of kickball
picked last at the park
we rented under the pavilion
we rented displaying our permit
to the nice park ranger
we rented did we think
for a minute he was a swinger?
and how dare he when he
works for the government?
I forgot how sad I was
watching her leap across
the stage unsure she
worked for the government.
The government opened
the box of knives you sent me,
of mold, of laryngitis, of anthrax,
of all the most violent gifts
I've gotten from the government,
folding all over each other
in the government, all the people
I never slept with in the government.
You said this was a movie

and I ran from all of the babies
who worked for the government.
All I say is stuff people say
when they work
for the government.
Do her legs go all the way up
in the government?
That little gnat's
in the government,

the roots, all the napkins
in the government, through
the blinds, the government
is cut into so many rectangles.

The Meat from the Dream the Heart Knows

I like that line about the city. The skyline's superficial fingering. The big black car making a comic strip of the road, paneling busyness. The derelict sequins: ruby then emerald then ice.

From space, the astronaut's untidy. His nipples dehydrate against his chest.
A bulb of orange juice bobs around the mess deck.

•

Yes, it's hard to understand why the butler's here, why the gun's in pieces, why Esme hates the pudding. In Tucson, we stole a wig from Wig-o-Rama and things

came together on Congress Street. Rides on handlebars. Stomping roaches into Rorschachs. A satellite crashes then London loses Singapore. Hello? Not really.

The heart knows one dream. You desperate in seawater prying a glued quarter from the sidewalk.

It's only a sin if no one laughs.

•

The sitcom is a prayer.

It is Inept Father's birthday. A woman jumps from the cake, tits affixed with tassels, spinning, persuading memory like noble wheat fields in good breezes;

good breezes—such good, good fields for hiding in. You know what the fuck the heart knows what hell what deep, brutal homework and it isn't that late.

•

Hate spiders through the office park. Rage like dominoes.
A matter of time before the whole place

goes. Agony like the Sicilian Defense.
Someone plays ping pong with your ennui, coward.

The phases shift, the wave delays, distant fuzz co-locates distortion. The whisper, then your eardrums into klieg lights. Pretty

is the flimsiest word to describe how pretty we were on the fraying rope bridge. So pretty. So pretty. So pretty. So pretty.

FROM FRIEND

Sommer, I'm dying. I get this message on my phone in line at Rite Aid. Sommer, I'm dying, you scream in my ear at the rock show. Sommer, I'm dying, you write in closing on a postcard from San Francisco. Sommer, I'm dying, it's my heart, Sommer I'm dying, can you feel this? Is it normal? as we stomp through the snow to get cigarettes. Jesus woke up, but who muscled the boulder away? Some prince kissed the beauty, but who wrote it all down? Let's go to the mummy exhibition, let's read aloud Fear and Trembling, let's slow the flow through our carotid. Sommer, I'm dying. Present tense. Subject. Verb. The thinning blood vessel, the soft pulsating stone, retina shriveled and rattling around in the skull. I can hear it when I jump. Then don't jump, I say.

Black Glass Soliloquy

There is nothing in my head today.
I think about you everyday.
My head full of blckkk glsss

My head full of bllllk sound.
I think about you every day.
I travel in my love for you.

An outline in the blckkk glsss.
Living in the blllckk glasss.
Time travels in my sound for you.

There is nothing in my head today.
Echo echo bl@@@k gl@{{.
To whom do I deliver sound.

To whom does the shudder render.
I think about you everyday.
I hang you in the B[][][][][] G[][][][][]

I hang you in my head today.
A ravel in the blccckkkkk soundd.
I think about you everyday.

My love for you is bla888888ck s####nd.
Echo echo bl&kk s((((()))))d.
I travel in my love for you.

I ravel in my love for you.
A bl>>>>K $(0)nd in my love for you.
I think about you every day.

There is nothing in my head today.
I hang you in my bLL^^CC// S_______---
][ravel in the B&&&&& S))))))))\d

I go out in the b::::::::::K G::::::::::ss
to see you in the <*++*> gIIIIIIs.
I hang you in my head today.

I ravel through the <<<ac>>> {oun}
Are you in my $[%&]d today?
An echo in my head today.

I think about you everyday.
An echo in the .
An outline in the .

FROM DARKLINGS

nothing solid clone
floating like music
the sound of music
fading in the dark
the dead part in everything
shining and dull
its hands are raised
like it's begging for food
sound gives life
death's sound too

nothing solid clone
pulses its swimming bells
a frozen lung tree
fading in the dark
the sound of static
music in the dark
the nails and the teeth
the shadows and the teeth
nothing solid clone
shaped like sleep

lost is the echo
that sleeps from the matrix
the dead part in sound machine
shining and dull
its hands are raised
like it's begging for food
motes of dark are functioning
the shadows and the teeth
filling the void
a frozen lung tree

nothing solid clone
floating like static
sleeping in time
to die at the hands of song
the dead part in everything
shining and dull
its hands are raised
like it's begging for food
sound gives life
wet with dew

Starts in Herds

I am a gateway drug
my problem is that I
get inside you and infect
you, I am infectious
my vocabulary is a curse
and my window, a harpoon
of light, I make your insides
rattle like tight rope-tension,
a tenor drum, I also drum
monkey-style in your head, that
beat for social dominance,
this art is not for sale
I've actually raised the stakes
for moving day, I'm selling all
my goods at twice the price
I paid, why, because I can and
I want to get laid and move to
Japan, there is no restaurant below
my apartment now, and I'd love
to dine on the dining room floor, what
a spectacular way to live far
from the pragmatic gluttony of
piracy, the web is really sucking
it all out of us people, there's a
horse cry

Poem With Scrutiny

I am obtrusive when alone
not only thinking of myself
with many questions
you are made entirely from assumptions
create panic in your main-dome
it's a hemispheric thing
I apologize for being so considerate
at night the lab-man calls with the results
I have a tiny tumor but it's only a ladder in mind
a day later it's reached the size of a pigeon's egg
I bludgeon all my problems and takeoff
wade into an Olympic sized pool
you are jealous of my notoriety
to be pinned-down by strangers
the pool has become thimble-sized
the water had to be drained, they kept saying
I was eager for the voices
to go away but not the medicine
in redundant time we lapse our mainstream
self-propulsion right up to the brink
making brave animals shy
making quarters spin on the bottom
if you shout it is because I am waiting
for you to love me
the way I want to be loved
night is generous with its blackness
and nobody to blame

Melatonin

My bus does well with your roads. Almost like a watery thing. Slipping where slippage is implied. It attends to your road, curves with your curves, breaks when you want it to. You're gonna have to be real patient with me, it can take a little time to get there. A little gas and oil. I don't mean to overuse the natural resources; I mean I too wish I rode by horse, bareback along the Chilean mountains. A quest towards over sized independence, blazing stars and saddleback lunches. Broad terrain, how we curve when you curve and still gleam hope from ridiculous dreams.

Getting Gas

Every time
A late 1980s pick up truck
With flat autumn colors
Comes into view

I feel the weird hope

That it's you
Anywhere in America

Wherever I am
I love you so bad that
I love you even worse.

In a past life,
Called rock and roll heaven,

You were a calico cat
Named Mona

Up in gawd's
Pumpkin patch
During my elementary school's Octoberfest,

It was always fall
And I always felt
Adventure,

And I fought until I won.

But it was just your potential I loved

Not who've you've become,
That you've always been,
Is who you really are,

And that's not fair.

That's all about me
And only what I saw.
The real one should rock on
Free, calm, and unhindered
Forever down the highway
With the suspicion and instinct
Of a calico stray.

But that potential one,
The one who never was,
She is mine, forever.

N4

I've got nowhere to go.

I have a place to sleep
Places that I like to eat at
Or sit and drink coffee at.

Places I can pick up pick-up work to pay for all the former.
Places I can park the van and sit for hours with the heat on

Awaiting the emails
Hiding from people.

But ultimately I have no place to go.

No hard place
To dig my hands in the funky clay and do my murders.
To steadily push imaginary eyeballs into the mud skull
And make a shape
I feel

It's dirty business
And I like to smoke while I do it.

Girls hate it. Employers hate it. Employees hate it.
Sometimes I hate it.
Stuck just sort of doing it a little bit all the time
For free with anything around me at 2/3 the level of quality
I deem "justified to exist."

I've even quit smoking again
Just for the lung capacity
To wrangle all this feline herd
called surplus nowhere

11 miles out town,
I cram it in a strip mall unit after 5pm
And keep the bodies on a hard drive
In the driver's seat back-pocket of the van.

The mornings are cold.
People still have their headlights on.
I watch their days start driving to my sleep place.

Everyone's life is like a tiny miracle.
I am fascinated by where they are going.
To somewhere, to no place? I don't know:
A weak observation, but that's what flies!

I will find myself somewhere.
Aggressively. Religiously,
Shredding the nicotine gum,
I win a decent song against the morning talk radio.
There is still magic somewhere. I chase her shadow.
Sweet baby Jesus
Let me crawl its shadow

My God!
My love!
My eyes!

All dart like a killer on the loose.

Moonlight on the Meadow

Day by day
I grow the hands of a man.
I walk the hills,
a view of the stars,
a heart below,
a heart above,
where water reserves
hold shelter.

I cross the river,
a passenger calling,
the words I utter
no less than a garden,
across the years
with what I please.

There is a patch of green,
a broken hearth
where seasons speak low
into the landscape's ear,
beckoning breath
from the birds of blue & yellow
& the swans & herons
that see me less & less.

Behind me a cuckoo calls,
the low distances,
the low thankful place.

I post my letter,
premonitions unseen
on either flank,
the country I knew,
white there, green here—
a tale of my time
broadening like a duck's bill.

Through it
I walk to the water's edge,
without regret,
with faith,
faith won in family,
a kingdom that is ours,
as familiar by moonlight
as it is by day.

Fire Animal

I jumped into the fire of making,
I remembered my own making,
making itself as I made,

Who or what was I
in this furnace
of action?

In white heat
I became defined,
defined in the stuff
a molten man.

I became it,
it became I,

Until I, me, we
were one burning mass

A fire animal.

DECEMBER 21, 2012; 11:23PM

I've got
some dope
lets get
some girls
and drive
to sevierville
and wait
for shit
to happen
we'll wear
black robes
and call
it mass
shoot up
and fuck
without rubbers
no armageddon
could equal
my actions
the end
has always
been within

JULY 19, 2013; 3:33AM

I'm beginning
to think
that satan
is my
spirit animal
his number
keeps calling
on my
cellular phone
I don't
know what
that means
but it
isn't frightening

Age & the Beat

A couple of months ago, the band I'm in played a show at an all ages venue on what could be called a school night. And due to it being a school night, the crowd was sparse, but it didn't stop us from having fun playing our songs. We finished our set but I stayed to watch all the other bands, too. I left exhausted.

To be clear, I have no sense of direction. I left going in the direction that I thought right but it turned out to be the farthest wrong possible. Soon I realized how wrong. I also realized my situation: I was a lone woman in a truck with easily a thousand dollars of music equipment in the cab, plus a bunch of beer cans in the bed. (At the show, my truck had been used as a trash can of sorts.) Now, I didn't want a cop to see me driving in circles on these sketchy dark roads, but I also didn't want anyone else to notice my driving in circles on these sketchy, dark roads.

I finally found my way out, but that night left an impression on me. The next day I thought about it as I waited on the bright-eyed moms and their sweet children at the library where I work. None of those women spent their previous night lost in a dangerous part of Birmingham with a cab full of music equipment and a bed full of beer cans. In fact, I would bet the $40 our band made on it.

I began to think about being a female, getting older and playing music. Do those three things go together? Can they? I guess they can just as easy as I can sit here and type out this story as I listen to my co-workers talk about home improvement, curtains and Crock-Pot recipes. It is not that I don't appreciate those things. I love a good Crock-Pot chili. I like a quiet night in with my boyfriend, watching movies. However, I also like to spend at least one night a week with a bunch of guys writing music in a storage space off Green Springs highway. I leave work, grab a bite to eat, a couple of beers and my bass, and head over to the storage space where I spend the next couple of hours writing music and drinking beer.

Nevertheless, I decided to write about this because I feel this pressure from my mother who likes to ask me when I am going to give up "all this music stuff." She tries to ask casually, but I hear the disdain in her voice. She still treats me like a 16-year-old who delivers pizza and holds on to the dream of being a rock star. But wait, I have my full-time job. I have my insurance—medical and dental . . . and I also have my closet full of skirts, blouses and pants that only my co-workers see.

I feel even more pressure from an internal dialogue; it comes from the social stigmas of what a 35-year-old woman is "supposed" to be doing. I work in a library in the middle of the wealthiest and most conservative community in Birmingham, and I see a lot of women my age whose lifestyles are so different from mine that we might as well speak two different languages. I see this opposite version of me so much that on some particularly gloomy days I question what I am doing. Where are my husband, my three kids, and my white picket fence? Where are my days that are filled with taking children to their piano lessons and preparing dinner? Truth is, I know my life didn't work out that way because of luck, or because somewhere deep down inside I designed it that way. If my life had followed that more conservative path, I know now that I would have become bored. I mean, what would I do after I made dinner?

It is also easy to let other paranoid thoughts sneak in that force me to ask myself if I am too old to get on stage and play music, or if others think I am too old to play music. Maybe people in the crowd are judging me by my frown lines and encroaching turkey-neck. Yet, I've made peace with those paranoid thoughts along with the random mornings when I shuffle to work with bags under my eyes. It is a hobby, but it is a fulfilling and passionate hobby, and I don't think I am too old to have hobbies, especially kick-ass ones that allow me to play shows, meet new people, and travel.

There was a time in my life from my mid-twenties to early thirties, that for many reasons, I did not play music, and I wondered, then, if I would ever play music with other people again. I questioned even if I should . . . since I was getting older. Somehow, one day, I still dusted off the guitar, tipped-toed over to a friend's house and timidly started playing.

Since I have started playing in bands again, I have noticed a trend. I see more people in their thirties and beyond return to music after years of silence. And I feel a sense of reassurance when I see someone older who's playing music. Maybe I feel a sense of solidarity. I know it's always inspiring. Some of these musicians have wives or husbands and children, yet they still find time to balance their life.

I think life should be celebrated at every age. When I use the word *life* I mean the things in life that you are passionate about. For me, it is playing music and writing, but it could be art, comedy, acting, writing a novel or a picture book or a poem, raising children—anything that allows you to live life and celebrate who you are.

My First Rehearsals with a Band

from *I Dreamed I Was A Very Clean Tramp*

The truth of our invention of our songs and our band preceded and transcended all the contentious opinions and stress and competitive junk that kept arising in the band, and that truth was the hilarious, incomparable intoxication of materializing into being these previously nonexistent patterns of sound and meaning and physical motion. It was as fraught and sublime as great Renaissance religious painting; Bellini's *St. Francis* . . .

The power and beauty of it was unimaginable until then. It can't be overstated, that initial rush of realizing, of experiencing, what's possible as you're standing there in the rehearsal room with your guitars and the mikes turned on and when you make a move this physical information comes pouring out and you can do or say anything with it.

It was like having magic powers. The ability to create action at a distance. The sounds that came from the amplifiers were absurdly moving and strange, the variety of them so wide in view of the fact that they came from flicks of our fingers and from our vocal noises, and the way that it was a single thing, an entity, that was produced by the simultaneous interplay of the four band members combining various of their faculties. We were turned into a sound, a flow of sound. I remember having a moment of weird revelation once, that each moment of a phonograph record being played, each millimeter of information conveyed via the needle to the amplifier to the speaker to the ear, is one sound. A whole orchestra is one sound, altering moment by moment, no matter how many instruments go into producing it. And, as our band rehearsed, in each moment we made the sound spray out in arrays we could instantly alter, emanating from inside us and our interplay and our inner beings combined, playing. And the sound included words.

All through this book I've had to search for different ways to say "thrill," "exhilaration," "ecstatic" to communicate particular experiences. Maybe the most extreme example of this class of moment is what I'm trying to describe here. What it felt like to first be creating electrically amplified songs. It was like being born. It was everything one wants from so-called God. The joy of it, the instant inherent awareness that you could go anywhere you wanted with it and everywhere was fascinatingly new and ridiculously effective. It was like making emotion and thought physical, to be undergone apart from oneself.

That's what makes the very beginning then in 1973 and 1974 different, and, in a way, more valuable than anything that came later in my music career, despite its shortcomings and problems and difficulties. It's that it was fresh and every moment had the surging astonishment and pleasure—even if in the service of anger and disgust, as it often was—of anything being possible to make happen. It was like creating the world, and the feeling could never quite happen again, or be sustained, anyway, because familiarity and habit take the edge off.

Avocados

Let's get wasted as avocados,
solemn and shapely
in their alligator skins, lucid, sweet-talking

lovers laid bare on rough blankets,
two-for-a-dollar magic
sacked and clutched

in a child's alleyway
hand. Let's get foamed, salty-eyed,
dismembered into smoothness,

gilded and glyphed
onto a retired stripper's back, smoked
and spooled, shucked

to a mineral glow. Let's get stupid. Opalescent.
God-complexioned. Viscera strangled
to a shimmer. Ghosted, vanquished,

sticky as hashish, lacquered and whispered
into the Guadalquivir's ear. Let's get squalid and romantic
in the squid-pink light

roughing up the tulips, then let's stumble
down the throat of 3 a.m.
to the titty bar

where Magda will stroke our faces
before breaking our jaws
with those ungodly breasts

and we will cry out with a tenderness
that betrays our hunger, our voices
thatched into a roof

that collapses under her weight,
twinkle like half-formed
hearts terrorizing

her vastness, green and wild as
        another country. Bearable
                music wincing between moans.

God is a Capitalist

I, too, want honesty in exchange for my good money, a warm body
to accompany me when I'm lonely,

feeling the way trees must feel absorbing the used-up light
along highways, a song whose human-less pulse undoes me

as kindness undoes me, sometimes getting what I want
and wearing the smug look of a road gleaming from within,

how you know when someone, without meaning to, is telling you the truth—
my sister hustling, her lucite heels steeped in cash,

each of us loaded with expired magic. I'm talking about a weariness of stars, crooked
hope, the kind perfected in southern hemispheres where tourists go

buying up the spirit of revolution. We all want a lap dance
to mean something, and now, watching her up there

I can't say where she got it from, the drive to keep making something
beautiful out of it, glittering beyond recognition,

and it rips my goddamned heart out, watching it unfold as it must
every night, the story of our naked life.

After the Poet from Kentucky Tells me my Poems Are Not Considerate to Their Audience I Try to Teach Him What I Know About Etiquette

When a lover waits for me to come,
I say thank you. When a lover
comes in my mouth,
I say you're welcome.
He runs his hand across
the pages like a priest,
breath full of bourbon
aftermath, crooked rows
of teeth like pews
in a musty tabernacle.
He jams his thumb again
at the misplaced simile
as if to say
straighten out darlin,
join the right side
and get a Camry.
Something about misogyny
makes my clit grow
seven throbbing inches.

Places Where I Would Like to Conceive

The cathedral outside Memphis
whose voluptuous seams
hold in a riot of prayer,
strung-out saints
washing away dusk's
graffiti. The steps
of the Imperial War
Museum, its arsenal
of leaves and rain,
thighs embroidered
with perpetual winter, glass
tanks of bullets, anemic
handwriting of soldiers'
letters home. I would like
to conceive inside money
factories. Exhibits
of expired maps. The glacier
I loved for its green arms
and misshapen mouth.
Django's pockets
of static. Stadiums
where silence bleeds
into history. I would like
to conceive atop
the world's tallest
elevator. I would like to
conceive holding hands
with your ghost
after drinking too much
and cavorting
with the stray dogs
of Cerro Alegre,
riding up and down
alleys of the city we love,
whose streets bear the gleam
of your ruinous face.

Pits

We go on and we tremble.
God says we can screw now.
God says to give up all your lovers,
Time to die.

When I was younger I drove a Lincoln.
God said to trade it in.
A tad lovely, then, and terrible,
And sick of my own kind,
I wanted to become a woman.
I wanted to wash the feet of other women
In public, I wanted his eyes
On me, olives on the ground.

I gave you my hand,
Now I go around with my sleeve
Tucked in my coat

I climb no trees, touch
One breast at a time,
Hold no hands myself.

I go on and I tremble
With your back in my blood
The clap my mother left me.

With me no more, and now,
And forever, and even always
The dust of my feet
In the desert
I give you stranger my sign,
My peace,
But God you remember
You fucked me out of my hand.

Translators

Blindfolded surveyors walking around a cliff
near the sea
looking for the cornerstones of death
brothers and sisters
fucking each other below on the sand
near the sea
near the sea
teachers stealing gum
from under shipwrecked desks
offices full of missals and T.V.'s
sad feet
no gas
checkbooks washed up on the beach
acre and acres of hogshit
every foot of which has to be stepped off

For Those Who Sleep And Those Who Die
Antonin Artaud

Return to the house where I drank pot liquor of love
Return to the field in evening where the mowing is laid by
To the lots of string without a kite or a hand
The same street the same dock of flanks
Dark river-beds where a fellow can piss
Where a man passes his dick turns into a rat

Man is so afraid,

he look down at cock, long ago many
centuries ships land on the enemy's beach, take down
mast in the dark, climb up cliffs in the fog, ram
enemy's door do bad things in castle, oh yea, man
go crazy play in blood like baby with duck in bathtub,
man think about favorite dog, got worms in heart, takes
dog to field trial, dog sniffs out man's life, point
at fool in frozen water, fool man, dead dogs, man look
at leaf frozen in pond, man think about woman in new
cabin beside fire, walls bleeding rosin, man forget about
dog, man want son, boy strong, call boy elephant, man
cannot sleep right, have bad itch in butthole, man think
cancer maybe, man wake up beside woman, moon come
in window, man glad he has no city, city can die for all
he cares, man smells fingers, smell bad, man gets up
to wash fingers, man steps on broken glass, sits down
on commode and sucks his foot, man thinks about God,
man says to God If I eat right will You take away cancer,
God no say, man flush pot, man decides go to India,
study other God, other God take away cancer, bring back
dog, make women go crazy, man go visit little
naked man on mountain, man give him all his money,
little naked man say go back home, stand on head with
fresh egg in asshole three times a day, man does what he
he says, oh yea, man think about troopships, man is so
afraid, man take chill, man get old real quick man nobody,
everything dark, man spit in papersack, man look at medicine
on table beside bed, man look at TV, Tarzan movie already over,
so sad so sad, man call doctor, say to make him young,
doctor look at secretary pulling up panties, say oh yea,
take man's money, man get young, man decide go to
Africa, man think everything swell when he get back
home, put many heads on wall, many skins, first night
wife run off, fool man, so man read book, man like,
so man read another book, soon man read book all time,
don't care about money, don't care bout woman, only
thing man remember is what he read, on weekends
go to old cabin, look at pine knots, think about what he
read, think about history, look down at cock,

man learn, once was another man become king, but king
had no sons, king get old, get sad, king get so afraid, look
at his cock, oh yea, one night king run everybody out of
castle, have private dinner, just with family, and favorite
dog, tell daughter to hop up on table, king takes pheasant
gravy, pours on daughter, rubs daughter's thighs with
gravy, picks up dog, tells dog like daughter, king tells daughter
not to be afraid, not be sad, tell daughter be strong, daughter
strong, daughter looks at mothers, says watch, daughter
takes dog by the mouth, breaks jaws, king says daughter strong,
man know lot about history, man afraid, man go crazy on
street one day, man go jail, man call lawyer
man like imagine too, man like to clip cut back of magazine,
man like sendoff, man also like guns,
life strange,

Cemetery Near the Sea
René Daumal

The word has no luck
And continues to wander

When it is almost morning
I drive a stake in the ground

The sea
The street where I tangled with your shadow

The sea
Like a great tent of sad tigers

The grave like a rope ladder
Left by a thief

The tide sifts out my eyes
Prison without hammers

Perhaps this is the root
Singing in time

And this is the crime
Living and dreaming

Bats

They will crawl out of the ashes of cold barbecue pits. Their wings will be cut from the backs of chimney sweeps. They will hang from the antlers of an elk like a congress of drowsy trapeze artists. At dusk above houses, they will appear and disappear and appear, weaving a jagged cotillion through the trees. Their songs will travel before them like aneurysms on strings, shattering streetlights, car alarms, nerves. When winter comes too early, we will see their faces in our frostbitten fruit. Insomniac, they will be your alphabet at the window. Sleeper, they will be the jewelry of your death, tangled in silk pajamas, in a wet beehive of hair.

Elk

They will outrun the arrow and the bomb. They will lean against abandoned jalopies and sleep. Their great antlers will be antennas growing back to God, clipping power lines, crackling with sheets of radio static lifting toward the stars. When they graze at night, their heavy heads will be like hornets' nests nodding in the breeze. In the darkness, slugs will test the air from the tips of their tines. On the first day of spring, they will walk the crumbling highways into the cities of man. They will sharpen their horns on cornices and cement. Everywhere they step will sprout grass.

Hippopotamuses

They will be the last behemoths of mud. Their heads will be like battered fedoras floating on the surface of a lake. Their torsos will be boulders percolating blood. When they haul themselves ashore, rivers will flow backwards, and cities, miles away, will blanch on the Richter. Their newborns will be like giant hardboiled eggs dredged in gunpowder. When they belch, fruit bats will glide from the caves of their stomachs and startle the moonlight. Their tiny ears will deceive. They will be deadly cartoons dancing a polka that disembowel man, woman, child.

Turkey Vultures

They will reek of tire fires and scorched fur. Their heads, shrunken by boredom, will be like desiccated beets skewered by the sun. They will descend forever, singed dirigibles corkscrewing blue skies, dreaming of the tart tartare of armadillo, the rank sinewy tangle of wolf. In a roadside ditch, they will bow their mummified faces into the steaming bowl of a body and eat, and raise them again, their blood-red hoods lacquered redder by blood. At night, they will roost in a forest of metal trees, black pineapples ripening in the moonlight, downy cocoons waiting to be kicked open by an angel. They will be the first and last foreboding: spangles of soot blown away in a gust.

Strong Man

Vivian hovered over the stove heating a cup of milk for the Strong Man convalescing in our bathtub. We found him at the edge of the woods behind the house, face down in the snow. A gang of children had scrawled obscenities all over his biceps and pecs, and a tiny row of blue blisters glistened on his upper lip like a mustache of radioactive lice. In those last hours of gravity, the night was a hush, except for the wooden spoon scraping the bottom of the iron pot. The cats sniffed the air beneath the bathroom door. When I peeked through the keyhole, I saw that he had switched off the lights. All I could make out were his shiny red tights rising in the dark, like a jellyfish billowing up from the bottom of the ocean.

Risk Management

The police officers were interviewing the neighbors about a dog that had been running roughshod through the town for days. It upset a checker game, chased a cat into a storm drain, knocked over garbage bins, dug up all of the potatoes from the community vegetable garden, defecated on the greens of the municipal golf course, and pilfered support hose and giant brassieres from the clotheslines of widows. It even interrupted a city council meeting, zipping up and down rows of the elderly and infirm sullenly waiting for some botched verdict. The policemen touched the tips of their pencils to their red tongues, as a lady with mascara smeared across her cheek said the dog must have been a pit-bull, yes, she was certain, a pit-bull frothing at the mouth with a giant chain around its neck, the kind you'd use to sink a body to the bottom of a river. A fat man beside her disagreed. He described the dog as lanky, with long hair and bangs, some kind of loping foreign hound that could track a pride of lions across the Sahara for days without any water. It was the middle of winter, but the heat kept peeling off the asphalt like black washcloths soaked in chloroform. One of the officers knelt in front of a girl holding a headless doll upside down by the foot. She said the dog was clear like water, like a ghost trying to get in out of the rain. She kept touching her throat, trying to show the man where it hurt.

Uncle Z's Toupee

Uncle Z wears a toupee to hide the hole in the top of his head. Years ago the secret police pistol-whipped him, down on all fours until the names rattled out, one at a time, like kidney stones into a metal bedpan. The hole they left never left him. When he lies down at night, the ghosts of names keep leaking from it, wafting like a chemical fog high into the atmosphere. On the bedside table, next to a glass of water and a little bottle of pills, bathed in the submarine glow of the alarm clock, the toupee rests, like the pelt of some extinct animal that whimpers softly in his dreams.

Field Recording

We knelt at the edge of the sinkhole and lowered the microphone down into the depths. Lewis fiddled with the dials on the reel-to-reel and pressed the headphones against one ear. We could smell the fires burning in the mountains, as the long shadows of dusk climbed down from the trees and rooftops. No one switched on any lights in the houses. No one parted the curtains to peek out at us in the field. Later that night, we hauled up the microphone and played back the tape. We heard the drone of bees, laughter, a train shoveling in the distance. We heard a woman talking to her dog about a soap opera and a large group of people singing "Happy Birthday" in French. We heard an old man praying to his dead wife. We heard a hailstorm pelting a cornfield and pigeons jostling in the rafters of an empty church. We heard a line of tanks advancing. We heard a roar rise in ecstatic waves from the bowl of a stadium. We heard a boy begging his papa to buy him a horse. When the tape clicked off, we drifted backwards through the silence that grew cleaner and colder by the second, like snow falling steadily all night, filling an empty swimming pool.

CONTRIBUTORS

Butch Anthony is an artist not easily defined, who collects bizarre objects and transforms them into strangely beautiful art for one of America's favorite roadside attractions, his "Museum of Wonder." His hand-built home was featured in the *New York Times* and is built from stones and the timber of an old cotton mill, elegantly decorated with Anthony's own artworks. At fourteen he was building birdhouses and stuffing his own taxidermy. His first building, a little log cabin on his grandfather's farm, would eventually became his shop. Butch resides on his 80-acre family property, a folk-art compound in Seale, Alabama, where his artistic career began after his long-time friend John Henry Toney dug up a turnip with a human likeness. After a drawing of the turnip fetched $50 in a friend's junk shop, Butch also began his artistic career. Butch's artistic spirit sees him apply his talents to a number of different modes and mediums, and he calls his specific genre of work "intertwangelism"—an ism of his own creation.

Rachel Ballard's first novel, *A Long-Forgotten Truth,* was published by Rozlyn Press in August 2011. Her poetry and prose have been published in *Poetry Walk: Sue C. Boynton Poetry Contest, The First Five Years*; *Jeopardy Magazine*; and *Pass the Fire: Stories of Service in America*. Rachel won "Best Writer" in *Cascadia Weekly's* 2011 "Best of Bellingham" issue and received a nomination for a Northeastern Minnesota Book Award. Rachel currently resides in beautiful Bellingham, Washington. "New Year's Day at Whatcom Creek, Far from the War" was originally published by the Sue C. Boynton Poetry Contest.

Brian Barker is the author of *The Black Ocean* (Southern Illinois University Press, 2011), winner of the Crab Orchard Open Competition, and of *The Animal Gospels* (Tupelo Press, 2006), winner of the Tupelo Press Editor's Prize. His poems, reviews, and interviews have appeared in such journals as *Poetry, Ploughshares, Quarterly West, American Book Review, The Writer's Chronicle, The Indiana Review, Blackbird, Pleiades, fugue, and storySouth*. His awards include an Academy of American Poets Prize and the 2009 Campbell Corner Poetry Prize. He has earned degrees in Creative Writing and Literature from Virginia Commonwealth University, George Mason University, and the University of Houston. He is married to the poet Nicky Beer and teaches at the University of Colorado Denver, where he co-edits *Copper Nickel*. "Bats," "Elk," "Hippopotamuses," "Turkey Vultures," "Strong Man," "Risk Management," "Field Recording," and "Uncle Z's Toupee" were originally published, respectively, in *The Cincinnati Review, Barrow Street, Southern Indiana Review, Plume, West Branch Wired, New South,* and *Indiana Review*. "The Last Songbird" was recorded live on KRFC radio in Fort Collins, Colorado.

Nicky Beer is the author of *The Diminishing House* (Carnegie Mellon, 2010), winner of the 2010 Colorado Book Award for Poetry. Her second book of poems, *The Octopus Game,* will be published in 2015. Her awards include a literature fellowship from the National Endowment for the Arts, a Ruth Lilly Fellowship from the Poetry Foundation, and a Discovery/*The Nation* award. She is an assistant professor at the University of Colorado Denver. "Mating Call of the Re-Creation Panda" was originally published in *The Southern Review.* "Nature Film, Directed by Martin Scorsese," "Scene 43, Take 1: Interior, Sushi Restaurant," and "Population," appear in *The Octopus Game.* Copyright © 2008, 2010, 2011 by Nicky Beer. Reprinted with the permission of The Permissions Company, Inc., on behalf of Carnegie Mellon University Press, www.cmu.edu/universitypress.

Pinckney Benedict grew up on his family's dairy farm in Greenbrier County, West Virginia. His two collections of short fiction (*Town Smokes* and *The Wrecking Yard*) and a novel (*Dogs of God*), were all named "Notable Books" by the *New York Times Book Review.* His most recent work is *Miracle Boy & Other Stories* (*Press 53*, 2010). "Joe Messinger is Dreaming" appears in *Miracle Boy & Other Stories.*

Jim Blanchard was born in Houston, Texas, in 1965, and he spent his formative years in Alaska, Ohio, California, New Mexico, Oklahoma, and Norway. In 1982, he edited and published the first issue of *BLATCH,* a punk rock and graphics zine, which lasted 14 issues and ceased publication in 1988. Blanchard has a Bachelor of Fine Arts degree from the University of Oklahoma, which he received in 1986. He moved to Seattle, Washington, in 1987 and worked a number of jobs: negative retoucher at a print shop, cover artist for books & CDs & records, editorial illustrator for magazines, copy shop "geek," technical illustrator, comic book artist, silkscreen poster artist, logo designer & art director for Fantagraphics Books, and inker for Peter Bagge's lauded *HATE* comic series. Since 2003, Blanchard has dedicated most of his time to large-scale graphic art paintings and commissioned portraits.

Dan Boehl is a founding editor of Birds, LLC, an independent poetry publisher, which put out his book *Kings of the F**king Sea.* He helps run the Austin reading series *Fun Party.*

Russell Brakefield is a poet, musician, and teacher. His most recent work appears or is forthcoming in *Bluegrass Today, The Indiana Review, NY Quarterly, Drunken Boat,* and *Poet Lore.* He teaches writing at the University of Michigan and works as the managing editor for Canarium Books.

Gaylord Brewer is the author of eight books of poetry, most recently *Give Over, Graymalkin* (Red Hen Press, 2011) and *The Martini Diet* (Dream Horse Press, 2008; winner of the 2006 Orphic Prize for Poetry), as well as the comic novella *Octavius the 1st* (Red Hen Press, 2008). Brewer has published over 800 poems in journals and anthologies such as *Best American Poetry* and the *Bedford Introduction to Literature*, and his plays have been staged in Chicago, Columbus, Nashville, New York, and Valdez, Alaska. In 2009, Brewer was awarded an Individual Artist Fellowship from the Tennessee Arts Commission. His 9th book of poetry, *Country of Ghost* (Red Hen Press) is due out in 2015. Brewer has also edited *Poems & Plays* for over 20 years. "Being Lon Chaney, Jr.," "Terminex," and "The Martini" appear, respectively, in *Barbaric Mercies* (Red Hen Press, 2003), *Exit Pursued by a Bear* (Cherry Grove Collections, 2004), and *The Poet's Guide to Food, Drink, & Desire* (Stephen F. Austin University Press, 2014).

Rachel Briggs is an illustrator and designer living in Nashville, Tennessee. Formerly the art director at *American Songwriter* and designer for *Time Out Chicago*, Briggs has since collaborated on creative material ranging from album art to animation for a slew of record labels. She has done work for bands such as Wilco, Pokey LaFarge, Jason Isbell, and Old Crow Medicine Show. She has been published in *No Depression, Rolling Stone,* and *SPIN*. Currently, her illustrated stage design can be seen on tour with platinum-selling artists Little Big Town. Her artwork is also featured on all the cans and brews of Wiseacre Brewing Company located in Memphis, Tennessee.

besmilr brigham (1913-2000), raised by farmers in the Rio Grande Valley of Texas, began writing seriously in Arkadelphia, Arkansas, traveled alone by freighter in 1948 to charred Europe, from 1950 to the late 70's with daughter and husband traveled by car to and lived in Nicaragua, Nova Scotia, Alaska, Honduras, Guatemala, Mexico, returning in intervals to the U.S. to work, writing relentlessly "putting away manuscripts" on her own terms, is the author of *Agony Dance: death of the (Dancing Dolls* (Prensa De Lagar, 1969), *Heaved from the Earth* (Knopf, 1972), and *Run Through Rock* edited by C.D. Wright (Lost Roads, 2000). She died in New Mexico. These poems were selected and transcribed from brigham's private archive in Las Cruces, New Mexico, by Robert Snyderman, a poet and independent scholar. "Flood Rain (Wind" was originally published in *University of Tampa Poetry Review #16*.

Nickole Brown's books include her debut, *Sister*, a novel-in-poems, and her upcoming collection, *Fanny Says,* which will be published by BOA Editions in 2015. Both "Fuck" (which originally appeared in *The Oxford American*) and "Go Put On Your Face" (first published in *JMWW*) will be in that second book. She graduated from The Vermont College of Fine Arts and was the editorial assistant for the late Hunter S. Thompson. She has received grants from the National Endowment for the Arts, the Kentucky Foundation for Women, and the Kentucky Arts Council. She worked at the independent, literary press, Sarabande Books, for ten years and was the National Publicity Consultant for Arktoi Books. She has taught creative writing at the University of Louisville, Bellarmine University, and at the low-residency MFA Program in Creative Writing at Murray State. Currently, she is the Editor for the Marie Alexander Series in Prose Poetry and is an Assistant Professor at University of Arkansas at Little Rock.

Sommer Browning was born on Sunset Boulevard in Los Angeles, California. She was raised in Venice Beach and has lived in Virginia, Arizona, Brooklyn, and now Colorado. She's the author of *Either Way I'm Celebrating*, a collection of poetry and comics, the forthcoming poetry collection, *Backup Singers,* both from Birds, LLC, and three poetry chapbooks. Her comics have appeared in *Drunken Boat*, *The Foghorn Magazine*, *The Stranger*, *past simple*, *H_NGM_N,* and *Octopus*. She has an MFA in poetry from the University of Arizona and a masters degree in Library Science. She makes books for Flying Guillotine Press with Tony Mancus and works as a librarian in Denver where she lives with the poet Noah Eli Gordon and the baby Georgia. She personally knows Jack Shit. "Federal Holiday" appeared in *Denver Quarterly*. "The Whistler" appeared on *Poets.org*. The first piece from "Friend" is unpublished, the second appeared on *BOMBLOG*. "The Meat from the Dream the Heart Knows" appeared in *Either Way I'm Celebrating* (Birds, LLC, 2011).

Ben Burr was reared in Ohio. He currently resides in Tennessee. "december 21, 2012; 11:23pm" appears in *jesus christ for now, maybe satan later* (Panama Red Arts, 2013).

Carlton Melton formed along the Mendocino County coastline in northern California on the weekend of July 17, 2008. The idea to play live, loud, improvised, experimental, instrumental, psychedelic music in a geodesic dome had been discussed for many years prior to this date. The opportunity came to fruition after the dome was completely rebuilt and the acoustic sounds inside were fully realized. The music is recorded live inside the dome to analog and digital sources using omni-directional microphones. All music is improvised in the sense that no one really knows who or what is going to be played at any given time. The song "Purer" was released in April of 2010 from the 12" split record by Carlton Melton and Empty Shapes on Mid-To-Late Records. Stay tuned . . . Long Live Dome Rock!

Jem Cohen steps out from behind the bass and his demanding main music projects (the Ettes, the Parting Gifts, JP5) and also from running Fond Object Records (record store, arts collective and record label) to showcase his own songwriting and multi-instrumental skills. Left to his own devices, Cohen disappeared down the solo worm-hole of writing and recording every song, performing every instrument, and producing 17 tracks in just a few weeks. Cohen's standout track "Happiness" is sure to bring you some . . . happiness. Enjoy. "Happiness" (Fond Object Music, 2013) was written and produced by Jem Cohen at Too Sweet Studios, Nashville, Tennessee. All instruments and vocals are performed by Jem Cohen except slide guitar by Adam Meisterhans.

Spencer Connell was born and raised in Nashville, Tennessee, but currently resides in Chattanooga. He studied poetry at Rhodes University and the University of Tennessee at Chattanooga. His work is soon to appear in the *Southern Collective Experience.* Aside from poetry, Spencer plays and performs traditional Appalachian music.

Larry O. Dean was born and raised in Flint, Michigan. His most recent books include *Brief Nudity* (Salmon Poetry, 2013) and *Basic Cable Couplets* (Silkworms Ink, 2012). Also a critically-acclaimed songwriter, Dean has numerous CD releases, including *Fun with a Purpose* (2009) with The Injured Parties. He was a 2004 recipient of the Gwendolyn Brooks Award. "Nixon Era Panda Dies" was originally published in *Poetry Super Highway.*

Kendra DeColo is the author of *Thieves in the Afterlife* (Saturnalia Books, 2014), selected by Yusef Komunyakaa for the 2013 Saturnalia Books Poetry Prize. Her poems have appeared in *Southern Indiana Review, The Collagist, Muzzle Magazine* and elsewhere. She is the recipient of an Individual Artist Fellowship from the Tennessee Arts Commission, a work-study scholarship from the Bread Loaf Writer's Conference and residencies from the Millay Colony, and the Virginia Center for Creative Arts. She is the founding poetry editor of *Nashville Review* and a Book Review Editor at *Muzzle Magazine.* "Places Where I Would Like to Conceive," "After the Poet from Kentucky Tells me my Poems are Not Considerate to Their Audience I Try to Teach Him What I Know About Etiquette," "God is a Capitalist," and "Avocados" appear in *Thieves in the Afterlife* (Saturnalia Books, 2014).

Destruction Unit is Ryan Rousseau, Rustin Rousseau, J.S. Aurelius, N. Nappa and A. Flores. "Night Loner" was recorded live under the moon and stars in Venice, Italy, by Stefano Scattolin. A small number of people were invited to attend. A different version of "Night Loner" appears on the *Deep Trip* LP released by Sacred Bones Records (Ascetic House, 2013).

Tav Falco is a musical performer, filmmaker, and photographer. He has led the psychedelic country group Tav Falco's Panther Burns (named after a plantation in Mississippi) since 1979. He moved to Europe in the late 1990s and since 2002 has been touring with a stable formation of musicians from Paris and Rome in his Panther Burns group. Falco was raised in the country, near Whelen Springs, and moved to Memphis, Tennessee, in 1973. With Arkansas poet Randall Lyon, he co-founded the nonprofit Televista "art-action" video group. Alex Chilton was impressed by a 1978 performance of Falco's at The Orpheum in Memphis that culminated in the chain sawing of a guitar. The two teamed up musically and evolved into the self-styled "art damage" band, Tav Falco's Panther Burns. Falco has said his main artistic purpose is "to stir up the dark waters of the unconscious." "Chapter the Thirteenth: Discourse of Rage, Conjuration, & Exile" is an excerpt from *Ghosts Behind the Sun: Splendor, Enigma & Death* (Creation, 2011).

Joshua Gillis was born and raised in Wayne County, Michigan. The poems herein are built using found text. Each poem has multiple anonymous and arbitrary contributors, both male and female, limited to one author per line. Each line was excised from separate and unaffiliated posts in the "Missed Connections" section of Craigslist, spanning numerous cities, internationally. His work has been published in *The Mall Mag*. These poems are previously unpublished. Please be encouraged to dissect and alter any and all poetry.

Noah Eli Gordon is the co-publisher of Letter Machine Editions, an editor with *The Volta*, and an assistant professor in the MFA program in Creative Writing at the University of Colorado-Boulder, where he currently directs Subito Press. His recent books include *The Year of the Rooster*, *The Source*, and *Novel Pictorial Noise*.

Richard Hell was a progenitor of the "punk" movement in the 1970's, forming Television with his high school friend Tom Verlaine in 1974, The Heartbreakers with Johnny Thunders in 1975, and then Richard Hell & the Voidoids in 1976. The excerpt we publish here describes his very earliest band rehearsals, in 1974. Since retiring from music in 1984, Hell has focused primarily on writing. He is the author of the journals collection *Artifact*; the novels *Go Now* and *Godlike*; and the collection of essays, notebooks, and lyrics *Hot and Cold*; as well as numerous other pamphlets and books. Hell has published essays, reportage, and fiction in such publications as *Spin*, *GQ*, *Esquire*, the *Village Voice*, *Vice*, *Bookforum*, *Art in America*, the *New York Times*, and the *New York Times Book Review*. From 2004 to 2006 he was the film critic for *BlackBook* magazine. He lives in New York. "My First Rehearsals with a Band" is excerpted from the autobiography *I Dreamed I Was A Very Good Tramp* by Richard Hell © 2013 by Richard Meyers. Courtesy of Harper Collins.

Carolyn Hembree's debut collection, *Skinny*, was published by Kore Press in 2012. Individual poems have appeared in *Colorado Review, DIAGRAM*, *Gulf Coast*, and *Verse Daily*, among other journals and anthologies. *Rigging a Chevy into a Time Machine & Other Ways to Escape a Plague* was a finalist for the 2012 Tupelo Press' and Switchback Books' manuscript competitions. Carolyn grew up in Tennessee and Alabama. Before completing her MFA, she found employment as a cashier, housecleaner, cosmetics consultant, telecommunicator, actor, receptionist, paralegal, coder, and freelance writer. She teaches at the University of New Orleans and serves as Poetry Editor of *Bayou Magazine*. "Old Sweetheart Slams White Russians and Mudslides on Ditmars Blvd., Astoria," and "The Goner" appear in *Skinny*.

JP5, a Nashville-based band, is the latest group fronted by Atlanta native Joseph Plunkett. It's also his most fully realized, the product of a guy who knows what he wants: a great rock-n-roll band fragile enough to fall apart, but strong enough to keep the method ahead of the mess. Plunkett's songs are full of clean pop hooks and classic rock arrangements, and just strange enough to surprise. The lyrics lean to the dark side of things, but there's enough light at the end of these tunnels to keep a party going. Plunkett is joined on guitar by Nashville native and way-Way Outsider, Cy Barkley, and Adam Meisterhans, a West Virginia transplant, and super shredder, who will soon be sucking it up and letting us all call him "Masterhands." JP5 also has one of the most solid rhythm sections going with Jem Cohen, also of The Ettes, on bass, and Rachel Hortman on drums, who plays with the authority of someone you suspect is secretly in charge of a lot more than the drum kit. Andrija Tokic recorded "Wait For It" at the Bomb Shelter in Nashville, Tennessee.

TJ Jarrett is a writer and software developer in Nashville, Tennessee. Her recent work has been published or is forthcoming in *African American Review*, *Boston Review*, *DIAGRAM*, and others. Her second collection, *Zion*, recently won the Crab Orchard Open Competition 2013. "After 40 Days" is forthcoming in *Zion* (Southern Illinois University Press, 2014).

Paul "Wine" Jones (1946 - 2005). Born John Paul Jones, Mr. Jones, a native of Belzoni, Mississippi, was a well-known farmer, welder, and electric blues guitarist. He is heard here playing the title track from his 1999 LP *Pucker Up Buttercup* (Fat Possum). Recorded live at Club Bart in Ferndale, Michigan, in January of 2004 by Matthew Smith. Wine Jones is accompanied by Craig Pickering (drums) and Matt Patton (bass).

Tim Kerr was a founding member of The Big Boys, Poison 13, Bad Mutha Goose, Lord High Fixers, Monkey Wrench, and others. All groups that have played an important role in what is known as the US indie/DIY scene today. He has helped record and produce countless numbers of bands for labels such as Estrus, In The Red, and Sympathy For The Record Industry. Not only has he been inducted into the Texas Music Hall of Fame, but Tim also earned a degree in painting and photography from the University of Texas in Austin, where he studied with photographer Garry Winogrand. His art has been shown in the U.S. and abroad in galleries such as PS1 in New York, 96 Gillespie in London, Slowboy Gallery in Dusseldorf, Hyde Park Art Center in Chicago, and the Artisphere in Rosslyn, VA. You can also see his art in his book *Your Name Here,* and his graphics on skateboards, clothes, records, and CDs.

Adrian Matejka was born in Nuremberg, Germany, and grew up in California and Indiana. He is a graduate of Indiana University and the MFA program at Southern Illinois University Carbondale. His first collection of poems, *The Devil's Garden*, won the 2002 New York/New England Award from Alice James Books. His second collection, *Mixology*, was a winner of the 2008 National Poetry Series and was published by Penguin Books in 2009. *Mixology* was subsequently nominated for an NAACP Image Award. His newest book, *The Big Smoke*, was published by Penguin in May 2013 and was a finalist for the 2013 National Book Award. He is the recipient of two Illinois Arts Council Literary Awards and fellowships from Cave Canem and the Lannan Foundation. His work has appeared in *American Poetry Review*, *The Best American Poetry 2010*, *Gulf Coast, Ploughshares*, *Poetry*, and *Prairie Schooner* among other journals and anthologies. He teaches creative writing at Indiana University in Bloomington. "Seven Days of Falling," "Wheels of Steel," "Tyndall Armory," "This Be The Verse," and "Language Mixology" are from *Mixology* by Adrian Matejka, copyright (c) 2009 by Adrian Matejka. Used by permission of Penguin, a division of Penguin Group (USA) LLC.

Brooke D. McCarley is a writer, musician and librarian who lives in Birmingham, Alabama She graduated with a journalism degree from Auburn University and is now seeking her Master's of Library Science at the University of Alabama. She is currently writing for the online site *I Am the F-bomb* and playing music with a Birmingham-based band called In Snow who has a record coming out on Step Pepper Records.

Andrew McFadyen-Ketchum is an award-winning poet, editor, and educator. His first book of poetry, *Ghost Gear*, is forthcoming with the University of Arkansas Press. Recent poems, essays, reviews, podcasts, and interviews appear or are forthcoming from *The Southern Poetry Anthology, Glimmer Train, American Literary Review, The Missouri Review, storySouth, and Blackbird.* "Stormdraining" and "The Year Hyakatuke Was Said" appear in *Ghost Gear* (University of Arkansas Press, 2014).

Joanne Merriam is the force behind Upper Rubber Boot Books, the small press that published *Apocalypse Now: Poems and Prose from the End of Days* and *Marilyn Monroe: Poems*. Her poetry has appeared in *Asimov's Science Fiction, Every Day Poets, Strange Horizons,* and *The Fiddlehead*, as well as in her collection *The Glaze from Breaking* (Stride Books, 2005; URB, 2011). She lives in Nashville with four angry rabbits and one friendly one. "Deaths on Other Planets" originally appeared in *Asimov's Science Fiction.*

Wayne Miller is the author of three poetry collections, most recently *The City, Our City* (Milkweed Editions, 2011), which was a finalist for the William Carlos Williams Award and the Rilke Prize. The translator and co-editor of several books, including Moikom Zeqo's *I Don't Believe in Ghosts* (BOA Editions, 2007) and the anthology *New European Poets* (Graywolf, 2008), Wayne lives in Kansas City and teaches at the University of Central Missouri, where he edits *Pleiades.* "Post-Elegy," "Allegory of the House," "The People's History," "A Bit About the Soul," and "Some Notes on Human Relations" were originally published, respectively, in *Granta Online, iO, Indiana Review, Lo-Ball,* and *Crazyhorse.*

William W. Miller teaches freshman composition courses at Murray State University. He will never leave Kentucky. The excerpt from his novel, *Grave Matters, Doctor Lamb*, is his first published work of fiction.

Ben Mirov is the author of *Hider Roser* (Octopus Books, 2012). He is also the author of *Ghost Machine* (Caketrain, 2010) selected for publication by Michael Burkard, and chosen as one of the best books of poetry in 2010 for *Believer Magazine's* Reader Survey. He is one of the founding editors of PEN America's poetry series. He grew up in Northern California and lives in Oakland. The first section of *darklings* was a finalist for *BOMB Magazine's* 2012 Poetry Contest, and published on *BOMBlog.* "Black Glass Soliloquy" is a collaboration with the artist Nick Almquist, and was published at *Poets.org.*

Mystery Twins is the guitar/drum duo of Doug Lehmann and Stephanie Brush. The Mystery Twins craft concise no-frills songs and perform them in similar fashion. Lehmann and Brush have been playing together as one half of the Nashville band The Clutters since 2001. They are like a cynical, co-ed Everly Brothers, brandishing razor-sharp songs that cut to the bone with the simplest of strokes. "The River" was produced by Doug Lehmann and Dexter Green, recorded and mixed by Joe Costa, written by Doug Lehmann and also appears on Mystery Twins debut album *Ghost In The Ground.*

Pamela Johnson Parker is a medical editor who also teaches creative writing at Murray State University. Her chapbooks are *A Walk Through the Memory Palace,* which won the Qarrtsiluni Prize, and *Other Four-Letter Words,* published by Finishing Line Press. A full-length collection, *Galaxies that Might Be You,* was a finalist for the Bruckheimer Award in 2013. Pamela's essays and poems have appeared in such journals as *Oranges and Sardines*, *Poets and Artists*, *Muscadine Lines, A Journal of the South*, and *Spaces.* One of Pamela's poems was chosen by D.A. Powell for 2011's *Best New Poets,* and a broadside of *"Odysseus: Uxoria"*, which won the Switcheroo Prize, is included in *Poets on Painting.* "Triage" and "It Pays to Increase Your Word Power," "First Person Plural, First Person Singular," *"In Ictu Oculi,"* and "Some Yellow Tulips" were originally published, respectively, in *Iron Horse Literary Review, Centrifugal Eye, Blue Fifth Review,* and *qarrtsiluni.*

Marquise Person aka "M-Dot Da Poet" is a twenty-five-year-old spoken word artist from Jackson, Tennessee, by way of Chicago, Illinois. Marquise has been writing since the age of nine but has been performing for the past two years after moving to Nashville. In those two years, he has been nominated twice for NIMA's (Nashville Independent Music Awards) "Best Live Spoken Artist," performed at local open mics as well as surrounding colleges and universities, and has held several writing workshops for young poets. His work has been featured in several anthologies, magazines, as well as read at local slam competitions. Marquise now hosts his own open-mic show in Smyrna, Tennessee, where he resides with his wife and three kids as he continues to write and spread the art of spoken word. Person's audio track "My Microphone Gets Around" was recorded with J. Reggaerica.

Dale Ray Phillips' short story collection, *My People's Waltz,* published by W.W. Norton & Company, was nominated for the 2000 Pulitzer Prize. His work has appeared in *The Atlantic*, *GQ*, *Harper's*, *Zoetrope: All-Story*, *The Oxford American*, and *Best American Short Stories.* He teaches creative writing at Murray State University. *The Oxford American* published a different version of "Creole" under the title "Having at It."

Benjamin Prosser was born in Bradford-On-Avon, Wiltshire, England, in 1974. He is a visual artist, musician and writer. His books include *Fire Animals, For the Fallen, The Cunt of Hope, The Sandman is Coming,* and *27 Reasons to Hate Me*, all published through his own Coffin Press Imprint. His work has been included in *Cannon Fodder* and *Sleep* magazines. He has exhibited/read in London, Edinburgh, Paris, Barcelona, Berlin and Helsinki and released records solo and in the bands Congregation and The TAP Collective on the Rim, Bronzerat, Velo and Fitzrovian Phonographic labels. Musically, he currently works under the solo moniker 'Black Spot' and in the found sound/improvisational unit "Unsui Trio," releasing CDRs through his own New Cross Committee of Vigilance Label. He is currently studying for an M.A. in Art Psychotherapy at Goldsmiths University London. "Fire Animal" was originally published in *Fire Animals* (Coffin Press, 1998).

Daniel Lucca Pujol is currently a touring musician, writer, and artist. He has released records via Saddle Creek and Third Man Records. His poetry, lyric, and prose have been featured in the *Nashville Scene*, *Rolling Stone*, and *Impose Magazine*. He earned an MA in Global Affairs from the University of Denver in 2012. He has a congenital hole in his left eardrum and double-jointed rotator cuffs. He can go from zero to sixty in a billion seconds. Demons watch you while you sleep. He lives in Nashville, Tennessee, with his partner, two rabbits, and a Chinese water dragon. His next album is titled *Kludge* and will be released in 2014 on Saddle Creek Records.

Sheila Sanderson is a rural Kentucky native who now lives in Prescott, Arizona, and teaches at Prescott College. She also serves as an editor for *Alligator Juniper* for both poetry and creative nonfiction. She is the author of a collection of poetry, *Keeping Even* (Stephen F. Austin University Press, 2011). Her work has appeared on *Verse Daily*, and in *One for the Money: The Sentence as a Poetic Form, a Poetry Workshop Handbook and Anthology* (Lynx House Press, 2012) as well as in various journals including *Crazyhorse* and *Southern Poetry Review*. "Though the End Be No Mystery" was originally published in *Spillway*. "Conspiracy in White" was originally published in *Crab Orchard Review*.

Zachary Schomburg was born in Omaha, Nebraska, and raised in Iowa. He earned a BA from the College of the Ozarks and a PhD in creative writing-poetry from the University of Nebraska. His books of poetry include *The Man Suit* (2007), *Scary, No Scary* (2009), and *Fjords vol 1* (2012). He has said of his work, which is known for its absurd, tender humor, "Mostly I want my poems to generate their own energy through confusion. I want my poems to confuse the reader. Not a confusion in a cognitive or narrative sense, but in an emotional sense." Schomburg co-edits Octopus Books and lives in Portland, Oregon. "The Killing Trees," "The Reckoner," and "Death Letter" appear in *Fjords vol. 1* (Black Ocean, 2012).

Frank Stanford's poems were reprinted with permission from C.D. Wright, Estate of Frank Stanford. They are from the unpublished collections: *Automatic Co-Pilot* (versions of poems from other languages), S*moking Grapevine*, *The Last Panther in the Ozarks* and *Flour the Dead Man Brings to the Wedding*, most of which are early works and had been cherry-picked by the poet for his published books. The latter title includes his most recent drafts and final poems. "Pits" was previously published in *raccoon*, #17, 1985, "Translators" and "For Those Who Sleep and Those Who Die," have no publication record; the anomalous "Man is so afraid," is on Poetry Foundation's *Poets.org*, and first appeared in *raccoon* #24/25, 1987, "Cemetery Near the Sea" was published in *Oxford American* #52, 2006. Gratitude to the editors of those print and online journals. Stanford's published collections are: *The Singing Knives* (1971), *Ladies from Hell* (1974), *Shade* (1975), *Arkansas Benchstone* (1975) and *Constant Stranger* (1976) all from Irving Broughton's Mill Mountain Press. *YOU* (1979*)*, and subsequent editions of *The Singing Knives* were published by the press Stanford founded in Arkansas in 1976, Lost Roads Publishers. The epic poem *The Battlefield Where the Moon Says I Love You* was first co-published by Mill Mountain and Lost Roads (1979); a subsequent edition was published by Lost Roads, now under the editorship of Susan Scarlata. *Crib Death* (1979) was published by Ironwood Press under the direction of the late Michael Cuddihy. *The Light the Dead See* was published by the University of Arkansas (1991). Copper Canyon is scheduled to publish a collected poems of Frank Stanford in 2015. Frank Stanford was born in Mississippi in 1948. He died in Arkansas of self-inflicted gunshot wounds in 1978 two months shy of his thirtieth birthday.

Sampson Starkweather was born in Pittsboro, North Carolina He is the author of *The First Four Books of Sampson Starkweather* and 5 chapbooks from dangerous small presses. He is a founding editor of Birds, LLC and works for The Center for the Humanities at The Graduate Center, CUNY. "I sense my own limit" was originally published in *Supermachine*. "our life, this temporary eclipse / to that other" was originally published as a limited-edition broadside by the Center for Book Arts, NYC. "Department of Defense" was recorded live at Third Man Records.

Steve Stern is the author of a number of novels and story collections, including *Lazar Malkin Enters Heaven*, which won the Edward Lewis Wallant Award for Jewish fiction, and *The Wedding Jester*, which won the National Jewish Book Award. His stories have been included in the Pushcart and O. Henry Prize anthologies, and he has received fellowships from the Fulbright and Guggenheim foundations. He's just completed a new novel that spans 300 years in the Pinch, a Jewish ghetto once situated on and around North Main Street in Memphis but has since gone to bonemeal and ashes. He is a writer-in-residence at Skidmore College in upstate New York.

Janaka Stucky is the publisher of Black Ocean, and its literary journal, *Handsome*. He is the author of *Your Name Is the Only Freedom* (Brave Men Press, 2009) and *The World Will Deny It For You* (Ahsahta Press, 2012), and his poems have appeared in publications such *as Denver Quarterly, Fence, North American Review*, and *Volt*. In 2010 he was voted "Boston's Best Poet" in the *Boston Phoenix*. "Writers like Stucky and imprints like Black Ocean . . . are at the forefront of an exhilarating revitalization of the poetic voice. *The World Will Deny It For You* speaks to a notion of quality so exceptional it makes everything shake."—The Denver Examiner.

You may know **Ben Swank** as a co-founder of Third Man Records. Or, as the founder of Hate Life. Or, as the drummer for Ultras S/C, Henry and June, and Soledad Brothers. Or, for his advice column "Swank's Guide to the Hate Life" in *The Nashville Scene*. Swank has a decade-plus of experience as a hard-livin' rock 'n' roll dude.

Paige Taggart lives in Brooklyn and is the author of three chapbooks. Trembling Pillow Press will publish her first full-length collection *Want For Lion* in 2014. She's an avid jeweler and co-founded the tumblr Poets Touching Trees. "Starts in Herds," "Poem with Scrutiny," and "Melatonin" appear in *Want for Lion*. "Split and Raise Forcefield on Deck" was recorded live at Third Man Records.

William Tyler is a Nashville guitarist and composer who strives to explore the spaces between the idioms of folk, classical, psychedelia, and pop melody. While largely a solo performer and always operating under the "banner" of instrumental music, he arranges his guitar-based compositions with particular attention to mood, melody, and often-times sympathetic instrumentations. Having released two critically acclaimed records under his own name, "Behold the Spirit" (2010) and "Impossible Truth" (2013), Tyler has established himself as one of the seminal players in the new solo guitar renaissance, but also remains curious as to how to expand the boundaries of this self-appointed genre. "Ghost Dancer" is a sound collage put together on cassette eight-track in 2007-2008 at home and mixed with the assistance of Lambchop's Ryan Norris. "Ghost Dancer" is a tribute to William Least-Heat-Moon and his cross-country trek on America's back roads chronicled in the now classic travel book *Blue Highways*.

Ken Vandermark graduated with a degree in Film and Communications from McGill University during the spring of 1986. His primary creative emphasis has been the exploration of contemporary music that deals directly with advanced methods of improvisation. In 1989, he moved to Chicago from Boston, and has worked continuously from the early 1990s onward, both as a performer and organizer in North America and Europe, recording in a large array of contexts, with many internationally renowned musicians (such as Fred Anderson, Ab Baars, Peter Brötzmann, Tim Daisy, Hamid Drake, Terrie Ex, Mats Gustafsson, Devin Hoff, Christof Kurzmann, Fred Lonberg-Holm, Paul Lytton, Lasse Marhaug, Joe McPhee, Andy Moor, Joe Morris, Paal Nilssen-Love, Chad Taylor, and Nate Wooley). His current activity includes work with Made To Break, Audio One, Lean Left, the Chicago Reed Quartet, Side A, Fire Room, the DKV Trio, duos with Paal Nilssen-Love and Tim Daisy, and work as a solo performer. In 1999 he was awarded the MacArthur prize for music. "Brown Rice" was originally composed by Don Cherry, (Eternal River Music/BMI), and arranged by Ken Vandermark, (Twenty First Mobile Music/ASCAP). The piece is performed by Jason Adasiewicz (vibraphone) Jeb Bishop (trombone) Pandelis Karayorgis (Wurlitzer electric piano) Nate McBride (electric and acoustic bass) Dave Rempis (alto saxophone) Chad Taylor (drums), and Ken Vandermark (tenor saxophone). Dave Zuchowski recorded the performance live on January 20, 2010.

Adam Vines is an assistant professor of English at the University of Alabama at Birmingham, where he edits the *Birmingham Poetry Review*. Vines has published poems in *Poetry, Southwest Review, Gulf Coast, The Literary Review, redivider, Barrow Street*, among others. His collection of poetry, *The Coal Life*, was published by the University of Arkansas Press. He was awarded the Individual Artist Fellowship from the Alabama State Council of the Arts for 2013. During the summers, Vines is on staff at the Sewanee Writers' Conference. "Anti-Aubade," "River Politics," "The Golden Years," "After Warhol's *Rorschach*, 1984," "After Tom Wesselmann's *Great American Nude #57*, 1964" were originally published, respectively, in *Southwest Review, Poetry, Mead, Gulf Coast, 32 Poems.*

Vox Arcana is a new music trio organized by prolific percussionist and composer **Tim Daisy** and includes two mainstays from Chicago's creative improvised music scene: clarinetist **James Falzone** and cellist **Fred Lonberg-Holm**. Drawing inspiration from a wide array of sources including the New York School of composers, and the pioneering work of Chicago's AACM, Vox Arcana explores the fertile borderline between composition and improvisation. "Soft Focus" is available from the full length of the same name released on Relay Records.

Calliope Blue Watford-Edelson is 8 years old and lives in Los Angeles, California. She attends the Citizens of the World Charter School, where she is a third grader. She states, "I like to do poetry because it's not a simple story. You can feel it through your ears going down to your veins transporting to your heart! It gives me feeling in what I need, like for instance math! I love writing because you can really feel it. I go to recess thinking what should I put in my poetry? Like sometimes I like to say 'the wind is blowing like a windstorm in Egypt!' I love having friends and family that support me! I hope you enjoy my poem." "A Poem is Everything" was recorded by her dad, Richie Edelson.

Chet Weise's writing has been published in *Copper Nickel*, *Bayou Magazine*, and *We Never Learn: The Gunk Punk Undergut, 1988-2001*. Also a musician, his work includes Estrus recording artists The Quadrajets and the Immortal Lee County Killers. Weise earned his MFA from Murray State University, lives in Nashville, Tennessee, and teaches at Middle Tennessee State University. Weise was banned from Canada during the calendar year of 2008 for playing rock-n-roll without a work permit. "In the Pines" appears in *Poems & Plays*, and "An American Prayer for the Second Coming" in *Apocalypse Now: Poems and Prose from the End Days* (Upper Rubber Boot Books, 2012).

Sharon Weise was born in 1947. She attended Southwest Missouri State College from 1966 through 1968 and majored in commercial art, but her passion was sketching and drawing people, mainly family and friends. She married in 1969 and concentrated on being a wife and mother and continues to do so. Her interest in drawing has been rekindled since her son, Chet Weise, asked her to illustrate his poem "An American Prayer for the Second Coming."

Stephanie Ann Whited's writing can be found online at *Verse*, *Sink Review*, and *The Rumpus*. She's an editor at *Coldfront Magazine* and lives in Ditmas Park, Brooklyn. "When Was Early" was originally published in *The Volta*, and "When the Cause is Lost" was originally published at *Spine Road*.

Joshua Marie Wilkinson (b. 1977, Seattle) is the author of several books, including *Selenography* (with Polaroids by Tim Rutili), *Swamp Isthmus*, *The Courier's Archive & Hymnal*, and *Meadow Slasher* (all from Sidebrow Books and Black Ocean). He's edited five anthologies (of poems, essays, interviews, and poetics), and, with Solan Jensen, he directed a film about Califone called *Made a Machine by Describing the Landscape* (Indiepix Films). He teaches at the University of Arizona, and runs a journal called *The Volta* (with Afton Wilky) as well as a small press called Letter Machine Editions (with Noah Eli Gordon). He lives in Tucson.

C. D. Wright is the author of numerous books of poems, including *One With Others* (Copper Canyon Press, 2011), winner of the National Book Critics Circle Award and the Lenore Marshall Prize. Wright is a chancellor of the Academy of American Poets, a MacArthur Fellow, and is the Israel J. Kapstein Professor of English at Brown University. "Imaginary June" was originally published at *Poets.org*.

Jake Adam York authored four books of poems: *Murder Ballads* (Elixir Press, 2005); *A Murmuration of Starlings* (Southern Illinois UP, 2008); *Persons Unknown* (Southern Illinois UP, 2010); and *Abide*, which will be published posthumously by Southern Illinois University Press in 2014. Originally from Alabama, he was educated at Auburn and Cornell. He received fellowships to serve as a Poet in Residence at the University of Mississippi (2009), to serve as the Thomas Visiting Professor in Creative Writing at Kenyon College (2011), and from the Mellon Foundation to serve as a Visiting Faculty Fellow at the James Weldon Johnson Institute for Advanced Study at Emory University (2011-2012). He was also a recipient of a fellowship from the National Endowment of the Arts. At the time of his death in 2012, he was an associate professor of English at the University of Colorado Denver and edited the journal *Copper Nickel*. "*te lyra pulsa manu* or something like that," "Letter Already Broadcast Into Space," "Postscript (Already Breaking In Distant Echoes)," "Letter Written On A Hundred Dollar Bill," "Tape Loop," "Cry of the Occasion," and "Dear Brother," will appear in a forthcoming collection of poems titled, *Abid*e; Copyright © 2014 by the Estate of Jake Adam York. Reproduced by permission of Southern Illinois University Press. Poet Adrian Matejka recorded York's "Letter Written On A Hundred Dollar Bill" via his laptop at the 2012 AWP bookfair.